UNIVERSITY LIBRARY
UW - STEVENS POINT

P9-AOY-210

THE COMMUNISTS IN SPAIN

# The Communists in Spain

**Study of an
Underground Political Movement**

GUY HERMET
*Fondation nationale
des sciences politiques, Paris*

*Translated from the French by*
S. SEAGO and H. FOX

SAXON HOUSE | LEXINGTON BOOKS

First published as Les Communistes en Espagne

© Librairie Armand Colin 1971

English Translation © D. C. Heath Ltd., 1974

All rights reserved. No part of this publication may be reproduced, stored in a retrieval system, or transmitted in any form or by any means, electronic, mechanical, photo-copying, recording, or otherwise without the prior permission of D.C. Heath Ltd.

*Published by*

Saxon House, D. C. Heath Ltd.
Westmead, Farnborough, Hants., England

*Jointly with*

LEXINGTON BOOKS, D. C. Heath & Co.
Lexington, Mass., U.S.A.

ISBN 0 347 01032 6
Library of Congress Catalog Card Number 74—3912
Printed in Great Britain by
Brown Knight & Truscott Ltd., London and Tonbridge

# Contents

JN
S395
C6
4L/3

v

275904

# Introduction

Even their opponents have paid tribute to the courage of the Spanish communists — hunted men who for more than thirty years now have been willing to sacrifice their freedom and sometimes their very lives out of loyalty to a political ideal. The dignity, verging on the tragic, of the exiled republicans — communists and non-communists alike — deserves admiration and sympathy, even though we may at times find it hard to understand why they acted as they did.

However, such feelings — shared not only by all whose political memory is scarred by the Civil War, but also by a younger generation to this day almost obsessively interested in Spanish politics — are not in themselves enough to justify the publication of a book about the Spanish communists.[1] Even less can such sentiments provide the subject-matter of such a work. Can a book like this be anything but an account of atrocities, matching the anti-communist slogans the Franco regime has been ceaselessly pouring out to justify its existence? Is there anything to be gained from a study of Spanish communism to add to our knowledge of the workings of political machines? Is the documentary material available to make such a study feasible and is this the right time to undertake a study of Spanish communism—seen not from a purely historical viewpoint, but examined as it is today?

We believe the answer to this threefold question is 'Yes'. The intrinsic interest of a study of underground communist organisations is obvious. The field of research offered by clandestine political groupings of all hues has in fact been much neglected by political scientists, who seem to concentrate virtually all their attention on political parties that operate legally. As for the specialists in communist studies, they have concentrated on three kinds of communist parties: great mass parties functioning openly in Western democracies[2]; parties in power in socialist countries; and parties operating in the Third World[3]. Communist parties of several other types have been virtually ignored by students of politics. This applies particularly to parties in opposition to authoritarian conservative regimes, to all underground parties as such, as well as to parties in capitalist countries which have attained a middle stage of development and are approaching the point of economic take-off.

This, then, is the justification for our study. The Spanish communist

1

movement is faced with just the situation marked by all the features noted above. That similar research projects are at present in progress under the auspices of the *Centre d'etude des relations internationales* can only add to the interest of this work.

The question remains of whether — having regard to the information available at this time — a study of the various Spanish communist groupings is in fact practicable. Studies of this sort into the background of political parties are rare, even for parties operating in Western democracies, where they are in no way threatened, and where adequate information is available. Such research projects are rarely, if ever, undertaken with regard to parties operating underground. This is the case in Franco Spain, where political parties are banned and where the 'Movement' sprung from the Falange claims to be the sole exponent of a fairly wide political spectrum.

No serious study has in fact been devoted exclusively to the Spanish parties, both as they are at present and as they were under the (Spanish) Second Republic, which allowed them to function openly. All there is consists of a good book on the Falange[4] (i.e. on a broad political movement and a particular phase in Spanish history, rather than on a political party); and some books of propaganda, put out either by the various parties themselves or by sources close to the regime.[5] A number of historical studies on anarchism or on the parties operating under the (Spanish) constitutional monarchy[6] may also be worth noting if only for the record.

Since our study deals both with an underground political movement and a Spanish party, it explores two virtually unknown areas. We were thus bound to have some difficulty in obtaining the necessary documentary evidence, due to the absence of earlier studies devoted to the Spanish communists and the obstacles which bar the way of anyone trying to observe at first hand the operation of underground political movements. However, a preliminary investigation confirmed that some sources of information, at any rate, were available, and also that the Spanish communist movement remains important enough to justify a study devoted exclusively to it.

On the whole, the amount of documentary material on the beginnings of the PCE is fairly substantial. The same applies to the period of its overt life under the Second Republic and in the Civil War,[7] and to a lesser extent to the years immediately preceding the triumph of the nationalists. Concerning this period, we can call on a body of evidence (though it is probably very biased) furnished by dissident Party cadres who left its ranks during the World War or soon after.[8]

As for official anti-communist propaganda literature, the supply is virtually limitless, put out by the press and other media of both the Franco regime and of the non-communist republican movements. Here, it is merely a matter of using one's judgement to select from the vast mass of publications that have appeared since 1936.

We are also able to make a more or less accurate assessment of the programmes and policies of the PCE as well as of the various splinter movements, thanks to the underground press[9] and to the various anthologies published in France by agencies connected either with the PCE or the French Communist Party. [10] Recent publications of this kind by Santiago Carrillo are particularly useful. [11] The work done by Michel Adam in his research into the background of the communist opposition in Spain during the period 1945-1963, though of a different kind, is also very valuable. [12] All in all, the only void of any consequence hampering research into communist ideology and policies is the absence of full published records of the three-party congresses held since the war — in 1953, 1960 and 1965. The only sources we can draw on in this respect are the fragmentary documents which have appeared in *Mundo obrero* and in a few other publications, produced either underground or abroad; and the works of Santiago Carrillo, noted above. ·

It is, on the other hand, much more difficult, and at times downright impossible, to obtain adequate information on the present influence of the PCE and the rival communist parties, and other matters concerning them. For security reasons, and perhaps also to blur the extent of their real importance, these parties, in their own publications, give practically no details of the numerical strength of their membership, the social background of their supporters, their organisation, circulation figures of their literature, and their day-to-day objectives. Moreover, it is impossible to put much faith in the reports that reach one about the actual influence of these parties on strikes, workers' and students' demonstrations, and other acts of opposition. Every movement seeks to exaggerate the part it has played in events of this kind, and even to claim sole responsibility for them at times. For the same reasons, it would be risky to give too much credence to the accounts published by various underground sources on the disputes and rivalries which divide the PCE and the dissident 'anti-revisionist' movements.

In this respect, the only remedy available to us is to rely, in part at least, on dubious information supplied from time to time by the official Spanish press, by underground publications and by foreign newspapers, reviews and some books. [13] For the rest, we have tried to compare and supplement the sparse data thus obtained with the impressions we have been able to obtain from our meetings with individuals we believe to be well informed, from the meetings of Spanish communists we have attended in France, and even from novels which deal, at least in part, with the communists.

From a scientific point of view, such methods are of questionable value and no doubt increase the chances of misinterpretation and factual errors. We are ready to run these risks, in the belief that they are inescapable when one is dealing with an underground political movement.

Finally, we must ask whether it is right to publish the results of such an inquiry at this time. Is there not a danger that we might depict what is in fact but a fleeting situation, that we might attach too much importance to mere coincidence or even to literary fancy? Moreover, is there not also another danger, namely that we may give away too much information and thus unwittingly help the Spanish communists' persecutors?

On the first point: to publish a study of the Spanish communist movement would, even a few years ago, have been premature, in view of the seemingly immutable political situation imposed on Spain by the Franco regime. Throughout the entire period from 1939 to 1960, any study of the various opposition currents in Spain did in fact seem irrelevant, because of the strength of the regime and the weak response to these movements among the people.

Today, we face a different situation. Spain's economic development, the rebirth of the working-class and student opposition, as well as the fact that what almost amounts to a public debate has now resumed in Spain — all these factors are beginning to have a marked impact on the political life of the country and are transforming, albeit very slowly, the nature of the regime that came to power as a result of the Civil War. It is thus no longer pointless to inquire into the role the communists could play in the process of renewal. It would also be useful to examine the various symptoms, within the underground organisations, of the crisis which now affects the entire world communist movement.

It is, moreover, possible to avoid indiscretion by taking certain precautions with the publication and presentation of the information we have been able to obtain. As for the exact identity of the various organisations or individuals, we have made a point of mentioning only those we have gleaned from published evidence — printed or cyclostyled, overt or underground — so long as such material is available to any person wishing to make a systematic study of the subject. On the other hand, the few pieces of information which are truly new, and which we have obtained in the course of interviews, or by other means, are reproduced in such a way as not to give away any secret, however innocuous it might seem.

Having outlined the background of this undertaking and the reasons for

4

setting about it in the way we did, perhaps we should now look in detail at the problems with which it deals. Studies concerned with political parties functioning in the open usually analyse their outward aspects — their membership and organisation — considering them more or less integral parts of a nation's political life. In particular, they tend to stress their subjects' organisation and structure, the composition of their membership, their propaganda and their performance at the polls. With clandestine organisations, such an approach would be futile. These organisations are, of course, in no position to contest elections; they have to make their propaganda furtively. They therefore regard it as one of their main preoccupations to conceal their true situation as effectively as possible.

Moreover, it seems clear that the impact a clandestine party makes on the individual citizen, and its image in the eyes of the people — whether the result of its own past actions or of the propaganda of its opponents — are at least as important as facts and figures. They are certainly more important than in the case of parties working in the open. The ideologies and programmes of such parties, not easily accessible except to people living outside the country, are in any case a matter of guesswork rather than of exact knowledge as far as the people at home are concerned.

The fact that the Spanish communist movement has to work underground means that we must give greater weight to its hidden workings within the framework of the Franco regime than to its more obvious role, which might seem negligible. The great symbolic function of Spanish communism, both negative and positive, should not detract from the value of a study of its ideology, membership and policies. To concentrate too much on the image of communism might well be a waste of time, for the public are familiar with its impact. There is a danger in not highlighting sufficiently clearly the relationship between concrete reality and its image, whether positive or negative. We have therefore tried to maintain a balance between the need to present, on the one hand, an overall picture of communism in Spain and, on the other, a detailed analysis of the organisations that profess it. Our subject thus falls into two parts: one deals with the general impact of communism and anti-communism under the Franco regime, and the other with the various communist organisations, which we have tried to analyse as more or less distinct entities.

Although our conclusions about the general political situation might at first glance seem to contradict one another, they are in fact, in our view, complementary. The first of these conclusions, arrived at by Salvador de Madariaga, [14] is that the repression imposed by the Franco regime, and the propaganda it has made, merely served to raise the prestige of communism: any total ban on political activity tends to favour the parties which

5

are best prepared for clandestine work. In the case of Spain, this applies to the PCE above all. At the same time, official propaganda has the effect of inflating the importance of the Communist Party, both by crediting it with all opposition activity — including acts for which it has in no way been responsible — and by indiscriminately accusing most of the opposition of being communists. Salvador de Madariaga also believes that by conditioning the Spanish people to the absence of free information and political activity, the Franco regime has accustomed them to a passive acceptance of political doctrines revealed 'from on high' — a basic characteristic of communist method. [15]

Conversely, it may well be that the regime's exaggeration of the communist menace, and the very fact that there is an underground communist movement, may provide it with a welcome reason to justify its own existence. The story of a 'Red plot' [16] is cited again and again by the regime as a reason for the intervention of the military leaders against the lawful Spanish Government in 1936. Ever since then, official propaganda has never ceased to argue that there is an enduring communist danger to justify repressive measures and the claim that the regime is the only effective answer to 'Marxist subversion'. [17]

The policies and attitudes of the two opposing camps have been less clear-cut in the last few years, following the process of liberalisation set in motion by the regime in .1962, and the emergence of new extreme left opposition groups, many of them set up by communist dissenters. However, these changes affect relations between the PCE and other revolutionary underground organisations rather than the general policies of the regime, which retains its authoritarian and anti-communist outlook, even though it has tempered some of its harsher aspects.

Theories developed for an analysis of the internal structure of the Spanish communist movement seem at first sight to lead to conclusions which, like those explaining its place in the general political system, appear contradictory. One would in fact expect the tendency, shared by all communist parties, to lean towards cultural and social isolation, to be even more pronounced in the case of clandestine parties; for the very fact that a party has to conduct its activities underground gives rise to particularly close links between its members, who face the same dangers and share the same beliefs, in virtual isolation from the rest of the population. Moreover, the prolonged exile of so many members of the PCE, as well as the ostracism to which they have been exposed by other republican refugees would also, one would have thought, have tended to strengthen the Party's cohesion and the loyalty of its members to the values they have shared and to the organisation which has protected them.

On the other hand, the many splits which have afflicted the PCE and brought about the movement's present state of disunity would seem to indicate the contrary. In other words, they suggest that a party forced to operate in secret is more prone to splits. The reason for this would seem, above all, to be the chronic tensions which invariably develop between the leaders abroad and the communists at home. The many divisions which have occurred on the home front in more recent times are probably due partly to the dogmatism and splintering that dog all underground movements.

To sum up, the propositions outlined above can be put in one simple thesis: the fact that the communist movement has had to operate underground in Spain has on the one hand enhanced its prestige, at least by comparison with the other opposition movements. On the other hand, it has harmed the Party, particularly its effectiveness and unity. The ambivalence of this starting point is bound to mean that the conclusions we may arrive at are bound to be equally vague and uncertain. The first two chapters, which deal with the history of the communist movement in Spain before and after the Civil War, merely give a rough outline of the most essential facts relating both to the policies of the Spanish communists and the attitude of the Spanish people to communism. They also deal with the political role of the PCE and dissident communist groups under the Franco regime.

As regards the distinction we make in this work between the Communist Party of Spain and the other communist movements, it ought perhaps to be said that in one sense it is only a semantic one. In actual fact, the book deals for the most part with the PCE alone;[18] not because there is nothing known about the rival movements — which are also discussed — but because the 'original' Communist Party for a long time accounted for virtually the whole communist movement in Spain; because to this day it has retained a fairly definite predominance within the movement; and because, in the eyes of the mass of the Spanish people, it remains the embodiment of communism.

## Notes

[1] This study has been undertaken by the *Centre d'étude des relations internationales de la Fondation nationale des sciences politiques*, headed by M. Jean Meyriat, who secured the necessary financial backing and included the project in the Centre's research programme. The author is also indebted to the communists — both exiled and those living in Spain —

who have assisted him, as well as to the Spanish students who braved the perils of collecting and taking abroad some of the clandestine leaflets and periodicals used in this study. He also wishes to acknowledge the help he has received from the library of the *Internationaal Instituut voor Sociale Geschiedenis*, Amsterdam.

[2]   Such a study was carried out, for example, at the seminar organised by the *Fondation nationale des sciences politiques* on 1 and 2 March 1968.

[3]   This was the subject of a seminar held in May 1968 under the auspices of the *Centre d'étude*.

[4]   S.G. Payne: *Phalange. Histoire du fascisme espagnol*, Ruedo ibérico, Paris, 1965.

[5]   For example, the official history of the Party published by the PCE (*Historia del Partido comunista de España (versión abreviada)*, Editora Política, La Habana, 1964); or the indictment of communism by E. Comin Colomer (Historia del Partido comunista de España, Primera etapa, 2 vols., Editora nacional, Madrid, 1967.

[6]   See: G. Fernandez de la Mora 'La estasiología en España' *Revista de estudios políticos* 116, March—April 1961, pp. 5—48. Also worth noting is a brief but excellent general study on the Spanish parties by J.J. Linz: 'The party system of Spain: past and future' in S.M. Lipset and S. Rokkan (eds) *Party system and voter alignments*, The Free Press, New York 1967, pp. 197—282; also C.M. Lorenzo, *Les anarchistes espagnols et le pouvoir*, Ed. du Seuil, Paris 1961; and J. Becarud and G. Lapouge, *Anarchistes d'Espagne*, André Balland, Paris 1970.

[7]   Note in particular D.T. Cattell, *Communism and the Spanish Civil War*, University of California Press, Berkeley, Los Angeles, 1955. The official history of the PCE and the 'counter-history' published in Madrid by E. Comin Colomer also provided a good deal of information on this period. Moreover, most of the very numerous works on the Civil War give a great deal of space to the PCE.

[8]   See E. Castro Delgado, *J'ai perdu la foi à Moscou*, Gallimard, 1950; El Campesino (V. González), *La vie et la mort en URSS (1939—1949)*, Les Iles d'or, Plon, Paris 1950; J. Hernandez, *La grande trahison*, Flasquelle, Paris 1953.

[9]   The official mouthpiece of the PCE, the bi-monthly *Mundo obrero* has appeared with great regularity. The PCE also produces the reviews *Nuestra bandera* and *Realidad*, as well as a range of specialised periodicals. The two pro-Chinese parties publish *Mundo obrero (ML)* and *Vanguardia obrera*; and a theoretical review *Revolución española*.

[10]   See, particularly, the publications issued in the 'Editions sociales'

series and those published as part of the 'Colección Ebro' of the Editions du Globe.

[11]   See general bibliography.

[12]   M. Adam, *Étude sur les thèmes de l'opposition communiste en Espagne de 1945 à 1963*, Paris 1965 (Mémoire DES science politique).

[13]   The most accurate source for this is 'Spain', *Yearbook on International Communist Affairs 1966*, Stanford University Press, Stanford 1967, pp. 144—8.

[14]   S. de Madariaga, *Spain, a Modern History*, F.A. Praeger, New York 1968, p. 630.

[15]   This theory applies especially to the period up to 1958.

[16]   See B. Bolloten, *The Grand Camouflage*, Pall Mall Press, London 1960. Like all fascist regimes, Franco's government at first presented itself to the world as the embodiment of 'anti-communism' (an expression borrowed from M. Duverger, *Institutions politiques et droit constitutionnel*, 10th ed., Presses Universitaires de France, Paris 1968, p. 379).

[17]   In his history of Franco Spain, Max Gallo mentions in every chapter official statements about the 'plot' M. Gallo, *Histoire de l'Espagne franquiste*, Robert Laffant, Paris 1969.

[18]   Divided since September 1970 into two factions, headed by Santiago Carrillo and Enrique Lister respectively.

# 1   Origins of the Civil War

Any mention of Spanish communism almost automatically calls to mind the Civil War and the *Frente Popular* — the Popular Front. This approach — born of the emotive impact of these events both on the Spanish people themselves and on intellectuals abroad — is at the same time too historical, and promotes the ends of the side which emerged victorious from the conflict, since the image it suggests of Spanish communism is that of a movement which has had its day and which was the perpetrator of violence and bloodshed. This view of the Spanish communist movement is moreover a distortion of the truth, since it ignores the present phase in the long history of the PCE and of the organisations which have sprung from it.

This chapter will not lay too much stress on the current period, nor give a detailed account of it. All it is meant to do is shed light on the attitudes and reactions of the Spanish people today, whether communists, anti-communists or uncommitted.

The Civil War is by no means 'ancient history'. The Spaniards of the seventies have in fact completed their political apprenticeship under the impact of its events, which remain alive in the minds of those who lived through them, or have been passed on, in conflicting versions, to a younger generation by the contending propaganda machines.

Nor must we neglect the years preceding the Civil War and the early days of the Spanish communist movement. Every group is linked by a shared vocabulary, by values, standards and experience acquired over the years. The history of the PCE does not go back far enough for the origins of this group 'culture' to have been forgotten, above all among the members of the Party's leading elite. For example, the fact that the anarchists have for a long time greatly exceeded the Spanish communists in numbers and importance is by no means to be overlooked today, despite the apparent — and perhaps real — setbacks the libertarian trend has suffered.

## The roots of the PCE

The Communist Party of Spain first saw the light of day at the close of a period of working-class and peasant agitation which has many traits in common with the situation in Russia at the same time — and which the

11

Spaniards incidentally know as the 'Bolshevik triennium'.[1] The difference in the situation in the two countries — accidental but of decisive importance — was the absence in Spain of the charge which set off the Russian revolution: the World War in which Russia was involved. Also, Spain lacked a team of revolutionary leaders comparable to the Bolshevik élite headed by Lenin.

The situation in Spain was thus calculated to produce a strong echo of the Bolshevik revolution, but without being such as to give rise to an exact repetition of those events. According to J. Díaz del Moral, who was one of the best informed witnesses of the working-class movement in Andalusia at that time, as well as being one of its most acute analysts,

> the news [of the October Revolution] had an explosive effect on the active elements among the Spanish proletariat, especially the syndicalists and anarchists . . . . The propagandists and leaders of the working-class movement, who had been greatly discouraged,[2] threw themselves into the struggle with renewed vigour. The anarchist and syndicalist press spread the good news . . . . And as always, the hearts of the Andalusian people were fired before those of the people in the other regions.[3]

Moreover, an agrarian movement inspired by the communists developed in Cordoba Province from 1918 onward[4] and nineteen papers that proclaimed their support for the October Revolution either came into being or announced their support for the new communist movement in 1918 and 1919.[5]

However, those who held the reins of political power — the ruling élite, the middle class and business circles — frightened by the menace of subversion, were all too ready to stand up to the revolutionary moves arising from the economic and social conditions in Spain at that time. Moreover, the Spanish army was fully at the disposal of these people, to be used as an instrument of repression, thanks to the fact that the country had remained neutral in the 1914—18 war. It was therefore easy to contain the violent agitation which marked the 'Bolshevik triennium' (1917—20), and this 'victory' was confirmed three years later by the establishment of General Primo de Rivera's dictatorship. The policy of class collaboration then adopted caused a good deal of confusion and disunity for some time among both anarchists and communists.

The Communist Party of Spain thus came into being at a time when the country's rulers knew how to make the best of the means at their disposal to block the revolutionary process sparked off by the Soviet example. It emerged, moreover, in a working-class environment greatly influenced by the traditions of anarchism and anarcho-syndicalism, which in other countries were beginning to disappear. The Socialist Party, moreover, from time to time adopted 'maximalist' positions, in contrast with the reformism of other European social-democratic parties. These two forces had a decisive influence on the PCE, both at the time of its birth and in later stages. Together with the influences which resulted from the Civil War and the Party's protracted underground existence under the Franco regime, these factors were largely instrumental in moulding the original character of the Spanish communist movement.

As P. Broué and E. Témine put it:

> The Spanish working-class movement is unique. In other European countries the struggle which began within the First International between the followers of Marx and those of Bakunin ended with a victory for the former, who were in those days known as 'authoritarians'. . . . In Spain, on the other hand, the 'libertarians' — friends of Bakunin, united in a secret society known as the Social Democratic Alliance — emerged victorious. This was to have lasting consequences, leaving the imprint of anarchism and anarcho-syndicalism on the Spanish working-class movement.[6]

This non-Marxist majority movement, organised in the National Confederation of Labour (CNT),[7] at first favoured the establishment of formal links with the Communist International. Lenin, for his part, was perfectly aware that the Spanish working-class movement was predominantly anarchist and that it was essential to gain the support of the CNT, rather than that of the socialists organised in the PSOE, should it become necessary to choose between the two. On 17 December 1919, the CNT did in fact decide to join the International provisionally; and a delegate, Angel Pestaña, went to Moscow in June 1920.

However, although the Russians gave him a warm welcome and although he met Lenin, Pestaña's reaction to the proceedings he observed at the Second Congress of the International was definitely cool.[8] He abstained in the vote on the twenty-one conditions for admission to the organisation. On his return to Spain he reported very unfavourably on the Bolsheviks.[9]

Taking advantage of the fact that the National Committee of the CNT, whose members had been arrested in November 1920, had become powerless, a minority faction, which was in favour of the CNT's participation in the Third Congress of the International as well as in the Constituent Congress of the Red Trade Union International,[10] succeeded in having a five-member delegation[11] sent to Moscow for these two meetings, held in

June and July 1921. These delegates, all of whom belonged to the 'pro-communist' minority, had good contacts with the representatives of the two Spanish communist parties which had just been established — one by the Socialist Youth and one by a minority faction within the Socialist Workers' Party; but since their mandate was very much open to question, they were in no position to enter into any commitments, either political or organisational. They therefore behaved with considerable discretion and confined themselves mainly to attending the meetings of the Red Trade Union International, at which their leader, Andrés Nin, played an important part.

The manoeuvre of the minority faction grouped around Andrés Nin and Joaquín Maurín caused the final rupture with the CNT, as well as a split between that organisation on the one hand and the Communist Internatio-nal and Red Trade Union International on the other. In August 1921, the representatives of the majority, gathered at a plenum at Logroño, retro-spectively annulled the decision to send delegates to Moscow. In February 1922, the National Committee formally rejected Maurín's proposal that the CNT should affiliate with the Red Trade Union International. Finally, on 11 June 1922, a national conference in Zaragoza brought the struggle between the minority and majority factions to an end:[12] the CNT reaf-firmed its 'apolitical' position and withdrew the commitment, entered into provisionally in December 1919, to join the International. Instead, the conference decided that the CNT should join the International Workers' Association, which was to be set up officially six days later in Berlin.[13] Nin, Maurín, Arlandis and Ibáñez thereupon left the anarcho-syndicalist organisation and established the *Comités sindicalistas revolu-cionarios*, whose official mouthpiece was the journal *La Batalla*. Later, they joined the PCE, after it had been reunited.

These changes in the CNT occurred at the same time as those in the German, Italian, French and Russian anarcho-syndicalist movements, fol-lowing the campaign of persecution to which the Soviet authorities sub-jected the Russian anarchists, and the suppression of the Kronstadt sailors' mutiny. These changes also reflected very clearly the reserve with which the most important anarchist movement left in the world after the dis-appearance of the Russian movement viewed the prospect of membership on unequal terms in the Communist International.

The Spanish anarchists shared Lenin's view, which regarded Spain as the country destined to be the venue of the world's second working-class revolution. However, they considered that this revolution should be con-ducted in accordance with their own views, rather than follow the Soviet model, and they stuck firmly to this line after the break of 1922.

The CNT's membership was much larger than that of the communist, and even of the socialist,[14] organisations. The Communist Party thus seemed to be — until the Civil War, or at least until 1934 — the vehicle of an alien type of revolution. It appeared bureaucratic and unsuited to Spain's society and mentality. As a result, it was bound to adopt a defensive attitude towards the predominant anarchist movement.

A number of anarchists, including the 1921 minority faction and, some years later, the members of the Seville group headed by José Díaz, stood out against this line and joined the PCE. However, most of them did not stay there long; and their presence merely helped to aggravate the divisions which rent the Party. Later, they were to become its irreconcilable enemies, having either resigned from it or having been expelled. Others, such as José Díaz himself,[15] were to make a brilliant career in the Party, though they were never to reach an understanding with the CNT.

In the absence of an agreement between the Communist International and the Spanish anarcho-syndicalists, the Communist Party therefore came into being, as was the case in most neighbouring countries, as a result of schisms within the social-democratic movement, itself a comparatively minor factor in Spain.

The Socialist Youth, which at that time had 2,000 members, had had differences with its elders in the PSOE[16] since the closing years of the First World War. While the officials of the main wing of the Socialist Party were divided into pro-Allied, pro-German and neutral factions, the young took a completely different view and tended to sympathise with the pacifist 'Zimmerwald' trend.[17] These differences grew more acute after the October Revolution. On 15 April 1919 they resulted in the Madrid branch of the *Juventud socialista* taking control of the *Federación de juventudes socialistas* and transforming it into the *Partido communista español* on 9 December 1919.

This first communist party to be established in Spain gained the support of half the members of the Socialist Youth, i.e. approximately 1,000 people.[18] Its official mouthpiece was the weekly *El Comunista*, the first issue of which appeared on 1 May 1920.

It immediately became apparent that the Socialist Youth initiative was premature. Above all, it provoked strong resistance from the pro-communist minority in the 'adult' socialist organisation and was condemned by the PSOE's Secretary-General, Daniel Anguiano, despite the fact that he was in favour of his party's affiliation to the International.[19]

All this did not prevent the extraordinary congress of the Socialist Party, held on 19 June 1920, from reversing its original refusal to adhere to the International, announced in December 1919. Two delegates were sent to Moscow to attend the International's Third Congress. The first, D. Anguiano, represented the party's pro-communist left wing; the second, Fernando de Los Ríos, supported the right. The two men returned from Moscow with conflicting views as to the response to be made to the twenty-one conditions for admission. De Los Ríos published a report opposing the conditions, while Anguiano was to become one of the leaders of the Spanish Communist Workers' Party, [20] set up by the minority faction after the official refusal to join the International, announced on 13 April 1921. [21] Since it could no longer use the party's premises, this second communist organisation set up its headquarters in the New School in Los Madrazo street. Its mouthpiece was the weekly *Guerra Social*.

The two rival communist parties thereafter engaged in polemics [22] until their merger, under the auspices of the International, which sent Professor Grazadei, an Italian Deputy and Marxist economist, to Spain to act as mediator.

The new unified party, established at a conference which took place from 7 to 14 November 1921, took the name of Communist Party of Spain, [23] which it retains to this day. Its first paper was the weekly *La Antorcha*, which replaced *El Comunista* and *Guerra Social* and the circulation of which is said to have been between five and six thousand copies. The Party had some 1,200 members. [24]


## A troubled childhood

The disputes between the various groups within the PCE continued after the merger. A succession of quarrels and schisms ensued and for over ten years prevented the Spanish communist movement from making any real progress.

A faction which, though a minority in the Central Committee had a majority on the Committee of the Communist Youth League, and was joined by a number of ex-members of the Socialist Youth, published a manifesto in 1922 attacking the incumbent Party leaders. The disciplinary measures taken against its members in March of that year made some of them leave the Party, to form the *Unión de cultura proletaria*. This organisation remained affiliated to the Communist International. Discontent also broke out among the majority that had left the PSOE to join the Party; García Quejido, Lamoneda and Anguiano left the Communist Party soon after the Congress held in the summer of 1923. [25]. The first two rejoined the party to which they originally belonged and were soon followed by the majority of ex-PSOE members. D. Anguiano henceforth remained outside any party.[26] Many members of the Socialist Youth and the majority of former PSOE members having quit the Party, it consisted from then on mostly of ex-anarchists and a minority group, made up of former members of the Socialist Youth who remained faithful to it.

This crisis forced the International to intervene in Spain once more. The man it entrusted with this task was Jules Humbert-Droz, its delegate for the Latin countries. A former Swiss Protestant pastor living in Paris, Humbert—Droz continued to act periodically as the PCE's mentor until the early thirties, when he was replaced by Palmiro Togliatti.

Small as it was at the outset,[27] the Party's ranks shrank even further as a result of these defections. Although it officially claims to have had 5,000 members in 1924 — the same membership as it had claimed for 1922[28] — it would seem that in fact its membership shrank from 1,200 in 1921 to a mere 500 in 1924.[29] The figure remained at this level throughout Primo de Rivera's dictatorship, and had risen to only 800 on the eve of the proclamation of the Republic in 1931.[30]

The ban imposed on the PCE in 1923 by the government of Primo de Rivera made its position even more difficult, and to some extent explains its rapid decline. Since the authorities had scant respect for the Party because of its weakness and its internal dissensions, it was hardly interfered with until late in 1923. The communist press was in fact not even banned. In addition to *La Antorcha*, mouthpiece of the Party Central Committee, a number of regional papers were published, such as *La Bandera roja* in Vizcaya province, *Nueva aurora* at Pontevedra and *El Comunista balear* in Majorca.

However, towards the end of 1923 many of the Party's members were arrested. More arrests followed throughout 1924 and 1925. As a result, the Party was virtually destroyed and those members of its Executive Committee who remained at liberty sought refuge in Paris. This flight to Paris followed a partial replacement of the leadership, which was accused of opportunism at the Fifth Congress of the Comintern in June and July 1924, an event which marked the start of the 'Bolshevisation' of communist parties. In this phase too came the rise in importance of a group of men who had originally belonged to the CNT, the leaders of which were J. Maurín, Martín Sastre and González Canet. However, the exile and subsequent arrest of these three leaders in 1924 and 1925 were soon to put an end to the growing influence of the group, which before long began to be suspected of Trotskyite sympathies.

Even before the expulsion, first of the 'leftists' and then of the 'Trotskyites', more and more people began, in the 1924—27 period, to quit the ranks of the Party and join all sorts of other organisations. In 1924, on their return from the Fifth Congress of the Communist International, two of the Party's delegates, Boyas y Valls and Grau Jassens, left its ranks. The former joined the CNT and the latter the Catalan *Esquerra* (Left). In the ensuing years the majority of ex-anarchists followed their example. In 1925, Oscar Pérez Solís — a former artillery captain who became Secretary-General of the PCE after the expulsion of the leaders who had formerly belonged to the Socialist Youth — quit the Party while in prison, having been persuaded to 'return to the true faith'. He later obtained a comparatively well-paid post in the oil monopoly at Valladolid. [31] The former leader of the Party faction whose members had originally belonged to the Socialist Youth, Ramón Merino Gracia, became one of the leading founders of a 'yellow' 'free trade union' when he came out of prison. Finally, in 1927, another ex-leader of the Socialist Youth, Juan Andrade, also engaged in factional activities, working hand in hand with Andrés Nin, who had failed in his bid for the post of Secretary-General because of his links with Trotsky.

J. Bullejos, who left France to settle in Bilbao, secured two successes in 1927–28. The first was that he managed to persuade a major CNT group in Seville, including the bulk of the port, transport, engineering and bakery workers, to support the Party. Led by Manuel Adame Misa, Antonio Mije, Manuel Delicado Muñoz, Jesús Bulnes and José Díaz Ramos, [32] these new recruits were soon to form one of the main strongholds of communist trade unionism. Their leaders experienced changing fortunes within the Party apparatus. M. Adame took his place at the side of Bullejos and Gabriel León Trilla in the leadership. Four years later, however, he was displaced by another ex-CNT man, J. Díaz.

The second communist success was the miners' strikes in the Asturias region, called in protest against Primo de Rivera's plan for a National Assembly. These stoppages were the first political campaigns of any importance the Communist Party managed to organise in Spain, and they reflected a certain growth in its internal cohesion. Not a single action taken by the Party had up to that time made any real impact. It confined itself in the main to self-defence and mutual aid and even practised anarchist-type *pistolerismo*, according to the anti-communist author E. Comín Colomer, who claims that this was how G. León Trilla succeeded in saving the anarchist murderer of Premier Dato, killed on 8 March 1921. Later he says, Trilla was involved in an attack on the Civil Guards. In 1923, it was by such means that he forced the workers of the Altos Hornos de Vizcaya company to proclaim a strike. A defector from the communist ranks, Jesús Hernández says that he and Trilla agreed to murder the socialist leader Indalecio Prieto by blowing up the offices of a newspaper in Bilbao of which Prieto was the editor. [33]

However, these relative successes achieved by Bullejos did not put an end to the Party's gradual erosion. Following the strikes in the Asturias region, arrests of Party members continued until the fall of Primo de Rivera in January 1930. Most of the members of the Central Committee were arrested and the Party leaders were once again forced to flee to Paris. It was there that the Third Congress of the PCE was held in August 1929. The restoration of civil liberties by the government of General Berenguer in 1930 did little to reduce the pressures on the Party, which remained banned.

In 1929, the Party suffered a further schism. A large section of the regional organisation for Catalonia and the Balearic Islands, the mouthpiece of which was the review *La Batalla*, [34] left its ranks. The leaders of this faction were Miratvilles and J. Arquer, who took with them a large part of the membership and soon formed the Workers' and Peasants' Bloc. [35]

José Bullejos also had difficulties with Moscow, relations with which had deteriorated. The difficulties started in 1927, when he refused to comply with a Comintern instruction that the communists should contest the National Assembly elections planned by Primo de Rivera. The elections, incidentally, never took place. Subsequently, his relations with the International were further strained, following the call for intensified class struggle issued by the 1928 Comintern congress. The instruction that the struggle should be waged on two fronts — that is, both against the bourgeois parties and the 'social-fascists' (in other words, the socialists) — forced the Secretary-General of the Party to withhold the PCE's support from the Republic, which had been proclaimed on 14 April 1931. The PCE thereafter fomented a whole series of pointless disturbances and strikes, and even attempts at revolution which did not stand the slightest chance of success. [36]

This policy was not calculated to improve relations with the socialists and anarchists, bad as they were already.[37] Armed clashes occurred with the socialists, in the course of which a group led by Jesús Hernández killed two UGT members. The anarchists' anxiety to counter PCE competition led them to establish the Iberian Anarchist Federation, better known by its initials FAI. Its role was to prevent the workers from drifting into either social-democrat reformism or Soviet-oriented communism. All in all, the seven years of the Primo de Rivera dictatorship and the first year of the Republic can be said to have led to the eclipse of the communists, whereas the socialists and anarchists emerged strengthened from this phase.

The Comintern, to undo the damage caused partly by its own inept orders (it officially cancelled them in 1934), decided to overhaul the set-up in Spain yet again. Foreign advisers were sent to carry out the reorganisation. In 1931 and 1932, the Argentinian Vitorio Codovila, the Frenchman Rabaté and the Peruvian César Falcón joined the Bulgarian Stepanov, who had been in Spain since 1928. [38]

On 23 August 1931 the PCE began publishing a new official organ, the weekly *Mundo obrero*, financed partly by the International. [39] From 14 November 1931, it was issued as a daily. *Mundo obrero* replaced the weekly *La Antorcha*, founded in 1929. [40] A theoretical review, *Bolchevismo*, also first appeared in 1931, but ceased publication the following year — after the expulsion of Bullejos — because of the lack in Spain of theoreticians of adequate calibre. [41]

The Fourth Party Congress, which met from 17 to 23 March 1932 in Seville, [42] was the prelude to the elimination of the leading group, consisting of Bullejos, Adame and Leon Trilla, which was meeting with increasing opposition from the Political Bureau, reshuffled the year before. [43] All three were expelled from the Bureau on 19 August 1932, following a stormy debate on the advisability of answering a summons to attend a plenum of the Comintern Executive Committee. Having in the end decided to go to Moscow, the three former leaders were kept in Russia until the beginning of 1933. Their expulsion from the PCE was announced during this forced sojourn, on 21 October 1932. Bullejos was replaced by José Díaz as Secretary-General. The ostensible reason for this was that the leadership had issued an 'opportunist' slogan by calling for the 'defence of the Republic' at the time of General Sanjurjo's anti-republican putsch on 10 and 11 August 1932. In actual fact, Bullejos was probably sacrificed in a tactical manoeuvre in favour of the Republic on which the International decided in 1932. It was felt this move would be easier if the Party leadership were replaced.

Even before the expulsion of Bullejos, the reorganisation of the Party gave rise to another important step: the setting-up of a communist trade union body, the CGTU. [44] Founded in 1931, this organisation resembled the French CGTU and pursued the same tactics of 'fighting on two fronts'. But it did not have the same strength, with a membership of no more than 50,000 to 90,000 at the end of 1932, [45] mostly concentrated among the railwaymen of the north, in Seville and in Asturias. At that time, the CNT and the UGT had 1,200,000 and 1,042,000 members respectively. [46]

This divisive move caused a total break-up, leading to overt opposition, with mutually hostile groups in which Nin, Maurín, Portela, Andrade, Arquer and Miratvilles were the leading spirits. It was at this time that J. Maurín joined the Workers' and Peasants' Bloc, which resulted from the merger of the *Batalla* group and Arquer's *Partit comunista catalá*. A. Nin and J. Andrade founded the Communist Left in 1931. Initially of Trotskyite inspiration, this group had few members but included some theoreticians of stature, whose mouthpiece was the review *Comunismo*. After Nin's break with Trotsky in 1934, all these people, urged on by J. Gorkin, drew together and eventually joined forces in the POUM [47] on 29 September 1935.

The communists' blunders prevented them from gaining a much larger following in the first three years of the Republic. True, the chance to operate legally for the first time since 1923 [48] allowed them to pick up some votes in the 1931 and 1933 elections as well as to increase their membership, but their showing in these two fields was in no way comparable to the socialists' or to the volume of abstentions organised by the anarchists. [49] Thus, in the Cortes elections of 28 June 1931, the PCE polled 190,606 votes, or 4·4 per cent of the votes cast, without securing a single seat. [50] Moreover, the elections showed that the communists had practically no following among the electorate, except in the areas where they had been established since before the Republic — in Andalusia, in Vizcaya and, marginally, in Zaragoza. [51] In the elections to the Legislative Assembly in 1933, the Party obtained 340,000 votes out of 8,000,000 but only one deputy, elected in Malaga. [52] Its percentage of the vote was no greater than in 1931. By comparison, the socialists won 116 out of a total of 446 seats in 1931 and 59 out of 473 in 1933.

Nor did the Party's membership grow very much in these three years. Its own claim was that it rose from 800 early in 1931 [53] to 16,000 in January 1933, no fewer than 20,000 in April of the same year [54] and to 30,000 plus 11,000 Young Communists in November, [55] dropping to 20,000 in March [56] and October 1934. [57] But it would seem that these official figures must be pretty drastically reduced to arrive at the truth. The first figure — that for 1931 — is probably the only genuine one. Comín Colomer estimates that the PCE reached a membership of 3,000 by the end of 1931 [58] and that it had somewhere between 5,000 and 10,000 members in the 1932–34 period. The progress it made was certainly quite marked, especially in Madrid, Seville and the Asturias, where considerable numbers of skilled workers in the CGTU were communists. The PCE, moreover, profited from the rivalries between the socialists and the anarchists, offering itself as mediator and playing the role of a party more given to careful thought than the PSOE. In this way it managed to attract a number of intellectuals and officials, including some regular officers, such as Lieutenant-Colonel Luis Barceló and Captain Márquez, a member of the President's bodyguard. Nevertheless, even if we accept the official figures, communist membership does not bear comparison with that of the socialists, which rose to over 50,000 in 1934. Although a similar comparison with the anarchists is difficult, since they refused to organise themselves as a party and joined either the CNT[59] or the clandestine revolutionary organisation FAI,[60] the contrast between their numbers and those of the communists is just as great.

Up to 1934, the PCE and its offshoot, the CGTU, thus amounted to a relatively second-rank political force, with its roots for the most part among the élite of the working class. Its tactical blunders, attributable largely to the Comintern's instructions, and the persecutions to which it was still subjected because of its extremist attitudes,[61] only partially accounted for this weakness. The anarchists were making mistakes at least as grievous at the same time, and were being even more fiercely oppressed, without losing their popular support to the same extent. A few months later, at the time of the Asturias rising in October 1934, the socialists likewise ran some pretty unsuccessful campaigns, but nevertheless retained the greater part of their support.

In fact, the weakness of the communists arose more from factors connected with Spain's political and working-class traditions than from the incidentals of the immediate situation. The first of these factors is the dominating influence of the anarcho-syndicalist tradition on the Spanish working-class movement. In the rural areas of the south in particular, the quasi-religious influence of the apostles of the anarchist millennium still fits best the thought-patterns and ideological needs of the rural poor living on the fringes of economic and industrial evolution. And, while it is true that anarcho-syndicalism also predominates in industrialised Catalonia, one should bear in mind that the Catalan working population includes a large proportion of recent immigrants from Andalusia and Murcia, working in technologically backward factories.

The socialists' success in preserving their prestige intact in Spain in the early thirties was another obstacle in the path of the communists. As J.J. Linz says:

> The brief period during which they took part in the republican government was not long enough for their followers to become disillusioned, the more so as the party, under Largo Caballero, very soon adopted maximalist positions, which, incidentally, led rapidly

to the inept and ill-fated revolution of October 1934. This maximalist policy of the socialists prevented the communists from presenting
themselves as radical competitors to the CNT, or even the
PSOE. . . . [62]

## Popular Front: the turning-point

After twelve years of impotence, stagnation and sometimes of retreat,
1934 marks a turning-point in the history of the PCE. In some respect it
was the take-off point of the Communist Party in Spain. It was the year in
which it acquired many of the characteristic features that distinguish it to
this day.

The first signs of a change can in fact be discerned in 1933, with the
attempt to launch a so-called working-class 'common front' policy, the
aim of which for the communists was to break out of their isolation, at
the cost of having to draw nearer to the socialists. This first attempt
misfired. The PSOE rejected the PCE's overtures. Likewise, it turned
down an offer that the two parties be merged, made by Vitorio Codovila
to Francisco Largo Caballero in 1934. [63]

The real coming together took place, as it were, in the heat of battle, in
October 1934, during the Asturias rising. Inspired by Largo Caballero and
the majority left wing of the Socialist Party, [64] this uprising was part and
parcel of a plan for a nationwide revolt, intended to put a stop to the
conservative measures of the government which came to power after the
1933 elections [65] and to replace it by a government of the people. With
the approval of the Comintern, which had shortly before adopted the
Popular Front formula, [66] the Spanish communists were willy-nilly carried
along in a course of action that was chosen by others and failed almost
immediately throughout virtually the whole of Spain. Like the socialists,
they played practically no part in the Barcelona rising — crushed almost
instantly by the army — which stayed loyal to the authorities in Madrid.
They played a bigger part in the preparations for a rising in Madrid. In the
event, this scheme was, however, abandoned, in view of the conspiracy's
failure in the remainder of the country.

In the Asturias, on the other hand, the communists, together with the
anarchists and the socialists, took on a considerable burden of responsibility. They took a particularly active part towards the end of the rising,
after the defection of the anarchist leaders, and took command of the
defence in a desperate situation. It was then — on 10 October 1934 — that
the Communist International made its appeal to the Socialist Workers'

International to defend the Spanish proletariat. The response was favourable, and a meeting between representatives of the two organisations took place five days later in Brussels.

Although the immediate cost of the Asturias rising was the arrest of a great many of the communist militants and leaders involved in it, and indeed also of many anarchists and socialists, this change of policy was to prove very worthwhile. First and foremost, it was good for the PCE's prestige. No longer was the Party ostracised by the other working-class organisations and the rank-and-file of the workers. In particular, it was from then on that Dolores Ibarruri became the idol of a large part of the working class. The outcome was also very satisfactory so far as the communist press was concerned: its circulation rose considerably with the lifting of the ban on it. The circulation of the daily *Mundo obrero* went up from 35,000 in October 1934, to 55,000 when it reappeared in January 1936. [67] Moreover, the underground press proliferated during the time of repression and reached a new type of reader. [68] The circulation of the Central Committee's clandestine paper *Bandera roja*, which stood at 5,000 at the end of 1934, reached 17,000 in the spring of 1935. [69]

Party membership also made considerable headway. If communist sources are to be believed, it rose from 20,000 in October 1934 [70] to 35,000 in February 1936 and 102,000 in May of the same year. [71] In actual fact, it seems probable that membership rose from less than 3,000 in 1934 to 10,000 in February 1936 [72] and 50,000 on the eve of the Civil War. [73]

But it is in the area of relations with the Socialist Party that the PCE's position improved most markedly. Its first move was to jettison the CGTU in order to strengthen the alliance. The merger of the communist trade union organisation with the UGT was officially announced on 11 November 1934. This sacrifice was largely cancelled out by the gains the communists made at the socialists' expense in the next two years.

Disillusioned by their experience of government at the outset of the Republic and by the conservative backlash of the *biennio negro*, the socialists were undergoing a 'revolutionary transformation' at this time, turning their backs on the reformism they had displayed during Primo de Rivera's dictatorship and up to 1933. They, and their left wing in particular, were consequently quite prepared to collaborate closely with the communists and even to forge some organic links with them. Their Secretary-General, F. Largo Caballero, had discovered Marxist theory during his stay in prison after the Asturias rising. Surrounded by young advisers, themselves Marxists of longer standing, [74] he began to dream of transplanting the Soviet revolution to Spain with the support of the USSR and the PCE.

The communists went all out to extract the maximum of advantage from these favourable circumstances. They flattered Largo Caballero, whom the socialists at that time saw as the Spanish Lenin, and stepped up the number of joint actions with the socialists, as well as contacts with those of their leaders who supported closer links with the communists, such as R. Llopis and the Marxist historian A. Ramos Oliveira. They saw to it that some of them, such as J. Zugazagoitia, J. Alvarez del Vayo and S. Carrillo were invited to the USSR. The communists also benefited from the merger of the CGTU and the UGT, which enabled them to gain a firmer foothold in the new single trade union organisation, especially in Madrid and Barcelona. Finally, they established ties of gratitude with many of the socialists who were helped by International Red Aid during the period of repression which followed the Asturias rising. Of 612 people who had suffered political victimisation because of their left-wing opinions and were helped in July 1935 by the International Red Aid, 220 were socialists, 206 communists, 23 anarchists, and eight left-wing republicans; 155 belonged to no party. [75]

This policy enabled the Party to draw closer and closer to the Socialist Youth. The latter proclaimed its adherence to Marxism in 1935 and merged with the Communist Youth in April 1936, to form the *Juventud socialista unificada*, or JSU. Before very long, the Secretary-General of that organisation, Santiago Carrillo, as well as the principal leaders of the Socialist Youth, F. Melchor and J. Cazorla, joined the PCE. [76] After those Young Socialists who had been opposed to the merger had left the JSU [77] it became a sort of appendage and membership reserve for the Communist Party.

The erosion of the socialist ranks by the PCE produced even better results for the latter in Catalonia, where communists, socialists and two other Catalan working-class parties [78] merged and established the United Socialist Party of Catalonia or PSUC. [79] This organisation was officially set up a few days after the outbreak of the Civil War, on 23 July 1936. The PSUC joined the Communist International in 1939, independently of the PCE. Nevertheless, despite some opposition, it soon became little more than the Catalan branch of the Communist Party.

The Communists also profited from the share-out of the seats won by the Popular Front coalition in the elections of 16 February 1936. The sixteen seats they were allotted [80] — out of 267 seats gained by the left — marked a big advance compared with the solitary seat the Party had won in 1933, and probably more than it would have gained had it not belonged to the coalition.

From the end of 1935 onwards, however, the progress the PCE was making began to worry the socialists. This disquiet became more pro-

nounced after the merger of the socialist and communist youth organisations — a move which annoyed Largo Caballero — and grew still more with
the establishment of the PSUC. Moreover policy differences also began to
appear: the left-wing socialists took up extremist positions [81] at a time
when the communists were beginning to moderate their stance as part of
their new policy, which called for an alliance of all anti-fascist forces,
adopted at the Seventh Congress of the Communist International in
August 1935.


## The Civil War: finest hour of the PCE

In the military uprising of 18 July 1936 and the subsequent Civil War,
which lasted until 1 April 1939, the Communist Party behaved even more
markedly as the most moderate, most trustworthy and most effective of
all working-class organisations. As a result, the PCE came to be considered
between 1936 and 1939 as a sort of 'party of order' in the republican
camp, anxious to defend parliamentary democracy rather than to promote
an immediate social revolution. As a close ally of the bourgeois republican
parties, linked ever more firmly to the right wing of the Socialist Party,
the communists obtained the support of a large section of the middle class
who had remained in the loyalist zone. While the motives of some of these
people were selfish, others were impressed by the PCE's efficiency. However, another side of the communists also began to emerge at that time:
that of an organisation dominated by 'mentors' from Moscow, ready to
resort to any means to rid itself of opponents and to get its hands on the
levers of power.

The Communist Party became a 'party of order' first and foremost
because it was militarily and politically effective — in marked contrast to
the ineptitude of the other working-class forces. Its efficiency was due to
a centralised organisation and the presence of a large body of advisers sent
by the Comintern. Another reason was the rapid growth of its membership in Madrid just before and during the first months of the war. The
Party's strength in the capital enabled it to buttress a succession of republican governments [82] at a time when it was virtually isolated. Later,
when Largo Caballero's government had left the capital, [83] it took over
the defence of Madrid.

In the political field, moreover, the PCE was the only working-class
party which genuinely supported the Giral government. In doing so, it was
obeying the advice of the Comintern, which considered it essential to keep
a republican regime of a largely liberal and bourgeois complexion in power

and to avoid a revolutionary break, which might have alienated the Western democracies, with these forces. As far as the communists were concerned, the republican government must stand for constitutional continuity; it must not be a 'Red' regime fighting the forces of conservatism. This was why they reacted to the formation of Largo Caballero's government with such scant enthusiasm and only agreed to join it after pressure had been put on them by their Comintern advisers. [84] Later, after some stormy debates, the same advisers made the PCE leaders withdraw their support from Largo Caballero and back the more moderate — and more easily controlled — PSOE. This too, is why they lent their support — decisive, as it turned out — to the establishment of the Negrín government.

The communists' moderation was also reflected in the policies they persuaded the governments they joined to pursue. Their immediate objective was to win the war in league with the middle classes and the peasants. For them, 'fighting for a democratic republic with a broad social content' was a secondary consideration. [85] As José Díaz declared in 1936: 'There can at this time be no question of establishing either a dictatorship of the proletariat, or socialism; only of fighting for democracy against fascism'. [86] After the augmented plenum held in Valencia from 5 to 8 March 1937, José Díaz reaffirmed this policy, mentioning only the need to set up a 'democratic republic of a new type'. [87]

In the event, this studiedly moderate policy of the communists led to occasional violent disputes with the anarchists and left-wing socialists, especially after the Negrín government had taken office. Backed by the communists, the latter launched a sort of 'counter-revolution' in May 1937 to restore its authority. The government's authority was threatened by the activities of the CNT and the plans for a joint UGT—CNT trade unionist administration — a scheme which led to the downfall of Largo Caballero. No longer hailed as 'the Spanish Lenin', Caballero was dubbed 'bureaucrat', 'machine politician' and 'saboteur of unity'. This was the turning-point which marked the end of the revolutionary course in land tenure and the collectivisation of firms.

In agriculture, the communists and republicans were opposed to the collective farming of land confiscated from the big landowners and the Church and favoured its division and free distribution among the peasants. The anarchists and socialists, on the other hand, advocated the nationalisation and collectivisation of large estates. It was this view which prevailed at first, the anarchists going ahead with immediate collectivisation in the area under their control, though it was in fact a communist Minister of Agriculture, Vicente Uribe, who promulgated a decree — dated 7 October 1936 — ordering the collectivisation of confiscated land. Before long, however, the PCE retracted its support for this measure and set up an anti-collectivist Peasant League, presided over by F. Mateu.

About collectivisation, José Díaz said, on 5 March 1937, that 'to plunge into such an experiment would be absurd and would amount to allying ourselves with the enemy'. [88] At about that time a dispute arose between Uribe and the Valencia branch of the CNT, which demanded the right to export for its own profit the oranges harvested in the area under its control. [89] The arrival of the Negrín government later enabled the communist Minister of Agriculture to launch an anti-collectivist counter-attack. This escalated as the summer went on, especially in Aragon. In this region, which had up to then been dominated by a Council of Defence of anarcho-syndicalist leanings and where 'libertarian communist' administrations had been set up in most villages, regular army units under the command of the communist Lister launched a systematic drive on 10 August to dismantle the collective farms. They restored the collectivised lands, implements, horses and cattle to their former owners or their dependants, dismantled any newly-constructed buildings specifically designed for collective use, arrested 600 anarchist officials and even went so far as to encourage small farmers who had retaken possession of their holdings to attack the remaining collective farms. [90]

The communists and republicans adopted a similar attitude to small- and medium-sized industrial and commercial undertakings, saying that they were not prepared to tolerate a situation 'where neither the individual citizen nor his property is guaranteed in the slightest degree'. [91] On 8 August 1936, only three weeks after the outbreak of the Civil War, Jesús Hernández was already saying: 'We cannot speak today of a proletarian revolution in Spain, for historical conditions do not allow it. We want to protect industrial enterprises of modest size which are in difficulties. In fact, we wish to protect them at least as much as the workers themselves'. [92] In his speech on 5 March 1937 in Valencia, José Díaz again stressed this aspect of the Party's policy, noting the need to defend the 'small industrialist' and 'small trader' and speaking of 'premature experiments' in collectivisation and socialisation. In a speech in Barcelona on 29 November 1938 at a meeting called by the Ibero-American Union, he again took the same line, declaring that the state was in no position to organise the entire market by itself. [93]

The communists put these principles into practice in the areas under their control, particularly in Madrid, where commercial firms, industry and even private banks retained a more important position than in Catalonia and in the Levante region. But the communists clashed with the anarchists in Barcelona, where they tried to give a freer hand in food distribution to private trade.[94] They helped the Negrín government to halt the socialisation of confiscated firms, some of which were in fact restored to their former owners.

As regards religion, the communists went out of their way to reassure liberal Catholics by adopting more subtle tactics than those of the socialists and particularly the anarchists. Even before the Civil War, they had been in touch with certain Christian groups which at a later date would have been called 'progressive'. As a result, they were able to persuade Father Juan García Morales — the 'republican priest' — to write articles for *Ayuda,* the journal of the International Red Aid. During the first few months of the Civil War, the Communist Party held out a protecting hand over members of the clergy who were in danger. At least one of these priests joined the Party, according to the paper *ABC* of 4 September 1936.[95] A few weeks before that, a Party card was issued to the statue of the *Cristo del gran poder* in Seville, to make sure it was not damaged.

The Party's advances to the Catholics became more urgent in 1937. Santiago Carrillo, Secretary-General of the United Socialist Youth, said that the organisation should establish by the end of the year 'links with young republicans, young anarchists and young Catholics fighting for freedom'.[96] In a speech to the Central Committee in Valencia in March 1937, the Party's Secretary-General, José Díaz, likewise took pains to say that he did not view all Christians in the same light. What needed to be done, he said, was to 'destroy the economic and political power of the Church, which has been at the heart of a conspiracy against the interests of the masses and has been one of the main pillars of semi-feudal Spain. To this end, Church property must be confiscated and nationalised'. But Díaz added: 'The struggle against the semi-feudal economic and political domination of the Church must on no account be confused with a struggle against religion as such. On the contrary: only a republican, democratic, free and progressive Spain will guarantee religious freedom in the country'.[97] In June, according to Louis Fischer,[98] the Communist Party was the first to call for the reopening of religious places and to protest against the violence to which Catholics had been subjected the year before.

Being the party of order for reasons of military efficiency and in response to the Comintern's instructions, and the party which called for a rapprochement with bourgeois parties and regimes, the PCE had no choice but to take up the position it did in the political spectrum. Its studied moderation was an almost inevitable response to the extremism of its anarchist, socialist and 'Poumista'[99] rivals. Its moderate stance, moreover, followed inescapably from the alliances it was forced to conclude with political groupings which were anything but in favour of revolutionary change.

The communists, in fact, had nothing to gain from trying to outdo the anarcho-syndicalists and Largo Caballero socialists in extremism. It would have been virtually impossible for them to have used more immoderate language than these people or to have been more precipitate in socialisation. Even had such a policy been practicable, it would have been most unlikely to detach any supporters from these two political movements in any significant numbers, since their popular following remained very substantial in the years 1936–39. By taking a moderate line, on the other hand, the PCE was able to gain the support of the mass of the 'non-party' public, frightened by the prospect of an immediate revolution and not at all confident of the power of the weak republican parties to protect them. At the same time, the PCE was the only more or less reliable ally of these parties, whose effectiveness depended almost entirely on the goodwill and material aid the communists alone could provide once the Soviet Union was the only foreign country helping the Spanish Republic.

The President of the Republic, Manuel Azaña – without a doubt the outstanding bourgeois politician to remain loyal to the lawful government – acknowledged this fact from the very outset of the war. Paying tribute to the assistance the communists were giving the Giral government, he told a visitor on 25 August 1936: 'If you want to understand the situation as it really is, and get to know men who know what they want, read *Mundo obrero*'.[100] A little more than a year later, in June 1937, the President of the Republic confided to the reporter Louis Fischer, who interviewed him in Valencia, that he would be sorely tempted to join the Communist Party were it not for the fact that such a move might well be misunderstood abroad.[101]

The socialists of Indalecio Prieto's reformist wing for some time maintained good relations with the communists, their chief allies in the Negrín government. At one time Prieto went so far as to advocate a merger between the PSOE and the PCE.[102] Not even the troubles that followed what became known as the 'Prieto incident' of November 1937[103] prevented the communists and Premier Negrín from working hand in hand, realistic politicians that they were, right up to the very last days of the war.

But, except for the factions headed by Dr Negrín and J. Alvarez del Vayo, the communists lost most of their moderate republican and socialist allies, as well as their followers of more recent vintage,[104] during the last days of the struggle. These new opponents joined hands with the

30

anarchists, the socialists of Largo Caballero's wing and the 'Poumistas' in opposing the PCE. They openly accused the communists not only of failing to keep good faith as allies of the moderate elements, but of being the tools in a plot to turn republican Spain into the Soviet Union's first satellite — a place where the Communist International was free to settle accounts with its opponents at will. These people held that the 'order' restored with the support of the communists would have been used by the latter, not for the legitimate purpose of defeating Franco, but as a cover for their own hegemonistic aims. The three reasons usually cited in support of this accusation are: (1) the communists' gradual assumption of control over the army and police; (2) the PCE's loss of independence to the Comintern and its emissaries in Spain; and (3) the brutal liquidation of the PCE's leftist rivals.[105] The Party was also accused of having been involved in the transfer of the Bank of Spain's gold to the USSR.

There can be no doubt that the communists gradually occupied positions of increasing importance in the republican army's High Command and Political Department. This was due largely to the fact that they made a greater contribution than any other political faction to the formation of new regular units (a move which the anarchists opposed on principle). They were also at one time able to gain the support of a great many loyalist regular officers. The Fifth Regiment, fielded entirely by the communists, was virtually the nursery of the Army of the Centre, the main pillar of the republican army. The International Brigades, forced on Largo Caballero[106] by the communists, were to remain under their control until their disbandment in the autumn of 1938. The Army Political Department was also set up at the insistence of the communists and, except for the period November 1937—April 1938,[107] was to all intents controlled by them.

In view of all this, it is hardly surprising that so many members and overt sympathisers of the Party should have been appointed to key posts in the military hierarchy.

It is equally true, however, that the communists did not confine themselves to taking the key positions to which they were entitled, and that in many instances they abused their power. They made the most of their control of the Political Department to conduct what amounted to forcible recruitment of Party members in the units under their control. According to J. Hernández, 50,000 members were thus recruited into the Party in the last three months of 1937 as a result of 'instructions given by Moscow to Togliatti, by Togliatti to the Political Bureau and by the Political Bureau to the whole of our vast agitation and propaganda machine. . . '. The former communist leader goes on to say:

At the front, in barracks, hospitals and staff offices, our men were in a position to offer promotion in exchange for the acceptance of a Party or United Youth League membership card. . . . Whoever showed the slightest sign of hesitation when presented with a membership application form . . . knew that he stood a very good chance of being sent to the most forward positions, held by shock units, and that his rank was at risk. The results were fantastic. Our numbers grew by tens of thousands. [108]

The communist commanders used even more questionable tactics in the army's military operations and in their relations with the government. They would refuse to carry out the orders of the High Command, interfere with the appointment or dismissal of officers, [109] and deprive of the support of their units, or withhold the supplies they controlled, from those whose politics they did not like. They had a monopoly of Soviet arms supplies, which they used for their own benefit, and, last but not least, they subjected the Largo Caballero and Negrín governments to a sort of permanent blackmail until, after the departure of Indalecio Prieto from the Ministry of National Defence, [110] the latter conceded to them virtual oversight of the army. At the end of the war, the Army of the Centre, the only one to remain at the republicans' disposal after the defeat of the forces in Catalonia, was to all intents and purposes under the communists' command. The latter controlled three of its four corps[111] and three-quarters of its command positions. This was the situation at the root of the anti-communist and anti-government *coup d'état* of Colonel Casado's junta. [112] The putsch put an end to the war, which the PCE officially wished to pursue to the bitter end; it was also a sort of settling of accounts between the anarchists and anti-communist republicans on the one hand and the communists on the other.

The communists were even more determined — and less justified — in their penetration of the army's counter-espionage service, set up by Indalecio Prieto on 15 August 1937. On communist initiative, the Military Investigation Service (SIM) soon became a political police, controlled by themselves, especially in Madrid. From 1938 onward it was little more than an appendage of the Soviet NKVD. With 6,000 agents and its own prisons and concentration camps, the service thereafter made it its business to eliminate the Communist Party's Trotskyite and 'Poumista' opponents.

The communists were, moreover, able to put pressure on the government and the President by giving them to understand that it was for the PCE, and not for the republican camp as a whole, that the USSR's moral and material aid was intended, and that should its influence be called into question this aid might disappear. This was how the communists engineered the downfall of the Largo Caballero government on 15 May 1937 after the Premier had refused to ban the POUM, the main opponent of the communists in the republican camp. [113] They went on to block an attempt by the leader of the PSOE's left wing to form a CNT—UGT trade unionist government from which the communists would have been left out. The President was thus forced to call on Dr Juan Negrín to form a republican coalition government made up of socialists and communists. [114]

According to their detractors, the communists' abuse of power in infiltrating the republican army and government with communist cells went hand in hand with the Party's transformation into a mere branch of the Comintern, and hence into an instrument designed to serve solely the ends of Soviet policy. There is some evidence to support this view, especially the influence exercised by the PCE's foreign advisers and the Russian experts placed at the disposal of the republican army and counter-espionage service. It was also only natural that the vitally necessary material support the USSR alone was giving the Republic should have resulted in a special relationship between Madrid and Moscow, with the communists — both Spaniards and foreign emissaries in Spain — acting as intermediaries.

At the end of July 1936, a number of foreign delegates were sent to Spain by the International. There they joined, and in some cases replaced, those already working with the PCE, including Codovila, Rabaté, Stepanov and Cesar Falcón. The most influential among them, however, was Palmiro Togliatti, then known by his *nom de guerre* of Ercole Ercoli. Togliatti's position was more or less that of a guardian of the Spanish communists. He attended regularly the meetings of their Political Bureau right up to 1939, and influenced vital decisions. In general, his was a moderating influence, opposed to the left socialists of Largo Caballero's wing.

The International Brigade was to all intents and purposes controlled by the French and Italian Communist Parties. The French, especially Vital Gayman, played an important part in the Brigade's military affairs, together with a number of German and Balkan communists, such as Ludwig Renn, Gustav Regler and Mate Zalka. [115] On the political side, the Brigade was controlled by Luigi Longo and, above all, André Marty. We also know that in 1937 and 1938 Klement Gottwald, László Rajk, Walter Ulbricht and Tito visited Spain. [116] None of these men — and this particularly applies to Marty and Longo — confined their activities to military matters. They intervened repeatedly in the PCE's internal affairs and on occasions took a hand in shaping its policies. According to D.T. Cattell, the Comintern began to play a decisive role after Soviet aid was stepped up in 1937. 'All the crucial work done by the communists in Spain was [then] taken over by foreign communists, appearances at public meetings and agitation among the public at large being the only exceptions'. [117]

The close dependence of the PCE on the Soviet Union can in any case hardly be denied. There were, however, some exceptions to this rule: on a number of occasions the Spanish communist leaders voiced their opposition to directives from 'head office'. Thus Jesús Hernández reports that he and José Díaz fiercely resisted Togliatti's order that the PCE should withdraw its support from the Caballero government. The two Spanish leaders, he says, did so at a meeting of the Political Bureau, attended in addition to Togliatti by Marty, Orlov, Codovila, Stepanov and Ernö Gerö. [118]

Despite these occasional shows of resistance, the communists did much to help the Russians conduct political purges in Spain. These purges, which were a sort of sideshow to the ones being organised at that time by Stalin in the USSR, were directed in the main against the leaders and militants of the POUM. [119] Accused of being Trotskyites and fascist agents at one and the same time, the 'Poumistas' were first evicted from the government of Catalonia in December 1936. Later, in February 1937, they were deprived, at the communists' insistence, of the newspapers and radio transmitters they controlled outside the province. Subsequently, the POUM's involvement in the May 1937 Barcelona rising resulted in its dissolution. Its members were disarmed; many were arrested. Knowing they could not persuade Largo Caballero's government to impose an official ban on the POUM, the communists first engineered the downfall of its leadership and then got President Negrín to approve a ban. Together with the republicans and moderate socialists, the communists were also instrumental in having the organisers of the rising tried in October 1938. On the other hand, there is some evidence to suggest that the PCE was not directly involved in the assassination of Andrés Nin. This crime, it seems, was committed without the Party's knowledge by a SIM squad commanded by the Russian Orlov and consisting of members of the International Brigade. [120]


### The Party during the Civil War — social composition

Outside Catalonia and the units under Catalan control, the accusations rightly or wrongly levelled against the PCE were largely unknown to the mass of the people in the republican zone. A considerable part of the

34

population continued to look upon the Party as a bastion against anarchy. The prestige it thus gained, together with the fact that the communists were in control of the information media and that they benefited both from the activities of the political commissars in the army and from the propaganda value of Soviet aid, helped the Party to grow rapidly between 1936 and 1938 — this at the very time when its catchment area shrank from fifty republican-controlled provinces to a mere twenty-two. According to the PCE's statistics, its membership rose from 102,000 in July 1936 to 249,000 in March 1937[121] and to 301,000 in June of that year.[122] From then on the membership is said to have remained static until the loss of Catalonia at the beginning of 1939. The ranks of the PSUC, the Catalan branch of the PCE, grew just as fast, especially after the elimination of the POUM. According to the leader of the PSUC, Joan Comorera, its membership rose from between 5,000 and 6,000 in August 1936 to 42,000 in 1937.[123] The Basque Communist Party is said to have had 22,000 members in March of that year.[124] In all, there were thus nearly 380,000 communists in Spain in mid-1937.

Although the PCE and the PSUC grew faster than any other political organisation in republican Spain,[125] these figures should come as no surprise. All the political groupings with their hands on the levers of power were able to attract a large opportunist following of people whose main purpose was to secure for themselves a political haven in uncertain times. Moreover, many of the new-found members of the various parties were soldiers whose freedom of political affiliation was limited.

The social composition of the newcomers to the communist ranks is of some interest. The statistics given below — the only figures of this kind ever made public by the PCE — show that in March 1937 55 per cent of the Party's members were peasants — mostly small farmers — and nearly 10 per cent were middle-class or professional people. Only 35 per cent were industrial workers. In March 1937, the membership of the PCE, broken down according to social origin, was as follows:[126]

| | | |
|---|---|---|
| Industrial workers (also independent craftsmen and shopkeepers) | 87,660 | (35%) |
| Farmers | 76,700 | (30%) |
| Agricultural labourers | 62,250 | (25%) |
| Middle class | 15,485 | (7%) |
| Members of the free professions and intellectuals | 7,045 | (3%) |
| Total | 249,140 | (100%) |
| Including: Women | 19,300 | (8%) |
| Servicemen | 131,600 | (53%) |

It should be noted that the category of 'industrial workers' includes an unspecified number of independent artisans and small traders whom the communists grouped together with the working class without saying so explicitly, to make the 'proletarian base' of the Party seem broader. In actual fact, industrial workers in the strict sense of the word probably accounted for a mere quarter of the Party's membership in the 1937—39 period.

The singular way in which the Party recruited its members among the troops — obvious from the proportion of servicemen in the PCE's total membership — is also reflected in these figures. True, the Republic was at war and the communists played an important part in the struggle. Nevertheless, the fact that 53 per cent of the Party's members were in the army shows beyond doubt that it recruited its new followers chiefly among the troops — sometimes in the manner described by Jesús Hernández in his account of the entry into the Party of 50,000 soldiers in the final quarter of 1937. [127] The dominant place held in its ranks by members of the armed forces helps to explain the comparatively small proportion of women members of the Party — a mere 8 per cent.

The preponderance of non-working class elements in the PCE was partly due to its comparative weakness at the beginning of the Civil War. The anarchists and socialists at that time had a vast working-class membership which they proceeded forthwith to enlist in the militia and later in the regular army units, which were politically fairly homogeneous. The communists, on the other hand, who at that time were few in number, were compelled to draw largely on 'unorganised' elements in Madrid and rural Castile. Later, regular units consisting of young recruits representing a cross-section of society, and particularly the countryside and the bourgeoisie, became the favourite catchment area for the Communist Party. These strata of society had provided comparatively few recruits for the militia. The PCE's chances, on the other hand, were nil in the socialist and anarchist regiments, in which most workers who belonged to a political party or trade union organisation were serving. This policy, dictated by circumstances and by the nature of Spain's working-class tradition, was, however, only one of the elements contributing to the PCE's 'ruralisation' and 'bourgeoisification' in the course of the Civil War.

There is no doubt that the Party's moderation also played a large part in helping to swell the number of its recruits among those sections of society which feared an immediate revolution or which wanted to make a career in the new republican state, while most workers remained loyal to the PSOE, UGT and CNT.

As P. Broué and E. Témime say: 'It was to the PCE and the PSUC that those who favoured the maintenance of order and the rights of private property in republican Spain turned. Judges, senior civil servants, members of the police — all saw in the Party a vehicle of the sort of policy they wanted, as well as means of safeguarding their own position and security.' In some cities, the communists attracted recruits even from among frankly conservative elements. Thus, in Valencia 'ex-members of the CEDA [128] as well as 'the most conservative sections of the republican bloc' [129] joined the PCE.

There can be no doubt that some of the people who joined the Party did so either out of sheer careerism or in the absence of any very definite political convictions. In Catalonia especially, the PSUC was to become a 'petty bourgeois' party as a result of the influx of new members seeking protection from anarchist pressures. One of the Goytisolo brothers explains, for example, that his father was, 'if anything right-wing, but he joined the PSUC in self-defence against the anarchists, who wanted to take possession of the factory where he was a member of the technical management'. [130] Others, such as the mayor of the village of El Toboso in New Castille, where the Popular Front polled only 200 votes out of a total of 1,100 in the February 1936 elections, [131] showed a marked lack of political commitment and joined the Communist Party by sheer chance — since it was as well to belong to some political organisation or other. Questioned by Mikhail Koltsov, the mayor described himself as a 'republican of communist convictions but also with anarchist sympathies, and at the same time an enthusiastic admirer of the Socialist Party. . . '. [132]

Should one go along with Joaquín Maurín, former leader of the POUM and a man of strong anti-communist views, in drawing a parallel between the evolution of the PCE during the Civil War and that of the Radical Socialist Party during the early years of the Republic? Maurín says:

> In every revolutionary phase there is a politically backward floating mass, eager to 'join' to protect their interests. Most of them make a rush for the group or organisation which to them seems the most radical and amorphous. It was this floating and uncertain mass of people which provided the Radical Socialist Party with its membership base during the early months of the Republic. In the Constituent Cortes, the Radical Socialists had fifty-six Deputies, compared with the mere three returned in November 1933. The mass of floating voters had swamped the party. Or rather — and what was even worse — they had voted for it in the belief that they were voting for the right. . . . The Communist Party in 1936 was in all but name a Radical Socialist Party, a demagogical party. The same politically

immature people who had gone Radical Socialist in 1931 went for the communists in 1936. [133]

This interpretation is probably wide of the mark so far as Maurín's views on the fragility of the communists' success, which he compares to the ephemeral triumph of the Radical Socialists in 1931, are concerned. Quite the contrary, it is virtually certain that had the Republic won, the Communist Party would have been one of the main political forces in Spain. On the other hand, his analysis of the social origins of the PCE's new recruits and supporters, and of their political motives, seems correct enough. There is no denying that in 1937 and 1938 the Communist Party really did contain a large bourgeois and rural element holding moderate views. Had the Republic emerged victorious, it would inevitably have had some trouble reconciling its revolutionary zeal with the conservative leanings of the majority of its supporters.

## Notes

[1]  There were certain similarities in the economic and social structure of the two countries, both of which were going through a time of rapid but chaotic industrial growth. Moreover, in both countries agriculture was dominated by large landowners and depended on the exploitation of the landless peasant masses.

[2]  As a result of the defeat of the working-class campaigns of 1917 and the effective repression which followed.

[3]  J. Díaz del Moral, *Historia de las agitaciones campesinas andaluzas*, Alianza editorial, Córdoba, Madrid, 1967, p. 277.

[4]  Ibid., pp. 278–9.

[5]  According to a survey carried out by the authorities on 1 February 1920.

[6]  P. Broué and E. Témine, *La révolution et la guerre d'Espagne*, Les Editions de Minuit, Paris 1961, p. 41.

[7]  Established in 1911, the CNT was to exert a dominating influence on the Spanish working-class movement until 1936. The anarchist workers' federations set up from 1881 onwards were affiliated to it. Its main strength lay in Catalonia, Andalusia and the Levante region.

[8]  No Spanish delegate attended the International's Constituent Congress in March 1919.

[9]  A. Pestaña, *Informe de mi estancia en la URSS*, Ed. ZYX, Santiago de Chile, Madrid, 1968; and *Consideraciones y judicios acerca de la Tercera*

*Internacional*, Ed. ZYX, Santiago de Chile, Madrid, 1968.

[10]   Or Profintern.

[11]   The delegation consisted of: Andrés Nin, Joaquín Maurín, H. Arlandis, Ibáñez and Gaston Leval.

[12]   With regard to this period, see in particular J. Maurín, *Revolución y contra-revolución en España*, Ruedo ibérico, 1966, pp. 249–67; J. Díaz del Moral, op. cit., pp. 162 and 178.

[13]   Founded on 17 June 1922 in Berlin, the International Workers' Association was the umbrella organisation of the anarchist trade unions.

[14]   The 437 delegates of the CNT who met at the Madrid congress in December 1919 represented 714,000 members. In 1918, the Spanish UGT trade union organisation had some 250,000 members, while the membership of the Spanish Socialist Workers' Party (PSOE) was approximately 50,000. The PCE had 5,000 members when it was founded; by 1931 its membership had shrunk to less than 1,000.

[15]   José Díaz was Secretary-General of the PCE from 1932 to 1942.

[16]   The Spanish Socialist Workers' Party was the heir to the Marxist movement which continued in existence, after the Congress of Córdoba in 1872, among Madrid printing workers organised in the New Madrid Federation. In 1879 this Federation gave birth to a small clandestine *Partido laboral socialista*, later replaced by the Socialist Party. This was officially founded in 1881, with Pablo Iglesias as its first Secretary. This Socialist Party assumed the designation PSOE at its constituent congress in Barcelona in 1888. The General Workers' Union (UGT), closely allied to the socialist movement, was established in the same year. The first socialist Deputy in the Cortes, Pablo Iglesias, was elected in 1910. Six socialist Deputies took their seats in 1920.

[17]   According to G. Sanz, 'Recuerdos de aquellos días' *Mundo obrero* 217, 13 April 1950, p. 20.

[18]   J. Maurín, op. cit., pp. 270–1.

[19]   This is why D. Anguiano attended a meeting organised by the pro-communist faction  of the Socialist Party on 7 November 1919 in Madrid.

[20]   PCOE.

[21]   By 8,080 votes to 6,023.

[22]   Cf. J. Díaz del Moral, op. cit., pp. 166–7 and 181.

[23]   *Partido Comunista de España (Sección española de la Internacional Comunista).*

[24]   That is, barely more than the membership of the PCE set up by the Socialist Youth, although the Party was also joined by the pro-Communist Anarchist elements grouped around A. Nin and J. Maurín.

[25]  The Constituent Congress of the PCE took place in 1921; the First Congress of the unified Party was held in October 1922 and the Second in July 1923.

[26]  See: P. Broué and E. Témine, op. cit., p. 54; and G. Brenan, *Le labyrinthe espagnol*, Ruedo ibérico, Paris 1962, p. 156.

[27]  In 1921 the PCE was really active only in the province of Vizcaya, thanks to the fact that the provincial branch of the Basque Miners' Union in the Asturias, headed by O. Pérez Solís, had joined its ranks. In this part of Spain the regional organisations of the PSOE followed the lead of the breakaway group. The Party was also active in Barcelona and had a handful of cells in Pontevedra, Madrid (ex-members of the Socialist Youth), Valencia, Toledo and Seville.

[28]  According to the reports submitted to the Fourth and Fifth Congresses of the Comintern (1922 and 1924), quoted by B. Lazitch, *Les partis communistes d'Europe*, Les Iles d'Or, Paris 1956, p. 183.

[29]  See J. Maurín, op. cit., p. 276.

[30]  B. Lazitch, op. cit., p. 183.

[31]  In 1929 O. Pérez Solís published a book on his experiences as a communist: *Memorias de mi amigo Oscar Perea*, Ed. Renacimiento, Madrid 1929.

[32]  The action of these workers seems to have been partly due to personal motives. Since it is a communist tradition to help members of all working-class movements in trouble with the police, J. Díaz got in touch with these men while he was in prison in 1925. After receiving help from the International Red Aid organisation, he joined the PCE in 1927 and reorganised the Seville branch. Following the strikes in 1928, many of his former anarchist comrades followed his example.

[33]  E. Comín Colomer, *Historia del Partido Comunista de España, Primera Etapa*, pp. 52, 135, and 145—8.

[34]  *La Batalla* in fact did not appear between 1925 and 1930. For further details of the secession, see J. Maurín, op. cit., pp. 266—8.

[35]  In October 1929 the Party was said to have had only six members in Madrid as a result of the split. Two of them made up the Regional Committee. L. Garcia Palacios, *Los dirigentes del Partido comunista al desnudo*, Imprenta de Juan Pueyo, Madrid 1931, p. 35.

[36]  The PCE supported an abortive rising in Seville in April 1931 and fomented disturbances on May Day. It organised more strikes during a 'Bloody Week' in July, when four demonstrators were killed. The communists were also said to have been involved in the ill-fated 1930 antimonarchist incident in Jaca (Comín Colomer, op. cit., pp. 242—6).

[37]  The socialists had earlier rejected a communist offer calling for a

common front against the Primo de Rivera dictatorship. They also refused to join the communists in launching a wave of protest strikes against the war in Morocco.

[38] According to J. Hernández, Stepanov was a Pole (J. Hernández, *La grande trahison*, p. 25). E. Comín Colomer reports the presence in Spain in 1932 of other men sent by the International, including Julio Rodriguez (Argentinian), Georg Martin Beck (German) and last, but not least, Ernö Gerö (Hungarian), known by his *nom de guerre* of Pierre or Pedro (E. Comín Colomer, op. cit., p. 485).

[39] According to E. Comín Colomer, the International's contribution amounted to 4,000 dollars.

[40] The average daily circulation of *Mundo obrero* was 20,000 in 1931–32; occasionally it reached 30,000. In Madrid, the paper is said to have sold an average of 6,000 copies.

[41] Comín Colomer, op. cit., p. 344. The review *Octubre,* established independently of the Party by Marxist intellectuals, survived a little longer.

[42] This Congress was attended by 257 delegates, representing 11,756 members.

[43] Notably by the inclusion of José Díaz and Dolores Ibarruri. In the official history of the Party, Bullejos is accused of having failed to grasp that the newly-born Republic was not dominated by the bourgeoisie, on which he concentrated his fire, but by the landed aristocracy, whose positions he had failed to undermine by a bold land reform (*Historia del Partido Comunista de España (versión abreviada)*, pp. 82–3). For the ideological debates in the Party from 1931 to 1939, see F. Claudín, *La crisis del movimiento comunista* I, Ruedo ibérico, Paris 1970, pp. 168–97 and 603–19.

[44] *Confederación general del trabajo unitaria.*

[45] 50,000 according to E. Comín Colomer (op. cit., p. 474); 90,000 according to J.J. Linz 'The party system of Spain: past and future' in S.N. Lipset and S. Rokkan (eds), op. cit., pp. 255–7.

[46] R. Lamberet, *Mouvements ouvriers et socialistes*. L'Espagne Les Editions ouvrières, Paris 1953, p. 167; G. Brenan, op. cit., p. 260.

[47] *Partido obrero de unificación Marxista.*

[48] In the 1923 elections to the Legislative Assembly which led to Primo de Rivera's assumption of power, the PCE obtained 2,000 votes and no seat (B. Lazitch, op. cit., p. 183).

[49] Nearly a million electors responded to the anarchists' call to abstain in 1931 and 1933.

[50] On that occasion, the PCE polled 48,694 votes in Oviedo, 43,119 in

Cordoba, 17,851 in Seville, 13,104 in the province of Vizcaya and 3,979 in Malaga (E. Comín Colomer, op. cit., p. 305).

[51]  The PCE is said to have polled 15·8 per cent of the votes in Malaga and 13·6 per cent in Andalusia. It polled 20·8 per cent in Vizcaya and 10·9 per cent in Zaragoza. Elsewhere its showing was much poorer (according to J.J. Linz, op. cit., p. 256).

[52]  According to N. Pla, 'José Díaz 1895–1942' *Nuestra bandera* no. 53, 1st quarter 1967, p. 127. Most other sources give a total of 40,000 communist voters in 1933.

[53]  *Correspondance internationale*, quoted by B. Lazitch, op. cit., p. 183.

[54]  Comintern and PCE sources, quoted by E. Comín Colomer, op. cit., p. 506.

[55]  Ibid.

[56]  Ibid, p. 202; see also B. Lazitch, op. cit., p. 183.

[57]  Ibid.

[58]  E. Comín Colomer, op. cit., p. 305.

[59]  Which had 1,200,000 members in 1932 (R. Lambert, op. cit., p. 167) and 1,577,000 members in November 1934 (according to the Directorate General of the Sûreté, quoted by G. Brenan, op. cit., p. 260).

[60]  Which is said to have had 10,000 members between 1934 and 1936 (ibid. p. 133). Some dissident anarchists, led by Pestaña, did, however, set up a small 'Syndicalist Party' during this period.

[61]  Communist papers were frequently confiscated or banned until 1936 under the so-called 'Law for the Defence of the Republic'. There were also many arrests, particularly after the Asturias rising. J. Díaz was arrested in the summer of 1932; Dolores Ibarruri was in jail from March 1932 to the beginning of 1933, and re-arrested in October 1934 and again late in 1935; she was released just before the 6 February 1936 elections. This harassment forced the PCE's leaders to cross the frontier illegally to attend the Seventh Congress of the Communist International in July 1935.

[62]  J.J. Linz, op. cit., p. 257. This writer also thinks that the socialists took from the communists the support of the agricultural labourers, who had turned their backs on the CNT, thanks to the immediate benefits Largo Caballero conferred on them when he was Minister of Labour in 1931 and 1932.

[63]  According to E. Comín Colomer, op. cit., p. 299.

[64]  The right wing of the Socialist Party, led by Indalecio Prieto, opposed armed action; however, the majority of the PSOE leadership approved it in principle early in October 1934.

[65] Radical Party governments under Lerroux and Samper blocked the reforms launched in 1931 and 1932. Lerroux's new government, formed early in October 1934, had even more reactionary aims, intending to amend the 1931 Constitution with the support of the Catholics, represented in the Cortes by the CEDA.

[66] The Popular Front formula differed from the Common Front and the Workers' Alliance, put forward earlier by the communists and socialists respectively, in that it advocated not only joint action by working-class organisations, but also collaboration with republican and 'anti-fascist' bourgeois parties. It implied unreserved loyalty on the part of the PCE to the Republic proclaimed in 1931. This new policy was followed by the Comintern from the summer of 1934, possibly to reassure Britain and France and to secure their support for the USSR against Hitler's Germany.

[67] E. Comín Colomer, op. cit., p. 577.

[68] According to José Díaz, the Party press had fifty-five papers and periodicals in 1935. There were nine legitimate papers, fifteen clandestine ones, eighteen works journals and thirteen other publications (quoted by E. Comín Colomer, op. cit., p. 565).

[69] *Historia del Partido Comunista de España (versión abreviada),* p. 114.

[70] B. Lazitch, op. cit., p. 183.

[71] Ibid. W.G. Krivitsky estimates that the PCE had just about 3,000 members at the beginning of 1936 (W.G. Krivitsky, *I was Stalin's Agent,* Hamish Hamilton, London 1939, p. 121).

[72] According to Hugh Thomas, *Histoire de la guerre d'Espagne,* 2 vols., R. Laffont, Paris 1961.

[73] D.T. Cattell, *Communism and the Spanish Civil War,* The University of California Press, Berkeley, Los Angeles, 1955, p. 21.

[74] Julio Alvarez del Vayo in particular; also Luis Araquistráin.

[75] E. Comín Colomer, op. cit., p. 429.

[76] S. Carrillo has been Secretary-General of the PCE since 1960. F. Claudín left the Party in 1964. Both had joined it in 1936 after a visit to the USSR.

[77] In March 1936, at the time of the merger, the Socialist Youth had 200,000 members and the Communist Youth 50,000. Half the Socialists left the JSU after the fusion, the membership thus shrinking to 150,000, virtually all of whom were pro-communist (D.T. Cattell, op. cit., p. 33).

[78] The Socialist Union and the Proletarian Party.

[79] *Partido Socialista Unificado de Cataluña — Partit Socialista Unificat de Catalunya.*

[80] Sixteen seats according to D.T. Cattell (op. cit., p. 31); seventeen

according to B. Lazitch (op. cit., p. 183); thirteen, plus two or three dissidents, according to J. Bécarud (*La Deuxième République espagnole*, Fondation nationale des sciences politiques, Paris 1962, p. 64).

[81]    The socialist intellectuals reacted to this situation on the eve of the 1936 elections with the sarcastic slogan: 'Save Spain from Marxism — vote Communist'. P. Broué and E. Témime, op. cit., p. 174.

[82]    After the victory of the Popular Front, four so-called 'out-and-out republican' governments took office one after another. None of their members represented any working-class party. They were the Azaña government (19 February—10 May 1936); the Casares Quiroga government (14 May—19 July); the ephemeral government of Martínez Barrio (19 July) and the Giral government (19 July—4 September). The next government (4 September 1936—16 May 1937) was the Popular Front one headed by Caballero, which fled Madrid in haste on the night of 6—7 November 1936.

[83]    The communists, whose Political Bureau stayed in Madrid to the end, virtually assumed power in the capital after the government's departure until their position was challenged by Colonel Casado in March 1939. In November 1936, the Party is said to have had 23,000 members in Madrid, of whom 21,000 were at the front (*Guerra y revolución en España 1936—1939*, vol. II Editorial Progreso, Moscow 1966, p. 153). M. Koltsov recounts with satisfaction how General Miaja, virtually abandoned by the government which had appointed him head of the military junta in charge of the defence of the capital, had only the communists to turn to for help. Koltsov reports: 'Miaja went out to look for the general staff which had been placed at his disposal, and for the Central Front staff. He could find neither. They had all taken to their heels. . . . He then set about looking for the Defence Junta, but could find no one. The representatives appointed to the junta by the various parties had left the capital without permission — all, that is except the communist Mije. . . . Miaja then appealed for help to the Fifth Regiment of the communist people's Militia. The Fifth Regiment placed itself unreservedly at the General's disposal, complete with all its units, reserves, stocks of ammunition and staff facilities, its officers and commissars. Checa and Mije made contact with Miaja on behalf of the Central Committee.' (M. Koltsov, *Diario de la guerra de España*, Ruedo ibérico, 1963, p. 190).

[84]    The two communist ministers in this government were Jesús Hernández (National Education) and Vicente Uribe (Agriculture). Jesús Astigarrabia became Minister of Public Works in the first Basque government in October 1936.

[85]  Quotation from P. Broué and E. Témime, op. cit., p. 175.

[86]  Ibid.

[87]  J. Díaz, *Por la unidad hacia la victoria*, Ediciones del PCE, Madrid 1937, pp. 13—15. A letter addressed by Stalin, Molotov and Voroshilov to the Spanish Premier on 21 December 1936 is also relevant in this context. They recommended Largo Caballero to exercise all the moderation 'necessary to prevent the enemies of Spain from being able to treat it as a communist republic' (quoted by S. de Madariaga, *Spain, a Modern History* p. 673).

[88]  J. Díaz, *Tres años de lucha*, Ediciones Euro-América, Paris, New York 1939, p. 298.

[89]  'Témoignages d'Espagne' *Noir et rouge* 39—40, December—January 1967, p. 16.

[90]  This account is taken from B. Bolloten, *The Grand Camouflage*, pp. 198—9.

[91]  This quotation was taken by P. Broué and E. Témime, op. cit. p. 137, from an article in *Frente rojo* of 14 August 1937 which violently criticised the policy of the anarchists in Aragon. It said among other things: 'Thousands of peasants have drifted from the land, preferring to abandon their holdings rather than put up with all the tortures they have suffered at the hands of the Council'.

[92]  Ibid., p. 175.

[93]  J. Díaz, *Tres años de lucha*, op. cit., pp. 288 and 675.

[94]  'Témoignages d'Espagne', loc. cit. (see note 89), p. 15.

[95]  Quoted by P. Broué and E. Témime, op. cit., p. 132.

[96]  Quoted by P. Broué and E. Témime, op. cit., p.,255.

[97]  J. Díaz, '*Por la unidad hacia la victoria*', op. cit., p. 14.

[98]  L. Fischer, *Men and Politics*, Jonathan Cape, London 1941, p. 397.

[99]  Member of the POUM.

[100]  *Guerra y revolución en España 1936—1939*, p. 259. See also: M. Azaña, *Obras completas*, vol. IV, Ed. Oasis, Mexico 1968, pp. 602—6.

[101]  L. Fischer, op. cit., pp. 397—8. However, M. Azaña was not greatly in favour of the setting up of the International Brigade and opposed the communists in 1938 and 1939.

[102]  P. Broué and E. Témime, op. cit., p. 245. The fact that relations were good in no way meant that Prieto and Negrín were pro-communist: if anything, the contrary was true.

[103]  In November 1937, the socialist minister, afraid, after various incidents in the preceding weeks, that the communists might attempt to take complete control of the army and of defence in general, dismissed 250 communist political commissars and called on Julio Alvarez del Vayo,

head of the Army Political Department, to resign. Del Vayo, though officially a socialist, in fact obeyed communist orders faithfully. In the end, the PCE came out on top in April 1938, when J. Hernández was appointed Commissar of the Army of the Centre. See I. Prieto, *Como y porque salí del Ministerio de Defensa Nacional — Intrigas de los Rusos en España*, Imprimerie nouvelle, Paris 1939.

[104]    For example General Miaja, Commander-in-Chief of the republican army, first joined the Party (according to L. Fischer, op. cit., p. 560), but eventually turned against it and threw in his lot with the junta of Colonel Casado in March 1939.

[105]    Anarchists, and more particularly members of POUM.

[106]    The Premier's response, in October 1936, to Luigi Longo, when the latter asked him for certain facilities in connection with the formation of the International Brigades, was said to have been very cool (see L. Longo, *Le brigate internazionali in Spagna*, Editori riuniti, 1956, pp. 43—4). In November it was the PCE and not the government which called on the Brigades to save Madrid (ibid., p. 71).

[107]    That is, in the interval between the dismissal of the 250 communist commissars by Indalecio Prieto and their reinstatement.

[108]    J. Hernández, op. cit., p. 122. As regards the position of the communists in the Political Department, see: D.T. Cattell, op. cit., p. 194.

[109]    Thus the communists were determined to get rid of General Asensio, military adviser to Largo Caballero.

[110]    The best known case of 'blackmail' was to do with the plan for a republican offensive in the direction of the Estremadura region in the spring of 1937. Although supported by Largo Caballero and the majority of ministers, this plan had to be dropped because the communists, who thought it too risky, opposed it. More than thirty years after the event, Santiago Carrillo himself admitted the extent to which the communists controlled the best units of the army and the best Russian weapons and equipment. In an interview with *Le Monde*, he declared: 'During the Civil War, the Communist Party could have taken power — it had the best units, it controlled the armour and the air force. . .' (*Le Monde*, 4 November 1970, p. 4).

[111]    Under the command of Barcelo, Bueno and Ortega. The Fourth Army Corps was commanded by Cipriano Mera, the CNT's best military leader (see: S. Casado, *The Last Days of Madrid*, Peter Davies, London 1939, p. 53).

[112]    Colonel Casado began his putsch on the evening of 23 February 1939 by banning *Mundo obrero*. Later, on 7 March, what was virtually a civil war broke out in Madrid between the communist troops and the

anarchists, led by Cipriano Mera, who had thrown in their lot with the junta. Togliatti, Claudín and Checa were arrested, then set free. The cease-fire proclaimed on 10 March enabled Casado to start negotiations with Franco on 19 March. The negotiations came to nothing and the war ended with the unconditional surrender of the republican forces on 27 March. The lawful government and most of the members of the communist general staff had left Spain on 6 March.

[113]    In due course, thanks to the provincial branches under its control, the PCE managed to eliminate Largo Caballero as leader of the UGT by causing a split in that organisation which lasted from 1 October 1937 to 2 January 1938. A few weeks earlier, on 17 August 1937, a unity pact had been concluded by the PSOE and the PCE.

[114]    There are indications that Manuel Azaña, the President of the Republic, was in favour of a trade union government without the communists, despite the value he put on their support.

[115]    General 'Lukács'.

[116]    Tito denies having visited Spain. José Amutio, however, the former socialist Governor of Albacete, claims to have met him at the International Brigade base, where, according to him, Tito spent two days.

[117]    D.T. Cattell, op. cit., p. 97.

[118]    J. Hernández, op. cit., pp. 67—70.

[119]    The result of a merger of Maurín's Workers' and Peasants' Bloc and Nin's Communist Left, the POUM's only real strength was in Catalonia, where it had between 5,000 and 6,000 members at the end of 1936. It advocated the immediate imposition of the dictatorship of the proletariat.

[120]    José Díaz is reported to have protested to the Russians against this 'operation'. He is also said to have protested when Antonov-Ovseyenko, the Soviet Consul in Barcelona, launched a drive against the POUM without consulting the PCE (H. Thomas, op. cit., p. 202). In assassinating Nin, it seems that the Russians acted in direct collaboration with the head of the SIM, the socialist Uribarri. The assassination of the POUM leader was not the only such crime committed by the SIM. Its agents, most of them communists, also took part in a large number of executions of foreign communists in the International Brigade 'condemned' by Orlov (see L. Fischer, op. cit., pp. 343 and 406; P. Broué and E. Témime, op. cit., p. 286; V.B. Johnson, *Legions of Babel*, University Press, London, and the Pennsylvania State University, 1967, pp. 109—11).

[121]    *Guerra y revolución 1936—1939*, vol. 1, p. 87; vol. 2, p. 267.

[122]    Figure quoted by D.T. Cattell, op. cit., p. 94.

[123]    J. Comorera, 'Catalonia, an Example for Unity' *Communist International*, April 1938, p. 376. Cattell says the PSUC had 64,000 members

at the end of 1937 (op. cit., pp. 94–5).

[124] D.T. Cattell, ibid.

[125] With the exception, however, of the Falange, membership of which rose from a few thousand in 1936 to one million in 1939. It must also be remembered that the anarchist and socialist–communist trade union organisations (CNT and UGT respectively) had a much larger membership than the political parties. Thus, the CNT is said to have had 2,178,000 members in twenty-two provinces in April 1937, compared with about 1,500,000 in fifty provinces in February 1936 (C.M. Lorenzo, *Les anarchistes espagnols et le pouvoir*, pp. 275–6). The FAI (Iberian Anarchist Federation) is said to have expanded its membership from between 10,000 and 30,000 in the spring of 1936 to 150,000 in April 1937 (ibid., p. 203).

[126] *Guerra y revolución 1936–1939*, vol. 2, p. 267; J. Díaz, *Por la unidad hacia la victoria*, p. 51; N. Pla 'José Díaz' *Nuestra bandera*, 1st quarter, 1967, p. 137.

[127] However, that particular recruiting drive took place after the above statistical table was compiled.

[128] Centre-right Catholic party under the Republic, headed by J.M. Gil Robles.

[129] P. Broué and E. Témime, op. cit., pp. 211–12. It would be wrong, however, to pursue this line of argument too far. The PCE also managed to attract a great many sincere intellectuals during the Civil War, most of whom subsequently chose exile.

[130] Account given by the poet José Agustín Goytisolo, quoted by S. Vilar, *Protagonistas de la España democrática. La oposición a la dictadura 1939–1969*, Editions sociales, Barcelona, Paris, Madrid, 1968, p. 310.

[131] This does not mean that the village was hostile to the Popular Front: the conservative landowners were still able to exert considerable pressure at the time of the 1936 elections.

[132] M. Koltsov, op. cit., p. 321.

[133] J. Maurín, op. cit., p. 287.

# 2 The Party Underground

Apart from the first few months of its existence, the Communist Party of Spain enjoyed only eight years of legality — from 1931 to 1939. During that time it experienced its 'finest hour', when it was the world's only Communist Party, apart from the Soviet Communist Party, to have a share in government. Throughout the remainder of its history, it had to function underground: first during the eight years of Primo de Rivera's and Berenguer's dictatorship, and then during thirty years or more of the Franco regime.

Despite this prolonged experience of underground existence, it is an open question whether the PCE has ever really been able to adapt itself to the mode of life forced upon it — whether it is not at heart a party yearning to work legally and in the open rather than a genuinely clandestine organisation. Such at any rate is the impression one gets when one examines the three principal phases of its history since 1939. Not unnaturally, the first phase could most aptly be called the time of 'squaring of accounts' — dominated by the conflicts which arose as a result of the decisive role played by the communists during the Civil War. The next period, that of rebuilding after the Second World War, was definitely marked by the Party's desire to maintain all the attributes of a major legitimate political organisation. It was only during the third phase of the PCE's clandestine existence — the start of which might perhaps be set around 1963 — that the communist leaders began to make a real effort to adapt themselves to the role of opponents of a mighty authoritarian regime rather than that of the main protagonists of an abortive political experiment.

## Squaring of accounts

The legal existence of the PCE came to an end on 6 March 1939. On that day the senior leaders of the Party — Dolores Ibarruri, Minister V. Moix, Nuñez Maza, Colonel Lister and the communist generals Cordón, Modesto and Hidalgo de Cisneros[1] — left Elda airfield near Valencia together with the members of the Negrín government.[2] They had suffered a double defeat — at the hands of the Francoites as well as of those of the junta of

49

Colonel Casado and his anarchist allies, who had put an end to communist rule in Madrid.

A few senior officials remained in Spain a few days longer: Pedro Checa, Secretary of the Party, visited Madrid briefly to try to set up an underground organisation at the last moment, the possibilities of such a move having apparently been overlooked by all concerned until then. In Madrid Checa joined Togliatti, Claudín and Carrillo, but did not stay long, since he wanted to catch the last plane to Oran, which was scheduled to leave Cartagena on 25 March. Togliatti, Dieguez, Zapiraín, Galán, V. Uribe, Hernández and some fifty other people, including numerous wives and children of Party leaders, shared the plane.[3] Santiago Carrillo, who did not leave Madrid until after the meeting of the defence junta during the night of 27–28 March 1939, was the last important leader to go into exile. Only the regional and local leaders stayed on in Spain (although some of these, too, left Catalonia in February) along with the mass of Party members.

The exiled leaders first sought refuge in France. Later most of them went to the Soviet Union, where they joined several hundred lesser Spanish communist fugitives from Catalonia. The vast majority of rank-and-file communist refugees stayed behind in the French camps of sad memory. Only a few hand-picked individuals were allowed to embark for Leningrad.

These refugees found a number of their compatriots who had preceded them to Russia, notably some republican pilots training with the Soviet Air Force, as well as a number of Spanish children who had been received in the USSR in 1937 and 1938.[4] Since there was no hope of the PCE's being able to accommodate all its exiled members in the Soviet Union, the Party sought to obtain a refuge for them in other countries, especially in Latin America. This effort gave rise to further complaints by its opponents in the republican camp, who accused the PCE of making improper use of its influence in the *Servicio de emigración para republicanos españoles*, set up on 31 March 1939 by the Negrín government as its last official act. France, however, remained the principal country of refuge for the Party's rank and file — and it was there that they were caught by the German invasion in May 1940.[5]

The views expressed as to the treatment the Spanish refugees received in the Soviet Union vary widely and caused yet more accusations to be levelled against the leaders of the PCE at the time. According to some, their treatment in the USSR was most satisfactory, considering the difficulties the country had to contend with two years later as a result of the German–Russian war.[6] But the accounts of defectors from the communist cause and some of the Spaniards repatriated from the Soviet Union[7] paint a very different picture of the life of the refugees during the war and the Stalin era. Jesús Hernández[8] and El Campesino[9] in particular, as well as a number of publications that appeared during the cold war period,[10] give a particularly gloomy picture of the life of the exiles.

These accounts blame not only the Soviet authorities and Stalin's police,[11] but also some of the leaders of the PCE, who, they allege collaborated closely with the Russians. This co-operation is said to have taken place at first within the committee responsible for selecting prospective immigrants into the USSR. This body was re-established in Moscow in May 1939[12] and consisted of six representatives of the PCE[13] and five of the Comintern. It was responsible for deciding all matters concerning the activity, place of residence and degree of liberty enjoyed by the refugees. Its instructions were carried out by central and local officials who, according to El Campesino, were no more than agents of the NKVD. In this way, the PCE leaders were forced to connive at the trials and deportations which were going on at that time and of which they could not help being aware.

The criticisms levelled at the Spanish communist leaders are partly due to the many cases of squaring of accounts which occurred between 1939 and 1945, both within the group in the USSR, and between this group and the ten or so fragments of the Party reconstituted in Mexico, Cuba, the Dominican Republic,[14] in Spain itself, and in a number of other countries. It should be remembered, however, that at that time this sort of conduct was commonplace among Spanish republicans in exile, both within the various parties, and among them.

The internal conflict was essentially between the central Party machine assembled in Moscow and Ufa around Dolores Ibarruri ('La Pasionaria'), and a rival group around Jesús Hernández. The latter was a former leading Party figure who had graduated from the Lenin School in 1933[15] and during the Civil War became Minister of Education and a close collaborator of José Díaz. Hernández clashed with Dolores Ibarruri in 1942, when she became the Party's Secretary-General, a post which had fallen vacant on the death of José Díaz. Sent on a mission to Stockholm, he made contact from there with a number of disaffected Spanish communist exiles in Mexico, denounced the personal intrigues of the leaders in Moscow and their attitude to the Spanish refugees in the USSR and accused La Pasionaria of seizing the Secretary-Generalship after bringing about the death of José Díaz.[16]

For their part, the leaders in Moscow blamed Hernández for his moderate policies during the Civil War and suggested that his attitude in 1942 was motivated by spite at his failure to get the post of Secretary-General after the death of Díaz. Jesús Hernández managed to leave Moscow at the end of the war and went to Mexico. There he became the leader of a group of Spanish communists and also tried to persuade other Spaniards, such as Enrique Castro Delgado, to leave the USSR. Delgado, too, eventually got out of the Soviet Union. [17] In 1946 Jesús Hernández published the only issue of the review *Horizontes* ever to appear. It voiced views close to those of the Trotskyites and left-wing socialists. He soon lapsed into silence, however, despite the fact that his pronouncements created a certain stir among communists in Spain itself.

This quarrel furnished the other republican groups, virtually all hostile to the communists, with fresh ammunition. They accuse the communists to this day of having been mere instruments of Soviet policy during the Civil War. From 1939 to 1945, the PCE was virtually put in quarantine by its former Popular Front allies, whom the Party in turn blamed for the common defeat. To counter this isolation, in 1939 the PCE established its own organisation to promote unity — the *Junta suprema de unión nacional*, which, after the USSR's entry into the World War, was transformed into the *Unión nacional de todos los Españoles*.

### First underground organisations

Another internal crisis in the ranks of the Party during these years was triggered by the differences between the leadership in Moscow and the underground apparatus in Spain. The Party machine at home, which was weak to start with, was repeatedly destroyed by the police, who managed virtually to eliminate the organised Party cells which had remained in existence in the country in 1939 or had been reconstituted in the early forties. The communists, denounced by Franco as the common enemies of the fascist Powers — despite the German—Soviet pact — became the object of a particularly brutal campaign of repression in the years 1939—44. In that time 200,000 republicans of all affiliations were either executed or died in camps or prisons. [18] This was a time when anyone who had attained any standing, however modest, in the republican army or state was presumed guilty and deserving the death penalty or prolonged imprisonment. A great many communists of course found themselves in this position.

The history of the underground organisations at this time is a long tale of martyrdom. Their sole preoccupation in this period was to maintain the cohesion of their members and to help those who were on the run or in prison. [19] The only genuinely active force consisted of the guerrilla units which remained in existence in the Asturias until 1941. Apart from these, the underground cells were mainly in the areas which had been longest under republican control, especially in Madrid. There was an even larger number of them in the prisons and labour camps. Most remained isolated, without regional, let alone nationwide, links; contacts with the exiled leaders in Moscow were of course virtually non-existent.

The first person to attempt to co-ordinate the activities of the underground apparatus was a middle-rank Party official, Heriberto Quiñones, who had escaped from prison in 1939. His task, difficult enough already thanks to the attentions of the police, was made even harder by the signing of the German—Soviet pact. Cut off from the Party Central Committee, [20] which was dispersed in a number of foreign centres, the communists inside Spain now found themselves ostracised by the non-communist underground.

This situation in the end led Quiñones to break with the leaders in Moscow, whom he accused of having fled the country. As a result, the underground Party apparatus went its own way. For example, it refrained from giving publicity to the slogan of 'National union of all Spaniards', issued in August 1941 after the German invasion of the USSR. Jesús Carreras, sent by the central leadership to re-establish contact with Quiñones, had to content himself with reporting that the breach was an established fact. This particular schism was to remain a chronic symptom in the relations between the PCE machines inside and outside Spain.

Lacking specific objectives, the organisation set up by Quiñones does not appear to have achieved anything, apart from giving the underground press a certain stimulus. Infiltrated by the police, the apparatus was all but totally destroyed in the winter of 1941—42: the majority of its members were arrested after their leader had been caught with all their addresses on his person. Jesús Carreras replaced Quiñones at the end of 1942 and reorganised what remained of the Party and the JSU with the help of a few people who, like himself, had returned from France. Carreras was in turn arrested in February 1943 and shot a few months later. The Party then virtually ceased to exist inside Spain, where the few surviving fugitive members were left without any organisation. [21] It was roughly at this time that Santiago Carrillo tried from outside Spain to save what remained of the Party's underground apparatus and to co-ordinate the activities of the cells in Valencia, Zaragoza, Barcelona, Cordoba and in the Basque country, newly established by communists released from Franco's prisons in 1942 and 1943. A group calling itself 'la Quinta del 42' (the 42 class) — one prominent member of which was the poet José Hierro — was set up in Madrid. However, it was soon smashed by the authorities.

## Disappointed hopes

From then on, the activities and resources of the PCE were in the main concentrated in France, especially in the *maquis* of the south-west, where the anarchists, and above all the communists, had more than 10,000 men in 1944, organised in six 'divisions', each with its own propaganda, supply and recruiting services.[22] It was also in France that the PCE tried to launch anew its policy of national unity. This was done at a conference said to have taken place in Grenoble in mid-1942 with the participation of representatives of the other republican parties and the liberal Catholics. But the attempt foundered on the opposition of the socialists and anarchists.

In November 1942, hopes of an early liberation of Spain, aroused by the Allied landing in North Africa, made the PCE revive the *Junta suprema de unión nacional*. In addition to a communist majority, it comprised socialists and conservative liberals. The move led in 1944 to the establishment of a rival junta by the anarchists and republicans exiled in Mexico, named *Junta de liberación nacional*. Although both these organisations sent emissaries to Spain to set up rudimentary guerrilla organisations and some 100 local juntas, neither succeeded in attracting much support in the country.

Despite this, urged on by the Spanish *maquisards* in the Ariège, Gard, Ardèche and Lozère departments, they launched an armed campaign against the Franco regime. Anarchists, and even more so communists – in spite of the Party's doubts – made up the bulk of these units. The main attack, kept up for ten days by 2,000 men who had crossed the Pyrenees into Spain by way of the Col d'Hospitalet, soon petered out. Receiving no support whatever from the local population, the guerrillas were surrounded by General Yagüe's troops. Santiago Carrillo, who had just returned from South America, ordered them to retreat to France. Some were captured; others remained in Spain, where they joined the resistance.

These resistance units, said to have been helped at first by the American Secret Service from North Africa,[23] operated mostly in the Asturias, Galicia, Catalonia, Aragon, Andalusia and the Estremadura. Pursued by the Civil Guard during the summer and autumn of 1944, they got no help from the mass of the peasants, who were afraid not only of official retaliation and imprisonment but also of a new civil war. In the mountains near Cordoba, the agricultural labourers called the guerrillas by their old nineteenth-century name of *bandoleros* and, just as they had done in those days, gave them fine funerals but very little else.[24]

Bereft of all hope of victory or of outside aid, especially after the failure of a last forlorn attempt to stage a landing on the coast of northern Spain in 1946, the guerrillas did little more than survive during the next few years. A new offensive by the Civil Guard in March 1947 all but wiped them out. However, in Catalonia and in the Levante region a few communist and anarchist guerrillas kept going until 1949; in Galicia and in the province of Granada some actually managed to survive until 1951. [25]

Throughout that time and until after 1950, the PCE officially stuck to the programme and aims it had set out at the end of the Civil War. The programme published in 1945 by and large reaffirmed the policies outlined by José Díaz in his speeches in 1937 and 1938. [26] He called for the distribution of the great estates among the peasants and agricultural labourers, with a promise of compensation for landlords 'not implicated in the crimes of the Franco regime'. As for industry and finance, the communists called for the nationalisation of the monopolies, credit institutes, the big banks and insurance companies, as well as of the mines, telecommunications, the railways, the merchant navy and shipbuilding. This list was even longer than the one presented in 1938, although shareholders were promised fair compensation.

The programme also contained a reference to the 'recognition of the national identity of the peoples of Catalonia, the Basque country and Galicia . . . within the framework of a democratic federation of the Hispanic peoples'. It proclaimed the need for respect for 'freedom of conscience and religious observance based on separation of Church and State' and outlined a plan for the establishment of a new democratic army similar to the regular army of the years 1937—39.

As to political institutions, the PCE called for the restoration of the republican institutions of 1936, following the elimination of the Franco regime. Unlike other opposition groups, the Party did not pin any hope on help from the United Nations or the Western democracies to bring this about. This view, largely justified by subsequent events, was in the years 1944—48 also rooted in the PCE's doubts as to what a Spanish Republic restored by the good offices of the United States, Britain and France might turn out to be like — perhaps a republic in which a government-in-exile dominated by anti-communist elements would return to power.


**The Party in exile — the cold war**

The liberation of France, the defeat of Germany and the restoration of international communications enabled the Party's leaders to resume contact with at least that part of its membership which was in exile. International events at that time seemed to point to an early collapse of the Franco dictatorship, and this encouraged both the communists and the other opposition movements to abandon their former indulgence in hopeful speculation and internecine quarrels and to come forward with clear ideas and policies. Alas, this hopeful period was not to last long. The regime, thought to be in its last throes, in fact found new strength in the cold war as well as in the 1953 rapprochement with the Americans. Franco was also helped by the fact that the Spanish people's memories of the Republic were growing dim with the passing of time. The old political parties now began to settle down to an exile of indefinite duration.

The Party's campaign to resume control of its apparatus was based on Paris and Toulouse, where the majority of the members of the Political Bureau had gathered in the course of 1945. The PCE's central apparatus was to remain in France until its expulsion in September 1950.

The operation was launched with a speech by Carrillo in Toulouse on 1 April 1945. Addressing a meeting of former guerrilla fighters, his main theme even at that early stage was the need for all-out political war. The first two post-war plenums of the Party Central Committee were held in Toulouse in December 1945 and at Montreuil in March 1947.[27]

Having re-established contact with the majority of exiled Party members — and expelled some of them — the PCE proceeded to outline a new policy which took into account the failure of its earlier attempts at waging an armed struggle and also of the Party's need to break out of its isolation. In July 1945, with this end in view, it joined the *Alianza nacional de fuerzas democráticas*, set up the previous year by the socialists and republicans. In January 1946 the PCE disbanded its own *Junta suprema de unión nacional* and then announced that it was ready to support the republican government-in-exile presided over by J. Giral. Santiago Carrillo joined this government on 10 April 1946 as Minister without Portfolio. V. Uribe was a member of the next government, with Rodolfo Llopis as Premier, from February to August 1947.[28] In September 1946, the communists unsuccessfully approached the anarchists with the offer of an alliance. This went unheeded, like their call for a National Front of all forces opposed to the Franco regime, made in March 1948. In October of that year, the PCE and its Catalan branch, the PSUC, announced their decision that henceforth they would combine legal with clandestine activity. Though both parties went on giving a good deal of publicity in their press to guerrilla activity — which in actual fact was well on the way to being totally suppressed — they did so only to underline their hostility to the idea of a recourse to the UN or to any other 'international' solution of the problem of how to replace the Franco regime. This was the approach

56

advocated by the socialists and moderates. The communists certainly attached much greater importance to their newly proclaimed policy of infiltrating the official 'vertical' syndicates. [29]

However, this new policy, to which the PCE has stuck ever since, produced little in the way of immediate tangible results. The underground
network was rebuilt in 1945 with cadres some of whom had returned to
Spain from France, [30] while others had managed to escape the 1940—44
campaign of repression; but it was almost totally destroyed again by the
police in 1946 and 1948. The collapse of the Party apparatus in Spain was
also due in part to a fresh dispute between the movement's clandestine
wing in the country and the leaders in exile. This quarrel was one of the
many episodes of the cold war, during which the PCE seemed less interested in fighting the Franco regime than in promoting Soviet foreign policy.
Jesús Monzón, who was in charge of the Party's clandestine apparatus, was
denounced as being responsible for all its setbacks in the country and
'Monzonist opportunism' became one of the deviations most frequently
invoked by the top leadership, headed by Dolores Ibarruri and Vicente
Uribe. [31] To make things worse, Monzón's successors in the underground
leadership were picked up by the police almost as soon as they had taken
office. One of them, Sánchez Viezma, was murdered, while another,
Zoroa, was executed by a firing squad.

Between 1948 and 1952 there were other accusations as a result of the
Yugoslav affair. Expulsions and schisms took place; and the Party, like
other communist parties, discovered in its ranks 'Titoite bandits' engaged
in 'disgraceful provocative manoeuvres' resembling the 'infamies of Kostov
and Rajk'. [32] Del Barrio and J. Comorera, [33] accused of being the spokesmen of the Spanish Titoites, were expelled from the Party in 1948 and
1949 respectively. At this time, the PCE's press, like that of the other
pro-Moscow communist parties, was full of denunciations of 'traitors',
past and present, such as Bullejos, Del Barrio, Cartón, Astigarrabia,
Bulnes, Lombardia, Adame and León Trilla, [34] not to mention Hernández,
Castro and Quiñones. [35] Stalin, on the other hand, was the object of
something not far short of religious adoration — a feature typical of the
entire communist press of the period — with Dolores Ibarruri and José
Díaz playing the role of minor saints in the Stalin cult. [36]

In its day-to-day activities, the PCE confined itself to publicising, both
in Spain and abroad, its opposition to the 'Atlantic' trends which were
beginning to emerge from 1947 onward in Spain as well as in the republican government-in-exile and in the other opposition groups. It was for this
reason that the communists left the Llopis government. In March1949,
they came out against the idea of Spain's accepting US aid, which was

then beginning to be canvassed. In June, a series of violent attacks was launched on Indalecio Prieto and the right-wing socialists, the latter having concluded a pact with Gil Robles's *Confederación de fuerzas monárquicas* the year before. The principal crime they were accused of was being well disposed towards the USA and NATO.

The eventual outcome of the PCE's anti-NATO policy was the transfer of its headquarters from France to Eastern Europe and Moscow, both for technical reasons and to escape police surveillance. The first to leave France, where they had been living since 1945, were Dolores Ibarruri, Santiago Carrillo and A. Mije, who moved to Prague in 1948—49. They were joined a year later by the majority of the other leaders and several hundred Party members, arrested and then expelled on 5 and 6 September 1950 by the French Ministry of the Interior in a round-up of foreign communists suspected of acting as a Soviet fifth column. [37] In all, 404 foreigners were expelled from France on this occasion, the majority being Spaniards living in Paris and south-western France. A further 150 — all Spanish — were deported to a spot south of Oran in Algeria, where they were made to stay in forced residence. They included the entire medical staff of the 'Warsaw' hospital in Toulouse, which had catered for Spanish refugees in the area, as well as for some men wounded in the Civil War and in guerrilla actions. [38]

This campaign of repression — the first since 1945 against the Spanish communists in exile — included searches of the Party's premises and the homes of its principal leaders as well as a ban on its papers published in France. *Mundo obrero,* which was published in the Rue Lafayette in Paris from 1946 to 1950, was forced to move to Prague, as were most of the other publications of the PCE, virtually all of which were at that time printed in France. [39] An arms cache is also said to have been seized at the time, near Barbazan, in south-western France.

From 1951 onward, however, two new factors were to counteract the Party's political and physical retreat to the USSR and Eastern Europe, to promote its reactivation as a political force in Spain and to help change its public image, notably among workers, intellectuals and students. The first was the fact that the French—Spanish frontier was fully reopened — a development which put an end to the separation of the underground activists in Spain from the Party leaders in exile. The second factor was the self-criticism to which certain leaders subjected themselves in connection with the strikes in Barcelona and the arrest of G. López Raimundo. [40]

The reopening of the frontier made it possible to send fresh cadres to Spain and to relieve those most immediately threatened in the country. It also made easier the dissemination of instructions and propaganda material by activists who did not figure on the police files, as well as by sympathisers posing simply as tourists. Later, new supporters recruited among the Spanish immigrant workers in France were used for this purpose. Efforts to reorganise the apparatus destroyed by the authorities between 1943 and 1951 proved in general successful, despite some inevitable setbacks, such as the arrest of G. López Raimundo.

The Party was thus able to go about two tasks it had set itself in October 1948, but which had remained a dead letter since then — the launching of mass campaigns and the infiltration of officially permitted organisations. To this end, the PCE got in touch with the socialists in the Spanish underground [41] and — for the first time — with militant Christian workers and left-wing supporters of the Falange. From then on the communists were to play an important, and sometimes decisive, part in the strikes and demonstrations, large and small, which became increasingly frequent from 1953 onwards. [42] They also tried, though with less success, to stage a number of actions of their own, such as the one on May Day of 1954. The only result of this was a handful of token stoppages and a few skirmishes with the police. In February of that year the communists were the only republican organisation to urge its supporters to take part in factory elections, the aim being to bring about the appointment of 'genuine representatives of the working class'. Moreover, making use of the ferment among the students which became apparent in Barcelona in March 1951 and took on unmistakably political overtones in Madrid in January 1954, the PCE renewed its attempts to infiltrate the student body, which up to then had been exposed exclusively to the propaganda of the Falange and the monarchists.

### Destalinisation

The second factor which helped the Party to recover arose from its 'destalinisation'. Stalin died in March 1953. In October of that year the PCE renewed its call for unity among all Spaniards in the struggle against the Franco regime. An article published in *Mundo obrero* in October 1954 called for the reinstatement of all unjustly expelled Party members. [43]

The same problem was discussed at the Fifth Party Congress — the first to meet since the one held in Seville in 1932. The Congress took place in Prague from 1 to 5 November 1954 and was attended by the leaders in exile, a small delegation of underground activists from Spain [44] and a number of PSUC representatives. Several decisions were agreed, foreshadowing those taken at the 1956 plenum and at the Sixth Party Congress in

1960. Some of these decisions concerned the Party's programme, notably the type of government the communists wanted in place of the Franco regime. The documents adopted in fact reiterated the policy the Party had outlined in March 1954, when it declared that it was in favour of a provisional coalition government but made no specific mention of the republican government-in-exile. [45] There was no explicit reference to the question of whether the 'bourgeois democratic republic' which the communists thought was the only possible solution in the prevailing situation should be a continuation of the 1936 Republic. [46] This matter was left in abeyance until November 1961, when the communist press publicly proclaimed itself in favour of a provisional government without defining its specific constitutional nature. The documents published after the Congress also repeated the call for unity in the struggle against the Franco regime which had already figured both in an appeal published in October 1953 and in a message addressed to patriotic intellectuals in April 1954.

The other decisions, which concerned the new statutes of the Party as well as the replacement of some of the members of its leading bodies, foreshadowed, albeit in a tentative way, the events that were to follow in 1956 and 1960. A number of representatives of the underground network, such as the bakery worker Simón Sánchez Montero, who is listed in the official documents under the pseudonym Vicente Sáinz and was at that time one of the chief leaders of the Party's Madrid organisation, were elected to the Central Committee. [47] Francisco Antón, whose rise in the Party's hierachy was the subject of some discussion – it was said to be due to his close friendship with La Pasionaria – was eliminated. She herself, however, retained the office of Secretary-General, and the Political Bureau still included several of the old leaders, such as M. Cristobal, M. Delicado and V. Uribe, who had joined it as far back as November 1932. The new members of the Bureau – S. Carrillo, F. Claudín, I. Gallego and E. Lister – all belonged to the generation of leaders who had first come into prominence during the Civil War and had then been in exile since 1939. The men of the underground, who had remained in Spain, were thus denied access to the highest authority in the Party. To put the matter in its correct perspective, however, it should be noted that, for all these formal changes, the Central Committee hardly ever met after 1939. In view of this, the new statutes adopted at the Congress, which emphasised the primacy of the Central Committee as a democratic decision-making body, must be seen as a declaration of intent rather than a practical measure.

The meeting of the augmented plenum of the Central Committee, held in August 1956, discussed frankly a number of questions which in 1954 had only been dealt with in a round-about way. Above all, it put an end to the personality cult and the 'errors' of the Stalin era.

A month after the opening date of the plenum, a six-page supplement to *Mundo obrero* dealt for the first time in detail with the revelations made at the Twentieth Congress of the Communist Party of the Soviet Union.[48] An account of the August 1956 plenum, published soon afterwards, included seven pages devoted to Santiago Carrillo's speech on the personality cult. In this report, submitted on behalf of the PCE's Central Committee, Carrillo welcomed the courageous self-criticism of the CPSU Central Committee[49] and placed on record 'its complete agreement with the latter's resolution concerning the cult of personality...'. Carrillo also admitted that the personality cult had 'existed to some extent and in certain forms' in the PCE.[50] He claimed that this had happened partly through the imitation of Soviet practices and partly as a result of the bad habits taken over from the Spanish bourgeois parties as well as from the PSOE and the CNT. In this connection, he spoke of the excessive emphasis placed on the role played by José Díaz and Dolores Ibarruri — albeit against their own wishes — 'since their modesty prompted them to oppose this type of propaganda'.[51]

La Pasionaria remained above criticism. In her closing speech at the plenum, she made it clear how far she thought the rehabilitation of the victims of the purges ought to go. According to her, Jesús Hernández and E. Castro were on no account to be rehabilitated. Bullejos, on the other hand, as well as Cartón, Astigarrabia, Bulnes, Lombardia, Comorera, Del Barrio and their 'Titoite' friends were eligible and could even be readmitted into the Party, provided they gave up their factional activities.[52] The error made in denouncing Tito had in fact been acknowledged before the plenum, which merely confirmed the policies adopted in June and published in the Party press in July[53] — at the same time as the supplement on the personality cult.

Echoing the line put forward at the Twentieth Congress of the CPSU, the Spanish communists blamed Beria for the unjust accusation.[54] At the end of the plenum, Dolores Ibarruri declared:

> The correction of an erroneous and unjust attitude ... in no way justifies the despicable conduct of those individuals whom the Communist Party had, for one reason or another, disciplined or expelled from its ranks before 1948 and who used the name of Yugoslavia as a slogan with which to attack and denigrate the Soviet Union and the communists ... .[55]

As regards personnel, the 1956 plenum continued the reorganisation of the leadership apparatus begun in 1954. In his stern criticism of the methods used by the leaders in the past, Carrillo gave details of the way the Party had been led since 1930. He spoke in particular of the arbitrary and often contradictory actions of certain individuals during the years 1939-45 and above all stressed the lack of democracy which had characterised the Party's actions between 1945 and 1950, when its leaders were in France. The fact that the Party was forced to function underground, he declared, was hardly an excuse, since the leaders were at that time quite free to meet both in Paris and Toulouse. Nevertheless, 'all the important questions were settled by the members of the Secretariat and the Political Bureau played but a minor role. The Central Committee, or rather what remained of it, did not meet once. We could have organised a Party congress but we did not do so'. Carrillo went on to say that this situation had not changed in any way until 1954, with the Secretariat making all the decisions, to all intents and purposes ignoring the Central Committee. Santiago Carrillo, himself the key figure in the changes made in 1956 and 1960, did concede, however, that 'a revolutionary party functioning underground is in no position to apply democratic practice on an extensive scale'. According to him, 'the needs of the clandestine struggle demand a large measure of centralisation, and this entails certain restrictions on democracy'. He declared that they also justified the continued primacy of the Party's apparatus abroad. [56]

The 1956 plenum undoubtedly helped the Party's underground elements in Spain to regain some of the influence they had lost to the leaders in exile. Senior officials of the underground were assigned higher positions in the PCE's leading bodies. Simón Sánchez Montero, in particular, became one of the working members of the Political Bureau, while Santiago Alvarez and Sebastián Zapiráin, who had made repeated visits to Spain since 1945, were appointed full and alternate members of the Bureau respectively. [57] An incident which occurred some months previously showed that the influence of the underground element could on occasion be decisive. It arose from a statement issued by Spanish communist exiles in Mexico, opposing Franco Spain's admission to the UN. At first this line was supported by some of the members of the Political Bureau, but when the leaders of the underground wing and their supporters in the Political Bureau opposed the statement, stressing the harm it was doing the PCE within the country, the Bureau decided not only to change its original policy but to come out publicly against it in an article in which Santiago Carrillo gave a cautious welcome to Spain's entry into the UN. [58]

The advance of the representatives of the 'internal front' went hand in hand with a decline in the influence of two veterans of the leadership in exile who, from 1956 onwards, were subjected to repeated attacks culminating in their virtual eclipse. Vicente Uribe, who had been a member of the Political Bureau for some twenty-four years, was ordered to surrender his control over the Party's clandestine activities at home, which he had wielded in autocratic fashion throughout the Stalin era. However, after an exercise in self-criticism, he was allowed to remain in the Political Bureau, where, if only because of the state of his health, he played only a nominal role. The other 'accused', Antonio Mije, was also compelled to confess his wrongdoings, notably his failure to support the new policy of national reconciliation vigorously enough. [59] In actual fact, the chief sin of both men was the bad grace with which they had bowed to the policies advocated by Santiago Carrillo, especially the rapprochement with the moderate opposition and the Catholics.

## National reconciliation: the peaceful road

On the tactical plane, the plenum approved the approach, outlined for the first time in the June Central Committee statement, on the policy of national reconciliation and the removal of the Franco dictatorship by peaceful means. [60] This policy has been maintained ever since, despite doubts following the events of May 1968 in France. It is based largely on the need for unity in the struggle against Franco and maximum use of the opportunities for overt action opened up since 1948. One new element emerged in 1958 — the watchword of 'reconciliation' among the Spanish people, divided since the Civil War. This made it possible for the Party to go beyond the constricting framework of the policy of unity among the working class and republican forces only. The new policy also laid stress on the need to employ 'peaceful means' — that is, legal methods rather than underground struggle. There is plenty of evidence to show that this change of heart did not occur in the PCE alone. It followed naturally from the recognition of the principle that there was more than one road to socialism, first proclaimed by the USSR in its declaration of 3 June 1955. It was this declaration which put the seal on the reconciliation of the USSR and Yugoslavia, and the basic principle was reaffirmed at the Twentieth Congress of the CPSU.

The first resolution adopted at the 1956 plenum made it clear that the PCE was ready to conclude pacts, agreements and alliances with all political groupings 'wanting national reconciliation'. [61] In their speeches at the plenum, Dolores Ibarruri and Santiago Carrillo laid great stress on the approaches the communists had made — and were prepared to make in the future — not only to the socialists and anarchists but also to the Catholics and even to Falangist workers. There was nothing new in this as regards the first two. In this connection the two speakers recalled the letter sent to Indalecio Prieto after his declaration of 1 May 1956 on the subject of 'national solidarity', as well as the agreements concluded in Catalonia between the PSUC and certain elements in the CNT. Ibarruri and Carrillo also made great play — a little clumsily, perhaps — with the sympathy which, according to them, the PCE enjoyed among anarchist and socialist workers. This was reflected, they claimed, in the decision taken the year before by a number of PSOE members, who had joined the PCE after having become disenchanted with the 'anti-revolutionary' policies of the socialist leaders. [62] Taking this line of argument one stage further, Carrillo declared that while it was altogether unthinkable for the PCE to wish to 'poach' members from the other working-class organisations, it was possible for a man 'to belong to the CNT and at the same time to the PCE or any other democratic party', since the CNT was a trade union organisation and not a political party. [63]

What was new in these statements were the references to a reconciliation and possible alliance with the Catholics, as well as to infiltration of the Falange as part of a policy of using all available means of overt action. In this connection Dolores Ibarruri noted merely how useful it might prove if there were 'people wearing the blue shirt, able to stand up openly, within the enemy camp, for the demands of the workers'.[64] This tactic was, in fact, nothing but an aspect of the policy of penetrating the official unions by getting PCE supporters elected on to works councils. More specific approaches to members of the Falange were made in the Party press the following year. Carrillo was at that stage prepared to go even further than La Pasionaria in this direction, acknowledging that some functionaries of the official 'vertical' unions had on occasion stood up courageously for the interests of their fellow workers. He went so far as to accuse the Basque communists of having failed to pay sufficient attention to such efforts by the *juntas sociales* in the region's unions. [65]

An alliance with the democratic Catholics was urged without reservation as a matter of immediate urgency. As far as they were concerned, it was no longer a matter of mere declarations of intent like those issued repeatedly since 1937. [66] Dolores Ibarruri, in particular, said that the Workers' Catholic Action must no longer be treated as a 'yellow' union, as some purblind Party members still insisted on doing. On the contrary, she declared, Christian workers were acting in closer and closer alliance with the communists, and the Workers' Catholic Action (ACO) was even in favour of legalising the PCE. In her view, therefore, Spanish Catholicism had ceased to be 'a monolithic force serving reaction and feudalism'. In another speech she went so far as to advocate the admission into the Party of any priests who might wish to join. [67]

However, in the coming years, internal opposition to these new policies continued to make itself felt, especially as regards the *rapprochement* with the Catholics. [68] During the following plenum, held on 13 and 14 September 1954, the need for the Central Committee to meet from time to time was acknowledged, but nothing was said about these differences of view. The plenum confined itself to underlining the 'success' of the Day of National al Reconciliation on 5 May 1958 — although it would have been more accurate to speak of its total failure. The Party had issued the directive for this campaign in September 1957. The peaceful national strike on 18 June 1959 was no more successful, since most other underground organisations apart from the Popular Liberation Front (FLP), held aloof from it.[69]

The partial failure of the peaceful national strike did not, however, prevent Carrillo from inflicting a final defeat on his adversaries in the Party. At the Sixth Congress — also in Prague, from 28 to 31 January 1960 — he managed to have the Political Bureau replaced by an Executive Committee which no longer included Vicente Uribe. [70] Carrillo, moreover, was appointed Secretary-General [71] in place of Dolores Ibarruri, who was 'kicked upstairs' to the purely honorary post of Chairman of the Central Committee

The Congress approved the principles of the 'peaceful national strike' [72] and the 'political general strike'[73], an extension of the former. These two types of strike, which in practical terms tended to be one and the same thing, have since then been invariably described as essential weapons in the struggle against the Franco regime, in spite of all the debates and schisms to which they have given rise since 1962. They were defined in 1959 in the following terms: 'A national strike is a general political strike of workers in town and country, with the support and participation in diverse forms of other sections and classes of society — peasants, petty and middle bourgeoisie, state employees and intellectuals — joining hands with the armed forces and the police against the dictatorship'. [74] Armed struggle plays a minor part in this context. In the Executive Committee's report to the October 1961 plenum of the Central Committee, armed struggle is endorsed only if the living conditions of the masses of the people 'reach the limits of what is intolerable'. [75] This definition allowed wide latitude to the proponents of the 'peaceful road'.

The success of this tactic implied a return to the concept of a mass party — difficult to pursue for a party functioning underground. [76] In practice, no attempt was made after 1939 to apply such a policy, which also called for structural changes in the organisation, to make it easier for middle-class people and intellectuals — who were expected to join in the national strike — to become Party membeis. It was to this end that the Sixth Congress agreed in principle that there must be an intense recruiting drive to attract new members into the Party as well as to regain the old ones with whom it had lost touch since the Civil War. With the same end in view, Congress ratified an amendment of Article 33 of the Party statutes, allowing individuals to enter without necessarily joining a Party cell.

The programme published after the 1960 Congress also stressed the need for closer links with the middle class. [77] The congress report says on this point that the PCE's aim was to defend 'the demands not only of the workers but also of social groups which are the natural allies of the working class'. As for the peasants, they were given the assurance that the socialist transformation of the countryside would be accomplished by slow stages, in accordance with the freely expressed desires of the peasants themselves. [78]

During the years which followed, the communist leaders issued more and more statements friendly to the 'middle strata', especially the 'non-monopoly bourgeoisie'. They even went so far as to praise the police and the army. An article published in 1960 dwelt on the almost friendly attitude of the Civil Guard men and of Major Pardo de Santayana — the guards and defence counsel respectively — during the trial in November of the arrested Congress delegates who had returned from Prague.[79] A little later, in a speech meant for the ears of the forces of law and order and made during the strikes of May 1962, the Secretary-General of the Party referred to the Civil Guards' apparent sympathy for the strikers and appealed to the army not to let Franco cast a slur on its honour any longer. [80]

The change in the Communist Party's line between 1956 and 1960 coincided with an important transformation in the Spanish political climate, which opened up for the Party excellent chances of action and recruitment. The regime, while not in fact menaced, as its propaganda media made out, was rejected by a growing segment of the population, which was shaking off the political lethargy it had displayed since the Civil War. Some people were beginning to reflect that there was bound to be a post-Franco period and that it would be best not to delay too long making some preparation for it. The regime itself was coming under the influence of a new generation of technocrats who wanted some degree of movement towards liberalism, and from 1962 onwards were making their mark on the economy and on the media.

After 1958, strikes — a rarity between 1947 and 1956 — broke out at frequent intervals. They have never since then died down, and sporadic outbreaks still take place. Moreover, they were from this time incomparably larger in scale and of much longer duration than they had been a few years earlier. [81] The students, too, were beginning to stir more and more, and, after 1956, to organise themselves into more distinct groupings. The first time a university incident took a violent turn was in February 1956 in Madrid, where one student was killed. There were more incidents, triggered by various causes in May 1957, March 1958 and January and May 1961, in Barcelona and Madrid. They grew more frequent still in 1962, and became virtually a permanent feature of the scene in the opening term of 1965, when the first of the 'free assemblies' was formed.

It was also at this time that the opposition of the intellectuals who had stayed behind in Spain at the end of the Civil War began to develop. [82] Some old Falangists, like Dionisio Ridruejo, who set up a Social Party of Democratic Action in 1956, [83] began at this time to voice openly their disagreement with the regime. [84] The University Congress of Young Writers, following which Rector P. Lain Estralgo and the Minister of Education, J. Ruiz Giménez, [85] were dismissed, took place the same year.

The Marxist philosophical revival, which occurred in these years, also benefited the communists. While not a single book on Marxist philosophy was published in Spain between 1939 and 1956 — apart from a few pages included in university textbooks or works of scholarship, [86] the few non-conforming reviews tolerated by the government now ventured to publish articles which discussed Marxist themes. In particular, there was the *Boletín informativo del seminario de derecho político* of the University of Salamanca, launched in 1954 by Professor Enrique Tierno Galván and his assistants Pablo Lucas Verdu and Raúl Morodo, which published thirty-two numbers before it was banned in 1964. [87] From this time, a relative relaxation of censorship allowed a growing number of the writings of Marx and Engels to appear, as well as a number of other books, beginning with simple introductions to Marxism and gradually progressing to Marxist philosophy proper.

This 'opening towards Marxism' was for many intellectuals but a first step in the transformation of the attitude of Spanish Catholics towards the authorities in power, a process given concrete expression in November 1965. On this occasion, a number of priests and laymen, gathered for a congress of the lay ministry, put their names to an 'Escorial Manifesto'. This document for the first time voiced the demands for the liberalisation of the regime and the Church's 'disengagement' from it that have been so often repeated since then. In the same year, the philosopher José L.L. Aranguren published the first book of Christian 'self-criticism' under the title *Catolicismo día tras día.* Also in the same the year, the group round Professor Manuel Giménez Fernández, a one-time Deputy representing CEDA, the Republican Catholic Party, and a Minister of Agriculture in 1934—35 under the Republic, founded the *Izquierda democrática cristiana*, whose programme, published in 1957, was inspired by the Italian Christian-Democratic Left. This clandestine organisation, which changed its name in 1965 to *Unión demócrata cristiana*, enjoyed a certain amount of success in student circles. Other Christian Democrat schools of thought, somewhat less left-wing in their politics, also tried to draw fresh strength in this atmosphere, which had become less unfavourable to political thought. The former CEDA leader, Gil Robles, gathered round himself some moderates opposed to collaboration with the regime; and the former Minister of National Education, J. Ruiz Giménez, became, via the review *Cuadernos para el diálogo,* the spokesman of a Christian opposition tolerated by Franco.

Other Catholic groups began from this time on to display much more radical attitudes. One of them launched the short-lived review *Praxis*, which had a frankly Marxist orientation, in Cordoba. In 1957—58, a number of progressive Catholics, including Ignacio Fernández de Castro, gained control of the *Servicio universitario del trabajo*, which was supposed to be subordinate to the official university Syndicate. They used the machinery of this body to organise the first militants of the *Frente de liberación popular*, which took shape in 1958. During its first two phases, in 1958—59 and from 1960 to 1962, the FLP was essentially an organisation of young progressive Catholics influenced by Marxist ideology whose aim was to bring about a 'Christian revolution', and who claimed to be generally to the left of all other underground organisations. While accusing the PCE of having become a conservative force, the *Felipes* [88] were in fact to some extent influenced by the Communist Party, which largely inspired their own organisation . They built up fairly quickly a following in the Workers' Catholic Action, and more particularly among the students, for whom, from 1962 onwards, they tended to take the place of the communists. But they worked closely with the PCE in practical action and were in fact virtually the only group to do so on the 'Day of National Reconciliation' in 1958 and during the 'Peaceful National Strike' of 1959.

The FLP tore itself apart and then reformed itself several times, partly as a result of police repression and partly because of ideological disputes. These differences resulted in the defection of many active members, several of whom joined the PCE. But even more joined the dissident or parallel communist organisations which began to appear from 1962 onwards. The FLP thus served as an ideological halfway house for young Christians undergoing the process of revolutionary radicalisation.

Despite the Hungarian rising and a campaign of persecution which hit the Party especially hard in 1959 and 1960,[89] the PCE benefited considerably from this climate, which remained until 1962. It rebuilt or consolidated its organisation in the working-class movement and among the students, particularly in Madrid, but also in villages in the provinces of Albacete, Badajoz and Seville. A number of Central Committee members, including Julián Grimau, were sent to Spain for this purpose. The PCE increased its strength quite substantially among workers, students and intellectuals.

Among the latter, and also occasionally among the students, recruitment often took place abroad, during trips by lecturers, painters or young writers to foreign countries, and France in particular. The communists' prestige made itself felt beyond the circle of their actual membership by virtue of their relative effectiveness compared with the other opposition groupings, and of their exemplary demeanour in the face of persecution, which bore even harder on them than on the others.[90] Many intellectuals like José María Castellet, Juan and Luis Goytisolo and Carlos Barral toyed at various times with the idea of joining the Party and have displayed warm sympathy for it on many occasions since then.

The communists' courage also contributed to their prestige among working-class militants thrown up by the series of strikes that had been taking place since 1959. For them, prison had been a recruiting ground and a privileged place of education ever since 1939. Another group that should not be overlooked is that of the Spaniards repatriated from the USSR in 1956;[91] these provided a fresh draft of members. Most of these repatriates kept away from all political activity, but some were soon arrested and involved in political trials. Thus eight of them were among the thirty-nine communists arrested in Oviedo in 1960. Julio Marín, leader of the Madrid university cell, who was arrested in 1959, was likewise a former refugee from the USSR; so was the electrician Aladino Cuervo, arrested after his return from the Prague Congress in 1960. The group of engineers and technicians arrested in Bilbao the same year had also been exiles in the USSR.

The Party was thus in a position to reinforce its clandestine machinery in Spain and to re-establish contact with veterans who had been isolated since the end of the Civil War, particularly in the Basque country, in the Asturias and in Madrid. In 1961 it even managed to set up again a *Unión de juventudes comunistas*, to take the place of the JSU, which had vanished practically without trace in 1945.

At the level of practical action, after the failures of 5 May 1958 and

18 June 1959, the communists concentrated on spectacular demonstrations. From 1960 onwards, their main interest lay in extending their influence among the workers, among whom activists of the Catholic Action had been busy for some years, and in arriving at an understanding with the other political opposition groups. Despite the increasingly moderate attitude they were adopting for this reason — which in 1963 even led them to reaffirm their desire to work with the bourgeois parties — these overtures met with only scant response.

They lost the support of those socialists in the country who favoured a rapprochement with the PCE. In August 1958, this group had seceded from the PSOE Executive Committee, which was opposed to such a move. But in November of the same year, Antonio Amat and the main leaders of the Socialist Party's clandestine organisation to be involved were arrested. In March 1961, the underground UGT and CNT trade union organisations, later joined by the STV,[92] formed the *Alianza sindical*, the true aim of which was to resist communist — but also Christian — penetration of the working class. In July of the same year, the PCE, together with the anarchists, the *Unión de fuerzas democráticas* — a left-wing Catholic body, made up of republicans, socialists and Basque nationalists — was excluded from the *Alianza*. Nor were they invited to the meeting held in Munich in 1962, attended by 118 monarchist, republican, socialist, left- and right-wing Christian Democrats and FLP members.

The communists were probably not surprised at the comparative failure of their attempts to collaborate with other émigré political organisations. However, they had more reason for satisfaction with the results they obtained 'in the field' from their efforts to infiltrate and organise the workers' councils which were beginning to spring up on the fringes of the old underground trade union bodies from 1958—60 onwards.

Here, too, the PCE stuck to a moderate line within the law, which enabled it to occupy a central place on the councils from 1962 to 1966. Later, this line landed the Party in difficulties which are to this day contributing to its troubles. In particular, the Party continued to advocate — as it has done almost continuously since 1948 — participation in the elections to the 'works arbitration committees', as some of the Christian and FLP activists were doing, and as the socialist, anarchist and Christian Democrat underground trade union federations were not. In 1961, the communists set up their own clandestine trade union body, the Workers' Trade Union Opposition, better known as OSO, but they seldom made use of it, being more prone to action within the workers' councils, the works arbitration committees and the official 'vertical trade unions'.

## The Party challenged from the left: divisions

Between 1964 and 1966, the PCE at last managed to establish extensive control in the workers' councils in Madrid and the Asturias. But the very extent of its penetration into these organisations, as well as its orders for the National Action Days on 27 October 1967 and 14 May 1968, which involved its followers in considerable risks, helped to isolate it once again and to provide the 'leftist' organisations which were springing up at this time with ammunition for criticism.

In 1966 there began a revolt, among Catholic, socialist and left-wing Falangist militants in the workers' councils, against the communists' methods, and more especially against their frequent recourse to votes of confidence giving them *carte blanche* to do as they pleased. One particularly serious crisis blew up in Madrid in June 1967, leading to the withdrawal from the councils of socialist delegates from the UGT and PSOE, and of Catholics and independent socialists from underground trade union bodies. As a result, the two sides set up their own trade union federations. [93] The same sort of difficulties arose in the Bilbao area, weakening the Basque workers' councils to such an extent that after the wave of arrests in the autum of 1967 they never managed to re-form themselves.

Although the great body of their members did not follow the Madrid breakaway group, from that time on the workers' councils tended to be looked on as a tool of the PCE — often with justification. The same applied to the youth and citizens' councils set up since 1967 with the object of reaching non-working-class sympathisers.

The PCE's moderate line led to its being outflanked on the left even before the crisis within the workers' councils. The first signs of this appeared in 1963, with the breakaway of the greater part of the Madrid students' organisation, which took the so-called 'Chinese' line. This rival 'Marxist-Leninist' movement took shape and spread among left-wing students — both communists and Christians who had discovered Marxism. On the other hand, at least until 1967, it hardly impinged on the Party's working-class following.

The first 'Marxist-Leninist' organisation cropped up in 1963. It was the *Partido comunista español,* which that year published a *Mundo obrero* of its own, parallel with the 'revisionist' PCE's journal. [94] In February and March 1964, there also appeared a single number of *El Proletario,* described as the mouthpiece of 'the Spanish Marxist-Leninists, as well as a single *Mundo obrero revolucionario*, claiming to speak for a *Movimiento obrero revolucionario'*. They were followed in April by the first edition of yet another clandestine periodical, *La Chispa,* [95] organ of the 'PCE Revolutionary Opposition'.

All these groupings, except for the first-named, which vanished when one of its leaders was arrested early in 1964, agreed to join together at a gathering held in Switzerland on 4 October that year. The merger took effect on 17 December 1964, with the creation of a *Partido comunista de España (ML)*, embracing the three trends represented by *El Proletario, Mundo obrero revolucionario* and *La Chispa.* Printed outside Spain, the new party's organ was distributed for the first time in January 1965 under the title *Vanguardia obrera.*

But the united PCE (ML) was short-lived. In March 1965, a new *Mundo obrero (ML)* was born. This gave an account of a split between the *El Proletario* group on the one hand and the *Mundo obrero—Chispa* combination on the other. The former stayed loyal to the united party and went on publishing *Vanguardia obrera.* The latter set up their own organisation which, however, kept the same name. [96]

There was little to distinguish the two parties in ideology and in their criticism of the bureaucratic, social-democrat and petty bourgeois character of the PCE. Moreover, at the outset both appear to have had links with the small anarchist group known as the *Federación ibérica de juventud libertaria.* [97]

What distinguished them was more clearly the provenance of their membership. The *Mundo obrero revolucionario—La Chispa* faction seems to have been recruited mostly among former PCE activists, many of whom were said to have left the Party after an 'extraordinary national conference' held on 15 and 16 February 1964. On the other hand, the *El Proletario* group, which controlled the 'united' PCE (ML), seemed to draw its support more from émigrés in Switzerland and Belgium, many of whom had never belonged to the PCE.

The second group began to strike root in Spain itself in 1966, thanks to the new strength infused into it by Paulino García Moya, a communist militant who had emigrated to Colombia in 1954 and who returned to Spain at the head of a small group at this time. Although García Moya himself was arrested soon after his return, the PCE (ML) did meet with some success at its own level, and maintained its lead over the other Marxist-Leninist organisations in the next few years. In 1966, it gathered to itself a new group which had left the PCE, known as the *Roja bandera;* and at about this time established close links with the *Ejército republicano de liberación* or ERL, which it hoped to turn into its military wing, within a National Democratic Revolutionary Front that it was just then trying to promote. In 1967, it even re-established a precarious union with the other PCE (m.l.). It managed, too, to hold three plenums of its Central Committee, in December 1964, December 1967 and December 1968. The last two took place in Spain itself, in Zaragoza and Malaga.

But these limited successes did not save the PCE (ML) from being in its turn torn apart by schisms; nor did they stop parallel organisations from springing up. These developments weakened the PCE (ML) more than they harmed Santiago Carrillo's PCE. An early breakaway faction, situated somewhere to the left of the Marxist-Leninist movement, was of the Trotskyite persuasion. Consisting of advocates of armed struggle and led by Francisco Crespo Méndez, and described by *Vanguardia obrera* as 'assassins in the pay of the CIA', [98] they were expelled from the pro-Chinese Communist Party in 1965 and took the name *Frente de acción revolucionaria*. Other Trotskyites broke away at about the same time, to organise the small groups of the *Partido obrero revolucionario (T)* at the universities of Madrid and Barcelona. [99]

The PCE (ML) underwent a more dangerous crisis in 1968, when some of its members at Madrid University — who were on the right rather than the left of the Marxist-Leninist movement — seceded from it. This group, who took with them a considerable number of the Party's student supporters, already reduced by the arrest of twenty-six members of the Party's central branch in February 1968, took the title *Movimiento comunista (ML) de España*. It published the underground journal *El Comunista* fairly regularly. Its programme, outlined in August 1968, was equally hostile to the Trotskyites, to the 'leftist' Marxist-Leninists and to the 'rightists' of the PCE. All were accused of 'plotting against the working-class movement to prevent the creation of its vanguard party'. [100] Its opposition to the orthodox PCE seems, however, to have been purely verbal. Even though it presented itself as 'Stalinist', just as did the pro-Chinese groups, the *Movimiento comunista (ML)* nevertheless advocated participation in the workers' councils, just as the PCE did. [101] In practice, its activists seem to have got on well with the mainstream communists, whereas their relations with the PCE (ML) were much more strained. They refrained from attacking supporters of Castro and Guevara, who enjoyed a great following at the university and who were being carefully cultivated by Santiago Carrillo. The other pro-Chinese groups, on the other hand were critical of Castro, whom they described as a 'petty bourgois revolutionary'. [102]

While benefiting indirectly, at least in Madrid, from the difficulties of its main Marxist-Leninist competitor, resulting from the defection of the *Movimiento comunista*, the PCE nevertheless continued to lose ground in other areas of Spain. In particular, its working-class base, until then little affected by the pro-Chinese movement, was for the first time under pressure. A new breakaway organisation, the *Partido comunista de España (Internacional)* had in fact been set up in Liège on 22 and 23 February 1969, attracting to its ranks a proportion of the communist following in Catalonia — intellectuals and students as well as workers.

The relative success of the PCE (*Internacional*) with proletarian members and sympathisers otherwise faithful to the orthodox Party is very largely explained by the history of the communist movement in Catalonia. In Spain, Catalonia has always been a bastion of leftist Marxist organisations, like the *Bloc obrer i camperol* and POUM in the days before the Civil War. When the PCE was trying to challenge the anarchists' predominant position there, it could only obtain a foothold in Catalonia by using the *Partit socialista unificat de Catalunya* as an instrument to gather some small moderate bourgeois left-wing parties — not unlike the French Radical Party — under its wing.

Convinced that the PSUC was destined for gradual incorporation into the PCE, the communist leadership had steadily tried to circumscribe its ideological and cultural independence. In 1943 or thereabouts, they even made an attempt to merge it completely with their own Party, triggering off a crisis which forced them to allow their Catalan branch at least a nominally separate identity, even if they did put it under a Secretary-General with a Spanish-sounding name (but who did speak Catalan). [103] On the other side, the original PSUC leaders and activists struck up only a conditional and tactical alliance with the PCE, as a defence against the anarchists during the Civil War; later, when they had gone underground, the PSUC's object was to have the use of the communist apparatus. It is in this spirit that the PSUC had asked for, and obtained, separate affiliation with the Communist International. Later, it was again in this spirit that it resisted the pressures which culminated in the departure of its first Secretary-General, Joan Comorera, in 1949. [104] Later the PCE managed to retain control over the PSUC only at the price of a *de facto* defection of a number of small clandestine groups dedicated to their independence.

In these circumstances it was not surprising that the divorce between the two, foreshadowed since 1967, [105] and formalised in 1969 under the banner of the PCE (*Internacional*) should have been welcomed by a fairly substantial proportion of Catalan communists, less marked by the sharp division between intellectuals and rank-and-file which characterised the rest of Spain. [106] By the same token, the somewhat regional character of the PCE (*Internacional*) helps to explain its poor showing in other areas. In Madrid, at one stage, it even had to dissolve its organisation for a while because it was unable to identify the police informers who had infiltrated its ranks; and in Seville, its local organisation was destroyed by the police early in 1969.

Allowing for its social make-up, it is surprising that the PCE (*Internacional*) should have presented itself in its two publications, *Mundo obrero (Internacional)* and *El Quehacer proletario,* as a Stalinist group demanding the bolshevisation of the PCE. By this it meant that the 'bourgeoisification' of the Carrillo apparatus made it imperative to transform the PCE into 'a proletarian organisation of the Leninist type' after expelling bourgeois elements from it, through an extension of the class struggle into the bosom of the Party itself. [107] At the tactical level, the PCE (*Internacional*) condemned both the law-abiding methods of the 'modern revisionists' and the Marxist-Leninists' undue preoccupation with theories. It demanded that the workers' councils should be recast in a revolutionary mould and advocated armed struggle, while condemning the prematureness of Latin-American guerrilla action in this context. [108]

The year 1964, in which the left-wing schisms formented by the intellectual and student base of the PCE began, was also notable for what Santiago Carrillo described as 'a right-wing liquidationist attempt aggravated by the fact that its promoters were Party leaders'. [109] This internal crisis, which blew up in the Executive Committee, was on the face of it caused by disagreement about the tactics used by the PCE since 1956 and about the Party leaders' analysis of the Spanish political situation. Fernando Claudín described the latter as 'subjective'. A member of the Communist Youth from before the days of the merger with the Socialist Youth, and a member of the PCE Secretariat and Executive Committee since 1956, Claudín at this time seemed to be third in the Party hierarchy, coming after Dolores Ibarruri and Carrillo. He had the support of two other members of the Executive Committee: Jorge Semprún, at that time known under the pseudonym Federico Sánchez; and at first also of Juan Gómez. In addition, he had the backing and moral support of some of the émigré intellectuals.

Signs of this group's opposition to various aspects of the policy followed under Carrillo's leadership had been discernible since 1963. What sparked the final break was a speech by Claudín at a meeting of the Executive Comittee on 27 March 1964. The report he submitted to the meeting recognised the tactical usefulness of the policy of national reconciliation as part and parcel of the struggle against the Franco regime, but took issue with the view that it could be the instrument of a democratic revolution. According to Claudín, the only way to achieve that end was a socialist revolution. [110] Claudín moreover condemned 'catastrophist' and subjective interpretations of the Spanish political and economic situation which, he alleged, had been accepted by the Party leadership in defiance of the facts. Claudín argued that the country's development, a reality largely denied by the leadership in the Executive Committee and the Secretariat, had made nonsense of their hopes of a change in the balance of forces in the country in favour of the opposition to the regime. Accordingly, he criticised his colleagues in the Party leadership — and himself — for having, through their failure to analyse the situation with sufficient vigour, sacrificed without good reason many underground activists who had been sent into action in pursuance of the policy of keeping Party activity within the law.

The reaction of the majority of the Executive Committee was to expel Claudín and Semprún first from the Central Committee and then from the Party itself, and to make Gómez perform a very unconvincing act of self-criticism. [111] More positively, the Committee also reacted to Claudín's criticisms by in effect accepting some of them. For instance, the imminent downfall of Francoism, continually harped on since 1963, was less frequently referred to after June 1964. This crisis had resulted, on the surface, from arguments about tactics and the PCE's alliances; but the roots of the conflict went back further and were partly a reflection of quarrels between veterans of the United Socialist Youth, going back to 1936. The United Socialist Youth (JSU), born of the merger of the two left-wing youth organisations, had ceased to exist fifteen years earlier, if only because its membership, recruited entirely between 1936 and 1939, was getting too old. It was replaced in 1962 by the Communist Youth Union, which was directly subordinated to the Party, in contrast to the JSU, which had enjoyed formal autonomy.

But it so happened that the current generation of PCE leaders who had been in their twenties in 1936 and were now aged between fifty and sixty, had originally come from the JSU and were divided among themselves by its dual origins. The quarrel which broke out in 1964 in the Executive Committee was thus but a continuation of those which had raged within the JSU between the ex-socialists, headed by Carrillo, and the former Communist Youth members, the most prominent of whom was Claudín.

All these difficulties cast doubt on the PCE's predominant place among the Spanish Marxist opposition forces. The Party's ability to attract support was reduced at the very moment when it had to cope with more competition from the left, when even Catholic groups were laying claim to the title 'communist', [112] and when revolutionary movements demanding autonomy were outstripping it in popularity in the Basque country and in Galicia. [113]

At first, Carrillo's team naturally tried to keep these quarrels to a minimum and to cover them up. Thus the Seventh Party Congress, held in 1965, was wrapped in a shroud of secrecy, the reasons for which went beyond the security considerations occasioned by the reverses the Party had suffered following the 1954 and 1960 Congresses. But the PCE, even though it controls to this day propaganda and communication resources beyond comparison with those of any other underground organisation, was struck a new blow in the form of the backlash of the Czechoslovak events.

The crisis unfolded in two stages. Its first tangible result was the expulsion of the 'Sovietophiles' from the Party in 1969. This group was led by the former Secretary for Organisation, Eduardo García, and by Agustín Gómez. They were followed out of the Party by some of the Basque communists and some Spanish communists living in France. In the second phase, Enrique Lister joined this breakaway group. He had been campaigning against the Carrillo line within the Party from the latter part of 1969 to the autumn of 1970. Lister, whose prestige among Spanish communists was second only to La Pasionaria's, and who was a Civil War hero, was expelled by the Carrillo faction in September 1970 together with Celestino Uriarte, the Party leader in the Basque country, and José Barzana, in charge of the PCE's financial affairs; as well as Luis Balaguer and Jesús Saíz, both responsible for Spanish communist refugees in the USSR. All were members of the Central Committee. [114] The expelled group, which received material aid from Czechoslovakia and Poland and support from the USSR, now controlled an independent and parallel organisation side-by-side with Carrillo's Party and published its own edition of *Mundo obrero*, the first copies of which it tried to distribute from the Spanish stands at the *L'Humanité* Festival in Paris on 13 September 1970. This group took with it out of the main Party the majority of Spanish communist refugees in the USSR and Eastern Europe, as well as some groups of refugees in France and of communists in Spain itself.


### The PCE in the international communist movement — impact of the Czechoslovak affair on the Party

The PCE's critical attitude towards the intervention of the Warsaw Treaty forces in Czechoslovakia did not merely coincide with that of other Western communist parties, notably the French and the Italian. The Spanish communists in fact went further than the French and the Italians, occasionally coming close to a complete break with the CPSU. This new line was a far cry from the almost total adherence to Soviet orthodoxy that had been so long displayed, before, during and after the Civil War. Like their French comrades, the Spanish communists on occasion even gave proof of a degree of discipline which exceeded the standards applied by other Western parties; thus, they changed their minds about the partial rehabilitation of Yugoslav revisionism which had taken place in 1956 and by 1959 were again castigating its virtual 'membership of the imperialist camp'. [115]

The PCE first gave signs of nonconformist reactions in 1964, immediately following Khrushchev's dismissal. In this instance, it did chime in with the French Communist Party. A long article in *Mundo obrero* praised the overthrown Party Secretary and stressed the 'considerable emotion' aroused by his removal. However, the article did go on to say that, in the opinion of the PCE leadership, 'Khrushchev's merits are shared by the CPSU as a whole, by its Central Committee, and of course by the men who now replace him – Brezhnev and Kosygin'. [116]

After this, the Spaniards conducted themselves most prudently; but their course was one of gradually embracing the principle of autonomy for each party within the international communist movement. This idea had been launched by Palmiro Togliatti in his speech at the Eighth Congress of the Italian Communist Party. After 1965, they maintained more regular relations with the Italians, who began to exercise a kind of tutelage over some of the progressive parties and movements in the Mediterranean region, while reducing their former special relationship with the French Communist Party and those of Eastern Europe. It is also worth noting that in 1966 a delegation headed by Carrillo went to Romania after attending the CPSU congress. A year later, to mark the fiftieth anniversary of the October Revolution, *Nuestra bandera* published an article in which the Secretary-General of the PCE declared that the Spanish communists considered themselves to be in sole charge of Spain's march towards socialism.

In January 1968, Carrillo made another visit to Romania. Soon afterwards, following the elimination of Anibal Escalante on charges of following a line too close to the Soviet one, he went to Cuba.

But the real turning-point in the PCE's attitude did not come until the Czechoslovak affair. On 1 May 1968, an article by Santiago Alvarez, considered fourth in the Party hierarchy after Ibarruri, Carrillo and Lister, voiced the 'profound sympathy' with which Spanish communists viewed the process of renewal taking place in Czechoslovakia, as well as their special interest in this process as a model for a future Spanish society. [117]

In July, in an interview broadcast by 'Radio Independent Spain', the Party Secretary-General added that 'the information we have about Czechoslovakia confirms that the replacement of the former [Novotný] leadership was a necessary step which could no longer be deferred, and that the new situation, even if it has led to the appearance of some anti-socialist groups, does not represent any real threat to the continued existence of a socialist regime ...'. [118] Finally, on 14 August, a week before the entry of Russian troops into Prague, a statement by the Party's Executive Committee, published immediately after the Bratislava meeting of Soviet, Polish, East German, Hungarian, Bulgarian and Czechoslovak representatives, declared that the statement issued at the conclusion of this gathering had endorsed 'the new course of the leadership of the Czechoslovak Communist Party towards greater democratisation of the country's life ...'. [119]

On 21 August itself, Dolores Ibarruri protested to the Kremlin against the military intervention which was taking place that day. Demands for an explanation, made by her on this occasion, as well as by Santiago Carrillo and by Longo and Pajetta, who happened to be in Moscow, are said to have been received with scant courtesy by the Soviet leaders. 'When all's said and done', Suslov is reported to have remarked to Carrillo, 'yours is only a small party'. [120]

A few days later, in a statement dated 28 August, the PCE Executive Committee put on record its 'negative attitude to the armed intervention in Czechoslovakia, being of the opinion that the solution of that country's problems is a matter for the Czechoslovak Communist Party and people, assisted by the socialist states and by the communist and workers' parties of the world'. [121] This statement, endorsed by the Central Committee in October by sixty-six votes to five, also revealed that 'on 22 August the PCE approached the CPSU Central Committee with a compromise formula for an understanding with the Czechoslovak Communist Party Praesidium, headed by Comrade Dubček, so as to find a positive political solution which would guarantee both the independence and sovereignty of Czechoslovakia and the strengthening of the socialist system in the country'. An article in *Mundo obrero* of 15 September made it clear, in addition, that Spanish communists could 'neither conceive nor accept the hypothesis, which our enemies are today in a position to put forward, that once the Communist Party has come to power in Spain in partnership with the forces of labour and culture, another socialist Power — no matter which — could dictate policies to us. Even less can we conceive or accept that such a Power could intervene militarily in our territory without the most energetic resistance on our part'. [122]

Like their comrades in most Western communist parties, the PCE leaders mitigated their attack by declaring that it did not affect in any way their appreciation of 'the decisive role played by the USSR and its Party

in the struggle against imperialism'. However, despite such savers, repeated
several times in the autumn and winter of 1968—69, the PCE henceforth
stuck to a position which has to all intents and purposes remained basically unchanged. Thus in October 1968, [123] it demanded that the international conference of communist parties, scheduled for 25 November of
that year, should be postponed. [124] And when the meeting did eventually
take place in Moscow, in June 1969, the Spanish delegation sided with the
twelve parties that were most critical of the main document submitted to
the sixty-nine delegations present. They signed it only with reservations —
at the urging of the Romanian, Swiss, Moroccan and Sudanese parties. [125]

Carrillo's team could hardly avoid criticising the Russian intervention in
Czechoslovakia; had it not done so, it would have isolated itself from the
other communist parties of Western Europe, most of which had condemned it. In the long run, the PCE was bound to benefit from its attitude. However, there is no denying that the immediate price was high —
high enough to jeopardise the internal cohesion of the Party, already
gravely damaged by the splits and quarrels of 1963.

Quite apart from the consequences of the PCE's attitude to the vital
facilities hitherto put at its disposal in the USSR and the East European
countries — the threat to which probably partly explains its approaches to
the Romanians, who might furnish the Party with a refuge in case of
difficulties with the other people's democracies — the condemnation of
the intervention in Czechoslovakia could hardly fail to arouse strong resistance, and to reawaken old quarrels in the highest reaches of the Party, as
well as in some of the area committees in Spain. As we have already
noted, the protest was the root cause of the expulsion of two leading
figures, Eduardo García, the Party's Secretary for Organisation, responsible for liaison with the underground apparatus; and A. Gómez, a member of the Central Committee since 1968, an engineer repatriated to Spain
from the USSR. Considered as a key figure in the PCE, García had spoken
out against the condemnation of the intervention and had earlier shown
his disapproval of 'Italian' tendencies, the persistence of which in the
Party after Claudín's removal he deplored. Instructed to reconsider his
position, though allowed to continue in his post until the autumn of
1968, he was eventually forced to resign in 1969, at the same time as
Gómez was expelled from the Central Committee. There was of course
also the 'Lister affair', leading to what was without doubt the gravest crisis
to have hit the Party in recent years. Despite Carrillo's denunciations and
his insistence that 90 per cent of Spanish communists living in the USSR
had remained loyal to his own organisation, the truth was that this latest

upheaval in the PCE made all earlier divisions and expulsions pale into insignificance.

The Party paper *Mundo obrero* did not give any account of the García affair until several months later — in its issue of 7 October to be exact. According to the paper, the two disciplined Party leaders had gone back on an undertaking given in October 1968 'not to destroy the unity of the Party' and had indulged in 'splitting activities on Spanish territory, losing all sight of the security rules incumbent on a party working underground'. [126] By contrast, *Mundo obrero* was unable to delay by more than a few days its report of the quarrel with Lister.

The impression persists that it is difficult to see how the émigré leadership could have found a position to satisfy all the leaders and 'elder statesmen' of the Party, as well as the majority of active members at home, who were in any case extensively divided among themselves. There was a sort of generation gap between the veteran rank-and-file, who bore the stamp of Stalinist discipline, and who were particularly numerous in the Basque country, in Asturias and of course in Eastern Europe, and the young, with their views more akin to the critical attitude of the New Left intellectuals. There was also a second conflict between the advocates of the peaceful and opportunist tactics favoured by Carrillo and those who wanted a more revolutionary line, better suited to the violent methods advocated by the leftists.

The García and Lister affairs were in one sense [127] only one episode in the longstanding rivalry between the two main 'strata' in the Party leadership: those dreaming of a return to 'monolithic communism' and those who preached polycentrism — themselves splintered into a multitude of factions, of which whoever had the support of the 'monolithic' communists at the time would momentarily prevail.

Today, there are signs that several of the most prominent members of the Executive Committee who may be fairly confidently classified as belonging to the 'monolithic' category now regret the direction in which the Party set out in 1968, even if they subscribed to it at the time in the name of democratic centralism. Besides Lister, who openly spoke out in this sense, after first subscribing to the Central Committee resolution condemning the Russian intervention in Czechoslovakia, it was noticed that Dolores Ibarruri did not join in the applause that followed Santiago Carrillo's speech at the June 1966 international conference of communist and workers' parties in Moscow. This discreet display of hostility, although possibly motivated by the Czechoslovak affair and its effects on the Party's internal life, is one aspect of the criticism directed against 'Italian' — i.e. 'opportunist' or 'rightist' — deviations.

In 1963, a coalition consisting of the 'polycentrists' round Carrillo, and the 'dignitaries', led by Ibarruri, took the field against Claudín and his followers. It now appeared that the Secretary-General was himself the object of attacks at the top level — attacks which perhaps indicated a reshuffle of alliances within the leading group. And after La Pasionaria had herself been attacked in the new pro-Soviet *Mundo obrero*, Lister and García were in danger of losing her support, still vital for the conquest of power within the party.

Moreover, Carrillo himself did not at this time appear to have a great deal of support outside that of the faithful majority of his own grouping and a few foreign sympathisers like Roger Garaudy. The Italian Communist Party of course came out on his side, by publishing, in October 1970, excerpts from the Central Committee statement announcing the expulsion of the 'pro-Soviet' group, accompanied by a commentary attacking the group.[128] But it remains to this day the only major communist party to have done so. Even leaving out of account the Soviet and East European parties (always excepting the Romanian party), who had no discernible reason to support Carrillo, the French Communist Party in particular took up a clearly 'non-interventionist' attitude to the conflict which was tearing the Spanish Communist Party asunder.[129]

## Notes

[1]  J. Hernandez, *La grande trahison*, pp. 174–5.

[2]  José Díaz, Secretary-General of the Party, had left for the USSR some months before, both for medical and political reasons.

[3]  P. Broué and E. Témime,: *La révolution et la guerre d'Espagne* pp. 492–3.

[4]  According to E. Castro, the Spanish colony in the USSR consisted of some 4,000 persons at the beginning of 1940, including 500 Party officials (E. Castro Delgado, *J'ai perdu la foi à Moscou* p. 348). According to Hernández, 5,000 children left for the Soviet Union (J. Hernández, op. cit., pp. 222–3). El Campesino says that 3,000 arrived in the USSR, in eighteen groups. They joined 1,700 children already there, as well as 102 teachers and 210 pilots who had gone there before 1939 (El Campesino, *La vie et la mort en URSS, 1939–1949*, pp. 183–4).

[5]  Departures for Mexico continued, however, from unoccupied France until 1942.

[6]  See the description given in 1946 by S. Carrillo, *Los niños españoles en la URSS*, Publicaciones *Mundo obrero,* Paris, pp. 11–31.

[7] The majority of Spaniards who returned to their native land in 1956, however, refrained from criticising the USSR's conduct. Many, in fact, remained staunchly loyal to the Soviet Union — as we were able to verify in interviews with some of them.

[8] J. Hernández, op. cit., pp. 22—224.

[9] El Campesino, op. cit., pp. 183—9.

[10] See, for example, 'Les Espagnols internés à Karaganda' *Bulletin de presse espagnol* 61, 16 February 1948, p. 18.

[11] These accounts are probably exaggerated, though undoubtedly partly true in view of the excesses committed under Stalin even during the war.

[12] The committee at first worked in Paris in March and April 1939. At that stage it consisted of Dolores Ibarruri, I. Falcón, Francisco Antón, Santiago Carrillo, A. Mije, J. Modesto, E. Lister, Martínez Cartón, J. Hernández, André Marty, Maurice Thorez and Palmiro Togliatti (El Campesino, op. cit., pp. 181—3)

[13] D. Ibarruri, J. Hernández, J. Modesto, E. Lister, I. Falcón, M. Cartón, F. Antón subsequently replaced Cartón.

[14] Where the Spanish communists took the lead in establishing the Dominican Communist Party in 1942.

[15] The highest qualification obtainable in any Comintern school. Hernández was the only PCE member to hold it.

[16] José Díaz had left Spain in December 1938 for treatment in the USSR. He had contracted tuberculosis the year before. This may well have suited the Russians, who considered both Díaz and Hernández difficult men to work with. In 1940, Díaz was in Moscow as a member of the Comintern Secretariat and shared with Dolores Ibarruri responsibility for directing the PCE. Later he was admitted to a sanatorium in Tiflis, where he died on 21 March 1942.

[17] E. Castro Delgado worked for the services which survived the defunct Comintern until 1944. In 1939 he was Secretary-General of the Political Department. El Campesino, the third prominent defector from the ranks of the PCE, left the Soviet Union later and does not appear to have had any links with the Jesús Hernández group.

[18] According to G. Jackson, *The Spanish Republic and the Civil War*, Princeton University Press, 1965, p. 539. Charles Foltz, quoting figures he claims to have obtained from the Ministry of Justice, says that between April 1939 and June 1944, 192,000 people were executed after due sentence. This figure does not therefore include summary executions. (From B. Crozier, *Franco*, Eyre and Spottiswoode, London 1967, p. 296.)

[19] The first such underground group on record was set up in 1939 by thirty-five members of the JSU in Madrid. All were shot in August of that

year, on charges of stealing legal documents compromising their comrades and of killing a military judge for the same reason. Rodríguez Chaos, however, denies this charge which, he says, was fabricated by the Falange. (V. Rodríguez Chaos, *24 años en la cárcel*, Colección Ebro, Paris 1968, p. 70).

[20] Several Central Committee members tried unsuccesfully to return to Spain from Mexico towards the end of 1939. Given away by one of their number, they were captured in Portugal and executed.

[21] At this time the anarchists were still stronger than the communists inside Spain. The police did not succeed in destroying their cells until 1945—46.

[22] G. Laroche, *On les nommait des étrangers ...*, *Les Editeurs français réunis*, Paris 1965, p. 186. From the end of 1942 onward, the PCE was able to use a 'rear base' in the Oran region, which had just been liberated by the Allied forces. It was manned by a large number of former soldiers of the republican army who had been interned in the labour camps of the Sahara.

[23] B. Crozier states that Spanish communists from Melilla were trained by the Americans near Algiers in sabotage and wireless communications techniques (op. cit., p. 351).

[24] J. Martinez Alier, *La estabilidad del latifundismo*, Ruedo ibérico, Paris 1967, p. 135.

[25] See the account of the Spanish guerrillas' activities in A. Sorel, *Guerrilla española del siglo XX*, Editions de la Librairie du Globe, Paris 1970.

[26] F. Antón, 'El programa de la victoria sobre el franquismo', *Mundo obrero* 217, 13 April 1950, pp. 10—11.

[27] The 'augmented' plenums of the Central Committee held in the USSR during the war were in fact only attended by the handful of PCE leaders then in Moscow.

[28] V. Uribe's resignation on 5 August 1947 led to the fall of the Llopis government. This event coincided with the beginning of the cold war, the disputes provoked in Europe by the Marshall Plan and the communist withdrawal from the French, Italian and Belgian governments.

[29] See S. Carrillo, *Nuevos enfoques a problemas de hoy*, Editions sociales, Paris 1967, pp. 43 and 45.

[30] Such as Cristino García, Santiago Alvarez and Salvador Zapiráin. Alvarez and Zapiráin were arrested in 1946 and released in the early fifties.

[31] Vicente Uribe was thereupon put in charge — from abroad — of the Party's underground activities.

[32] I. Gallego, *'Salvaguardar el Partido de los zarpazos del enemigo'*, *Mundo obrero* 217, 13 April 1950, p. 12.

[33] The former leader of the PSUC during the Civil War and the years of exile from 1939 to 1945 tried at that time to set up a new united socialist party.

[34] Gabriel León Trilla had to face worse than insults: according to E. Comín Colomer, he was executed in Madrid on 6 September 1945 by a squad headed by Cristino García and under orders from the PCE (E. Comín Colomer, *Historia del Partido comunista de España*, p. 52. The communists claim that it became necessary to execute Trilla, allegedly the leader of a gang of common criminals masquerading as guerrillas (A. Sorel, op. cit., p. 130).

[35] The term 'quiñonismo' was coined at that time to describe those accused of wanting the Party to be led from within Spain.

[36] Santiago Carrillo paid glowing tribute to Dolores Ibarruri's 'mastery of Marxist-Leninist historical science and her exercise of stern criticism and self-criticism, worthy of a great proletarian leader cast in the Stalin mould' (S. Carrillo, 'Es possible poner freno a la locura agresiva de los imperialistas' *Mundo obrero* 21 (2), 15 December 1951, p. 1). José Díaz, for his part, was described as 'Spain's greatest living politician' ('José Díaz' *Nuestra bandera*, 5 April 1950, p. 263).

[37] 'Vaste opération de police contre la cinquième colonne établie en France par les partis communistes étrangers' *Le Figaro*, 8 September 1950, pp. 1 and 8.

[38] 'Près de 300 antifranquistes espagnols et démocrates immigrés sont arrêtés' *L'Humanité*, 8 September 1950, p. 6.

[39] Notably the reviews *Cultura y democracia* and *Nuestra bandera*. The communist exile press had also gained a foothold in Mexico, especially the review *España popular*, which appeared from 1940 till 1948. However, towards the end of the forties, the paper's circulation was clearly on the decline.

[40] New Secretary-General of the PSUC, arrested in 1952.

[41] The anarchists had already repulsed the PCE's advances. They had in any case lost most of their support, which in the early forties had still been considerable. In fact, they never quite recovered from the defeat of the guerrilla campaign and the authorities' effective drive against them in the years 1945—47. They had, moreover, been divided since August 1945 over the question of collaboration with the republican organisations and the government-in-exile. One faction, the so-called 'apolitical' group, had the support of most of the anarchist exiles but enjoyed only minority support in Spain itself. The situation of the other faction, which favoured 'co-operation against Franco', was exactly the reverse. It was 1960 before the two were reconciled.

[42] To mention but a few, the strike in Barcelona in 1953; that in the Euskalduna shipyards in Bilbao in December of the same year; the strikes in Barcelona in 1955, followed by the major strikes which occurred in 1956, first in the footwear factories in Pamplona and later in Bilbao, in Guipuzcoa Province and in Barcelona.

[43] 'Recuperemos para el Partido lo que pertenece al Partido' *Mundo obrero* 23 (23), 31 October 1954, p. 5.

[44] A police informer infiltrated this delegation, as a result of which its members were arrested on their return to Madrid. The delegates came from the capital, Valencia, the Estremadura region and Catalonia. Luis Goytisolo was one of them.

[45] The republican government-in-exile has remained in existence continuously since 1945. The Llopis government, which resigned on 6 August 1947 following the departure of its one communist member, was followed by the Valera caretaker government. The latter was replaced by that of Alvaro de Albornoz, in turn succeeded in July 1951 by Gordón Ordas and in 1958 by Herrera. The government at the time of writing, formed in January 1962, is presided over by Claudio Sánchez Albornoz. Since 1947 these governments have consisted exclusively of representatives of the republican and Catalan parties. Since the death of the former Speaker of the Cortes, Diego Martínez Barrio, who exercised the functions of President of the Republic from 17 August 1945 till 1961, the Presidency has been held by Luis Jiménez de Asua.

[46] 'Por una republica democratica' *Mundo obrero* 24 (2), 31 December 1954, p. 2.

[47] The Central Committee appointed in November 1954 comprised thirty-nine full and twenty-two alternate members. The Political Bureau consisted of: S. Carrillo, F. Claudín, M. Cristobal, M. Delicado, E. Lister and V. Uribe. The Central Committee comprised, in addition to the above, S. Alvárez, J. Ambou, F. M. Arconada, L. Balaguer, J. Barzana, L. Carro, L. Fernández, I. Gallego, E. García, J. Gómez, J. Grimau, D. Ibarruri, A. Jimeno, G. López Raimundo, J. J. Manso, F. Melchor, P. Méndez, R. Mendezona, A. Mije, J. Modesto, J. Moix, A. Moreno, C. Pérez, N. Pozuelo, W. Roces, R. Romero Marín, A. Roncal, V. Sáinz, J. Semprún, J. Sandoval, R. Sergio, J.-A. Uribes, V. Velasco and R. Vidiella. The alternate members were: J. Bonifaci, J. Cárdenas, E. Casas, A. Cordón, D. Cuesta, E. Fabregas, J. García, A. Guardiola, I. Hidalgo de Cisneros, J. Izcaray, L. Lacasa, E. López, D. Malagón, J. Planelles, P. Prados, E. Ramírez, J. Rejamo, J. Román, J. Sáiz, M. Sánchez Arcas and L. Segundo. Those working in the Spanish underground are listed under pseudonyms

('Elección del comité central' *Mundo obrero* 23 (24), 15 November 1954, pp. 1 and 3).

[48] 'Sobre la lucha victoriosa contra el culto a la personalidad y sus consecuencias', *Mundo obrero* 25 July 1956 (supplement to issue no. 7).

[49] Central Committee of the Communist Party of the Soviet Union.

[50] At that time, at its Fourteenth Congress, held in July 1956, the PCE rejected the accusation so far as it was itself concerned. The PCI (Italian Communist Party) took a more cautious line.

[51] *Informes y resoluciones del pleno del comité central del Partido comunista de España*, Ediciones Boletín de Información, Prague 1956, pp. 153—4, 241 and 245—6.

[52] Ibid., pp. 274—5.

[53] M. Azcárate, 'Un gran paso en bien de la paz y del socialismo' *Mundo obrero* 25 (7), July 1956, pp. 7—8. This article was written in the very month when Khrushchev received Tito in Moscow.

[54] The French communists continued for a long time to maintain a much more unyielding attitude towards Tito. The Italians, on the other hand, resumed their contacts with him when Togliatti visited Belgrade on 28 May 1956.

[55] *Informes y resoluciones del pleno* ..., pp. 131—2.

[56] Ibid., pp. 162—9.

[57] The eleven members of the Political Bureau appointed on 31 August 1956 were: S. Alvarez, S. Carrillo, F. Claudín, M. Delicado, I. Gallego, D. Ibarruri, E. Lister, A. Mije, V. Sáinz [S. Sánchez Montero], M. Sánchez and V. Uribe. In addition, there were three alternate members: J. Gómez, F. Romero Marín and R. Sergio [Sebastián Zapiráin]. The Central Committee remained virtually unchanged, except that V. Velasco was replaced upon his death by D. Cuesta.

[58] *Informes y resoluciones del pleno;* ..., pp. 158—9.

[59] Ibid., pp. 252—3. Mije, whose name does not appear on the 1954 list of members of the Political Bureau, was so listed in 1956. He was also mentioned as one of the members of the Executive Committee which replaced the Political Bureau in 1960.

[60] 'Por la reconciliacíon nacional, por una solución democrática y pacífica del problema español' *Mundo obrero* 25 (7), July 1956, p. 1.

[61] *Informes y resoluciones del pleno* ..., p. 235.

[62] 'Veteranos militantes socialistas ingresan en nuestro partido' *Mundo obrero* 24 (10), 30 April 1955, p. 5.

[63] *Informes y resoluciones del pleno* ..., pp. 88—103 and 209.

[64] Ibid., p. 110.

[65] Ibid., pp. 183—4.

[66] The same theme was taken up in two subsequent articles, published in 1954, 'La Iglesia se prepara ...' *Mundo obrero* 23 (17), 31 July 1954, p. 2; 'Nuestra posición: respecto a los católicos y sus creencias' *Mundo obrero* 23 (18), 15 August 1954, p. 3.

[67] *Informes y resoluciones del pleno ...*, pp. 106 and 277.

[68] See F. Claudín, *Informe sobre el proyecto de programa*, 1960, pp. 83—8. and 96—7.

[69] This campaign, confined virtually to the communists alone, resulted in nothing more than scattered strikes and demonstrations in Madrid and Valencia. According to a British ethnologist who happened to be in the capital on the day, 'the attitude of the people in the quarter generally was that they were almost desperately anxious to avoid getting into trouble; in fact they did not even want to be drawn into any discussion'. Mr Kenny added that the students, who were on holiday at the time, could thus take no part in the campaign and that absenteeism in the factories was less than usual. (M. Kenny, *A Spanish Tapestry*, Harper, Colophon Books, New York 1966, p. 140)

[70] The Executive Committee set up in 1960 consisted of S. Alvarez, S. Carrillo, F. Claudín, M. Delicado, I. Gallego, J. Gómez, D. Ibarruri, E. Lister, R. Mendezona,, A. Mije, J. Moix and J. Semprún. Alternate members were: S. Sánchez Montero, G. López Raimundo and F. Romero Marín.

[71] Carrillo was assisted in the Secretariat by F. Claudín, I. Gallego, A. Mije and E. García. The latter held the vital post of Organisational Secretary.

[72] *Huelga nacional pacífica*, or HNP.

[73] *Huelga general política*, or HGP.

[74] *Declaración del Partido comunista sobre la huelga nacional*, July 1959, quoted in F. Claudín 'La via española al socialismo' in *Horizonte Español 1966*, vol. I Ruedo ibérico, Paris 1966, pp. 70—1.

[75] *Sobre algunos problemas de la táctica de lucha contra el franquismo*, 1961, p. 30.

[76] As shown by the arrest of eighteen participants in the Congress on their return to Spain. As in 1954, there was an informer among the delegates.

[77] This programme was published shortly before the Conference of eighty-one Communist and Workers' Parties, held in Moscow in 1960, at which the concept of 'national democracy' was put forward.

[78] *Programa del Partido comunista de España*, 1960, pp. 26 and 57—62.

[79] 'Los comunistas ante los tribunales militares' *Mundo obrero* 31 (1), 15 December 1960, pp. 7–8.

[80] *Dos meses de huelga*, French Communist Party, Paris 1962, pp. 114 and 141–2.

[81] During the Asturias miners' strike in March 1958, the number of strikers reached 25,000 on the 18th. The strikes of April and May 1962 are said to have involved nearly 300,000 in the Basque country, León Province and Catalonia, as well as in Asturias, and even affected farm workers in the Cadiz area and the Province of Badajoz. These strikes lasted over two months. But the longest strike was in 1966, at the 'Bandas y Laminaciones de Echevarría' works which went on for five months.

[82] Very many academics chose exile at the time; most of those who stayed behind were 'purged'. The teaching staffs in the faculties were almost entirely replaced by conservatively-minded people close to the Falange or to Opus Dei, all too often recruited in haste, and without any real professional qualifications. The students, too, were extensively recruited into the Falange machine. This helps to explain why intellectuals and academics were so passive during the fifteen years that followed the Civil War.

[83] In 1964, this party took the name *Unión social demócrata*. For a while it published a review, *Mañana*, in Paris.

[84] Ridruejo was one of the first 'opposition' Falangists, his resistance to some of the prevailing tendencies in the movement going back as far as 1941.

[85] At the time, Giménez belonged to the liberal wing of Catholic Action, and during his tenure of office followed a policy of 'opening intellectual windows'. He awarded bursaries for foreign travel to many young academics who subsequently joined the opposition. He now belongs to the Christian Socialist movement and is the moving spirit behind the review *Cuadernos para el diálogo*.

[86] On this subject see E. Díaz, 'La filosofía marxista en el pensamiento español actual' *Cuadernos para el diálogo* 63, December 1968, pp. 9–13.

[87] Those running this review, however, had no connection with the PCE, though they did have some contacts with the PSOE and Ridruejo's group. Another Marxist review that appeared at this time was *Litoral*, published in Pontevedra, fifteen numbers of which appeared before the censorship became aware of its leanings and banned it. Marxists were also working at this time on the reviews *Insula* and *Indice*.

[88] As the students called the FLP militants.

[89] Julio Marín, who was leader of the Madrid University cell, S. Sánchez

Montero, member of the Central Committee, and Lucio Lobato were arrested in 1959. Abelardo Grimeno Laza, also a Central Committee member, was caught shortly afterwards. The sixteen militants who had returned from Prague after the Sixth Congress were arrested in 1960; a trial of PSUC leaders rounded up in Barcelona took place the same year, as did that of thirty-nine prominent Party members in Oviedo. Furthermore, a decree promulgated on 21 September 1960 lent the law of 2 March 1943 added force by making all political activity against the regime equivalent to military rebellion. Spanish communists were also subject to persecution in France, where arrests took place in 1960.

[90]  A comparison of the sentences handed out to communists with those imposed on members of the Catholic opposition bears this out. In the 1959 and 1960 trials, for example, the communists received sentences of up to twenty years' imprisonment, while the maximum sentence imposed on socialists and Catholics arrested at the same time did not exceed eight years.

[91]  These repatriates had been children at the time of the Civil War, or fathers or mothers of families who had been evacuated from the Basque country, from Santander and the Asturias in 1937. The first shipload of them arrived in Valencia on 29 September 1956. The 532 passengers included thirty-one Soviet women married to Spaniards. The total number of these repatriates eventually reached about 800. A score or so returned to the USSR in later years. Most were manual workers and middle-grade technicians — fitters, skilled men in the building trade, electricians, and so on — but they also included five pilots, as well as some economists and engineers.

[92]  *Solidaridad de trabajadores vascos*: a Basque Christian trade union organisation which went underground in 1937.

[93]  J. Blanc and A. Gabel, 'Un syndicalisme de classe; les CO' *Le Semeur*, 1, 1967—1968, p. 112.

[94]  On 'Marxist-Leninist' groups up to 1965, see L. Santiago de Pablo, 'El marxismo entre los exilados comunistas españoles' in *Situación y revisión contemporánea del marxismo,* Centro de estudios sociales de la Santa Cruz del Valle de los Caídos, Madrid 1966, pp. 176—8.

[95]  'The Spark'.

[96]  The names of the two parties which resulted from this break is distinguished only by the typography of the initials 'M' and 'L' in brackets after the main title of each. The briefly 'united' organisation run by the *El Proletario* group, which probably remains the stronger and continues to publish *Vanguardia obrera* at fairly regular intervals, retains its title of

*Partido comunista de España (ML).* The breakaway faction calls itself *Partido comunista de España (m.l.).*

[97] According to the *Yearbook on International Communist Affairs 1966,* p. 148.

[98] 'Denuncia de un provocador' *Vanguardia obrera* 3 (22), March 1967, p. 7.

[99] In Barcelona these groups had been rounded up by the police in January and February 1969 during the state of emergency.

[100] 'Derechismo — Izquierdismo — Sinpartidismo' *El Comunista,* 5 December 1968, p. 2.

[101] 'Las comisiones obreras ...' in *'Sobre el movimiento obrero y la táctica de los comunistas (marxistas-leninistas),* p. 4 (no date or place).

[102] *Adulteraciones del equipo de Santiago Carrillo,* 2nd, augmented edition, Ediciones *Vanguardia obrera,* Madrid, p. 10.

[103] Namely Gregorio López Raimundo.

[104] Comorera was relieved of his post in Paris on 2 September 1949. He returned to Catalonia secretly on 31 December 1950. Arrested in Barcelona in 1954, he died in Burgos jail on 8 June 1958. The Comorera version of the crisis in the PSUC is given in the monograph *Partit socialista unificat de Catalunya (CE) — Aportació a la història política, social i nacional de la classe obrera de Catalunya,* Publicacions Treball Modern.

[105] A constituent 'pre-conference' of the PCE *(Internacional)* took place in December in Catalonia; a second, 'national', meeting was held in July 1968. The first number of *Mundo obrero (Internacional)* appeared the same year.

[106] It is known that during the Civil War, PSUC recruitment took place in circles untouched by the anarchists — in other words, not among workers but among the white-collar sections, technicians and members of the liberal professions. Traces of this petty bourgeois make-up of the membership are discernible to this day, and have helped to reduce the gap between the rank-and-file — which is in any case much more educated than elsewhere — and the intellectuals.

[107] 'Existe el Partido de la clase obrera? '*Mundo obrero (Internacional),* December 1968, pp. 1–7.

[108] *'La línea divisoria'* ibid, pp. 8–9; *'Sobre la lucha de clases y la insurreción armada'* ibid, pp. 13–16.

[109] S. Carrillo, *Après Franco ... quoi?* , Editions sociales, Paris 1966, p. 173.

[110] The report was published in mimeographed form in 1964 under the title 'Las divergencias en el Partido' (no date, place or pagination). It was

republished by the PCE journal *Nuestra bandera* in January 1965. A later version, used here, was published by the PCE (ML) in 1968: F. Claudín *El subjectivismo de la política del Partido comunista de España (1956–1964)*, ENP del PCE (ML), Madrid, (no date).

111 See J. Gómez, 'Problemas del desarrollo económico de España' *Realidad* no. 8, February 1966, p. 27.

112 Such as the *Acción comunista* group, breakway from the Popular Liberation Front.

113 Particularly the Basque organisation ETA (*Euzkadi Ta Askatasuna* – Basque Homeland and Freedom) and the Union of the People of Galicia, to which the PCE tried to provide some competition by reviving the *PC de Euzkadi*. However, this move was compromised by the expulsion of E. García from the Party (see below), and by the setting up of a *PC de Galicia* in 1969.

114 'Se ha reunido el pleno ampliado del comité central' *Mundo obrero* 40 (15), 30 September 1970, p. 1.

115 *Le bilan de vingt ans de dictature fasciste*, Rivet, Limoges 1959, p. 68.

116 '*Sobre el reemplazamiento del camarada Kruschov*', *Mundo obrero* 34 (18), 15 October, 1964, p. 1.

117 S. Alvarez, 'La renovación en Checoslovaquia' *Mundo obrero* 38 (11), 1 May 1968, p. 11.

118 'Une déclaration de Santiago Carrillo' *L'Humanité*, 31 July 1968, p. 3.

119 'Declaración de nuestro comité ejecutivo trás la Conferencia de Bratislava' *Mundo obrero* 38 (16), 15 September 1968, p. 5.

120 K. S. Karol, 'La déchirure des partis communistes européens' *Le Monde*, 23 October 1970, p. 7.

121 'Declaración del PC de España sobre los acontecimientos en Checoslovaquia' *Mundo obrero* 38 (16), 15 September 1968, p. 5.

122 'La cuestiòn de checoslovaquia' *Mundo obrero* 38 (16), 15 September 1968, p. 4.

123 See S. Carrillo, 'Más problemas actuales del socialismo' *Nuestra bandera* 59, 3rd quarter 1968, p. 4; and N. Pla 'Juventud: lo pro-soviético y lo anti-soviético' *Nuestra bandera* 59, 3rd quarter 1968, p. 30.

124 '¿Adónde vamos?' *Mundo obrero* 38 (17), 1 October 1968, p. 4; 'Resoluciones aprobadas por el comité central del Partido comunista de España' *Mundo obrero* 38 (18), 15 October 1968, p. 1.

125 The Dominican Communist Party rejected the document absolutely; those of Britain and Norway postponed signing it, pending approval by their Central Committees; the Italian and Australian parties, as well as

those of Réunion and San Marino, would endorse only one of its four chapters.

[126] 'Le Parti communiste espagnol ...' *Le Monde*, 2 and 3 November 1969, p. 3.

[127] However, the dispute was not merely about the PCE's attitude to the USSR but also about Carrillo's tactics of alliance with all groups opposing Franco, no matter who they were.

[128] See 'La lotta unitaria dei comunisti spagnoli' *Rinascità*, 27 (42), 23 October 1970, pp. 23–24.

[129] The fact that Carrillo has managed until now to withstand Lister's onslaughts seems, however, to have slightly modified the attitude of the French communists in Carrillo's favour. Evidence of this is the publication by Editions sociales, which is controlled by the French Communist Party, of the report presented by the PCE Secretary-General at the September 1970 augmented plenum (S. Carrillo, *Libertad y socialismo,* Editions sociales, Paris, 1971).

# 3 Organisation of the Spanish Communist Movement

The dichotomy of the historical experience of the PCE — today an underground party without access to the levers of power, but yesterday a mighty party which had the decisive say as regards the exercise of it — is without exact parallel in any clandestine communist organisation in Europe. The imprint of this twofold experience on the Party's command structure and on the sub-culture of its militants remains clearly visible and decisive. They help to explain some of the Party's misjudgements in both action and organisation — often over-ambitious in relation to its resources. But this background has also helped to ensure the cohesion of the Party, by keeping green the memories of the faith and courage of its followers.

True, the gradual replacement of the Civil War generation by new members or sympathisers who have not experienced the era of the PCE's glory has in the past ten years or so cast some doubt on the appropriateness of total dedication to a corps of leaders whose principal credentials may seem to be nostalgia for a power that has vanished. Some progress has been made towards giving up prestige gestures which have proved to be both ineffectual and dangerous. Nevertheless, the fact remains that the structure of the Party's formal organisation, its operations in practice, the composition of its leadership apparatus, its methods and its propaganda style still hark back to past attitudes. The same applies to the way the Party recruits its membership and educates its militants. Moreover, it seems that this attachment to a certain grandness in organisation is not entirely unknown even to the dissident communist groups, despite their attacks on the old Party, which they nevertheless continue to imitate.

## Formal structure

On paper, the organic structure of the underground PCE does not differ much from that of great parties enjoying lawful status. It is based on a hierarchy of bodies, at the bottom of which is the factory, neighbourhood or 'nucleus' cell, to use the terminology of the Spanish Party. The pyramid then rises through the local,[1] factory or university committee, the

95

sector committee, and the provincial and regional committees to the Central Committee and the Party Congress. In accordance with the concept of democratic centralism, the members of the Central Committee are in theory appointed by the Party Congress. The Party Congress consists of representatives of the provincial and regional committees, themselves elected by the committees below them. These latter in turn are supposed to draw their mandate from the cells, which form the base of the communist institutional edifice. In practice, however, co-option procedures are also employed.

The Central Committee, the Party's supreme body between Congresses — and the total duration of Congresses has not exceeded a dozen days since the outbreak of the Civil War[2] — appoints the members of the Executive Committee, which in turn acts as the Central Committee's standing body in the intervals between plenums. The Central Committee likewise appoints the Secretary-General of the Party, whose duties, in theory purely technical, are supposed to be limited to the preparation of projects commissioned by itself or by the Executive Committee, and to carrying out the decisions of these two bodies. In addition to its plenums, which are very difficult to organise and take place every eighteen months or so,[3] the Central Committee also occasionally holds augmented plenums by co-opting a certain number of Party officers or outside activists. Because of the practical difficulties attendant on clandestine work, the Central Committee is sometimes consulted by correspondence on important subjects. Such was the case, for example, during the recent debates which preceded the expulsion of E. García.

According to a list published in December 1965, after the Seventh Party Congress, the Central Committee at that time consisted of forty full and forty-six alternate members.[4] Vacancies arising from deaths, as in the case of Juan Modesto and Ignacio Hidalgo de Cisneros, or from expulsions — García, Gómez, Lister, Uriate, Bárzana, Balaguer and Saíz — were filled by co-option. According to Santiago Carrillo, in October 1970 the Central Committee had altogether 111 members, of whom ninety were resident in Spain. Twenty-nine of them had been promoted the previous month to make possible the expulsion of Lister and his group.

The Executive Committee and Secretariat each had thirteen members — two of them being alternate members — and six secretaries, according to a list published in 1960 after the end of the Sixth Congress. It was also at this time that the honorary post of Party President was created especially for Dolores Ibarruri, after her replacement by Santiago Carrillo as Secretary-General. Since that date, there have been extensive changes in the composition of the Executive Committee and Secretariat, as a result of

96

the expulsion of Claudín and García. Although the list of the new members of both bodies has been kept secret, it would appear that there has been a slight increase in their total numbers.[5]

In addition to all these echelons, which make up its vertical structure, the Party also controls a variety of fringe organisations which enjoy a nominal autonomy. The most important of these is the *Unión de juventudes comunistas*, or JCU. There is also the *Oposición sindical obrera* (OSO), and there was the *Frente nacional de ayuda a los presos,*[6] which existed between 1940 and 1945. More recently, there has been the *Unión democrática de mujeres*.

Three parallel organisations: the *Partit socialista unificat de Catalunya*, the *Partido comunista de Euzkadi* and the most recent, the *Partido comunista de Galicia*, perform regional and linguistic functions. They cater for the three provinces in which there is regional nationalism. In practice these parties enjoy only a limited autonomy, hardly going beyond that of a regional or provincial committee, and this despite the relative complexity of their structure, based on the pattern of the PCE.

The United Socialist Party of Catalonia (PSUC) does, however, wield a measure of autonomy a little wider than the parties of the Basque country and Galicia, at least as far as appearances are concerned. In particular, its press gives considerable prominence to directives and resolutions from its own command bodies, unlike the mouthpieces of the Basque and Galician Communist Parties, which by and large content themselves with reproducing PCE pronouncements.

But even for the Catalan party, autonomy is limited to matters of detail. One reason for this is that the Secretaries-General of all three parties — Catalan, Basque and Galician — are mere functionaries delegated by the PCE Central Committee, such as Gregorio López Raimundo in the case of the PSUC. The same picture emerges at grass roots level in the basic organisations, whose members are automatically attached to the appropriate regional Party unit of their place of residence whenever they change their address.

The organisational structure described above may seem to be out of keeping with the real scale of the underground communist apparatus in Spain. And in fact only three concessions have been made to the need to operate in clandestine conditions. These are: the appointment of a 'Central Committee delegation' to function in the interior; a relaxation of the rule that each individual member must belong to a cell; and the admission of the existence of groups of sympathisers unable for practical reasons to join the Party.[7] The device of the Central Committee delegation to the interior is largely a reflection of the PCE's concern not to appear to be led entirely from abroad. The relaxation of the Party cell membership rule, which had been enforced fairly rigidly until 1960, originated from the Sixth Congress, which abolished the rule that every member must belong to a cell, by amending Article 34 of the Statutes. Since then, individual direct membership of the Party has been permissible, at least on a provisional basis, particularly for intellectuals and candidates of non-working-class origin, who could not be conveniently included in the existing cells. On the third point, the Central Committee has ever since 1956, recognised the advantage of having a category of quasi-members made up into local groups seeking contact with the Party without always managing to establish it. Such groups would occasionally receive some propaganda material and listen to 'Radio Independent Spain'. In his speech to the augmented plenum in 1956, Carrillo took pains to stress the more or less emergency character of these *ad hoc* groups;[8] but one wonders whether they are not in fact at least equal in strength to the properly enlisted Party members, particularly during the difficult times that follow police drives against the Party.

**Power in the Party — work in practice**

The exercise of 'democratic centralism' produces similar results everywhere. In the Spanish Communist Party, as in others, it secures the effective predominance of the Secretariat and Executive Committee over the Congress, the Central Committee and the other organisational echelons. The instructions and ideological directives issued by the Secretariat and Executive Committee to these bodies are difficult for them to question. Thanks to the appointment procedures used for the top positions — candidates being subject to the approval of lower-ranking committees — the practical effect of democratic centralism is that the position of the Party's leaders, whose tenure can only be challenged by their peers, tends to be a stable one.

These characteristics are well known and have been extensively analysed; it seems therefore pointless to examine in detail the entirely stereotyped forms they take in the PCE. Using this situation, which is common to all communist organisations, as our starting point, our intention is rather to discover what effects its underground existence has had on the operations of the PCE beyond those which normally result from democratic centralism.

Some of these consequences are admitted, at least partially, by the leadership itself. The Party's leaders have been concerned, in particular, to justify the continued location of its headquarters abroad, as well as the centralisation made necessary by the clandestine conditions of the Party's work. Thus, Carrillo has repeatedly insisted that hard facts obliged the Party apparatus to keep its most senior officials out of the reach of Franco's police: otherwise the Party would be continually 'decapitated' and rendered incapable of reconstituting itself.

However, in April 1964 the Secretary-General refined this explanation, when he said:

> With the exception of a very few comrades, all the leaders of the Party, whether they are at home or abroad, have worked and fought, or are working and fighting, in the country itself. Those who, much against their will, have not yet done so live in close touch with the everyday efforts and struggles that go on within the country; and whenever the Party considers that the time has come, they will go home without hesitation.[9]

Accordingly, Carrillo has refused to recognise that serious conflicts could arise between the Party's organisations at home and abroad. Any clashes, he argued, would be resolved by the fact that 'most of our leadership is working at home, or goes to Spain as often as necessary'. [10]

In the same speech, Carrillo also dashed any hopes that the democratisation drive launched after the 1956 augmented plenum would continue; he said the democratisation experiment tried out at the time of the Sixth Congress, held in Prague in 1960, had been a mistake. The arguments he deployed to make his point, based in the first instance on the admittedly unacceptable risks to which activists had been exposed by the excessive publicity given to this Congress, are worth examining in some detail.

Carrillo begins with the initial thesis that 'as long as there is fascism, centralism will override democracy', and then goes to the heart of the matter:

> With the Sixth Congress of the Party, we undertook an experiment. We aimed for a congress that proved too democratic — with too many delegates who had come straight from the factory — so that no one might be able to say that the Congress was an officials' congress, a congress of the Party's leaders only. You can see the result. We have suffered a very severe blow. The fact of the matter is, Comrades, that as long as we have fascism and as long as we remain on the Central Committee, we shall not have another congress like the Sixth Congress. We shall henceforth watch our step carefully when we have a congress and shall insist first and foremost not on formal democracy in the Party but on the need to protect the security of the Party's organisations.

In his peroration, Carrillo took an apparently eccentric, though not altogether surprising, course by pointing in advance, and in a not very flattering manner, to those who, he thought, would resist this centralistic policy most stubbornly. He identified them predictably as intellectuals who found Party discipline hard to bear because, unlike their worker and peasant comrades, they had not experienced 'the harsh discipline of labour'. [11]

These thoughts on the discipline and secrecy indispensable in a clandestine movement shed no light on the specific function of each regular Party body. This applies particularly to the higher echelons, such as the Central Committee, the Executive Committee and the Secretariat. The time seems gone when the PCE was showing signs of nostalgia for the outward manifestations of a past greatness, as in the period of the 'open underground' it enjoyed in France between 1945 and 1951. Its organisation no longer has a home of its own as it did in Paris immediately after the liberation. Instead of offices on the Boulevard Montmartre or in the Rue Lafayette, it now has to make do with modest premises in Prague or one of the suburbs of Paris. A nascent tradition of grand public rallies at the Mutualité, the Maison des Syndicats or the Toulouse stadium is less in evidence nowadays. As for Central Committee meetings, they remain as few and far between as in the past, and the Central Committee itself continues to play the role of a sounding-board for decisions taken elsewhere. Much the same would seem to apply to the last three Congresses. The approximately 150 to 160 participants — 80 per cent of them representing organisations in Spain itself [12] — did not presume to question any significant aspect of the policies laid down by the Secretariat.

The Executive Committee, too, seems to be playing a less important part than the tiny command team made up of the permanent members of the Secretariat. The fact that the Executive Committee's members are scattered — some living in the USSR, some in Eastern Europe, and others in France or Spain, or even in Spanish jails — prevents the holding of properly constituted plenary meetings, and thus leaves the Secretariat with a pretty free hand. So it was that the expulsion of García could be decided without the explicit agreement of all members of the Executive Committee. Moreover, the compartmentalisation of spheres of responsibility and the secrecy surrounding the Party's organisation, which is a fundamental rule of underground life, gives the Secretariat a virtual monopoly of information about the real position of the Party. This privilege gives it an extra card to play against the Executive Committee, which finds itself asking questions, the material for the answers to which is furnished and selected by the Secretariat and, more particularly, by the Secretary-General.

True, the Secretary-General and his assistants do not have access to all the levers of power. Secretaries who specialise in propaganda, general administration and financial affairs, or in liaison with the clandestine Party machine in Spain, have special sources of information and freedom of manoeuvre in their own particular sector, by virtue of the very compartmentalisation of the Party and of the delegation of authority resulting from it. To see this clearly, one need only recall the García affair, in the course of which the Secretary for Organisation, dismissed in 1969, was able prior to that event to maintain a correspondence with the provincial committees in the country and afterwards to organise meetings of various local PCE committees in France.

In their turn, the Party's permanent cadres in Spain enjoy in practice considerable autonomy *vis-à-vis* the émigré leadership. Because of the sheer difficulty of communication, they cannot always submit their decisions for the leadership's approval, and the latter allows them a wide margin of initiative and of interpretation of directives in the light of local conditions. These permanent cadres, amounting to about thirty people, [13] include a large proportion of Central Committee members and, on occasion, a few members of the Executive Committee. Some, like Simón Sánchez Montero, [14] Horacio Fernández Inguanzo [15] or Miguel Núñez, [16] who represents the PSUC, are militants, working in the country itself, who have been promoted to this status.

The extent of responsibility shouldered by the cadres working in Spain, and the specific *modus operandi* of the Party organisation in the country, have led to a clear-cut division of authority within the PCE. The formal structure of authority, embracing all echelons, from the cell up to the Central Committee, has been reflected in reality only among the émigrés, particularly in France and Mexico, and even then has been limited to some extent by the incorporation of a considerable proportion of them in local organisations, such as the French Communist Party in the case of the émigrés in France. The Party bodies inside Spain are much more on the pattern of groups formed and inspired by full-time Party officials, rather than being strictly modelled on structural blueprints which have remained unaltered since the time of the 'bolshevisation' of communist parties. In practice, the backbone of the underground organisation in Spain consists of a number of provincial leadership centres based on a nucleus, or several nuclei, of militant members concentrated in industrial towns or universities.

However, the effects of this duplication are less serious than one might suppose. The cell structure characteristic of communist organisations, particularly in conditions of illegality, means in effect that the regional command centres communicate only with the Secretariat and have practically no contact among themselves. The isolated Party cadres in Spain are, therefore, unable to coalesce into anything larger than provincial, or at most regional, units. They do not have the benefit of the material support and the advantages of foreign asylum provided by the method of leading the Party from abroad. Moreover, the policy of systematically promoting to the Central and Executive Committees Party officials who have proved themselves in the field has contributed further to defuse potential conflicts between the Party's external and internal organisations.

The Secretariat thus wields sufficient control over the underground organisations — more easily, perhaps, than over émigré elements which are less dependent on it and more exposed to the examples of 'indiscipline' which so proliferate in France, Italy and Latin America. Crises, when they happen, tend to happen at the summit, as in the Claudín, García and Lister affairs; in émigré circles; or in special categories inside the country, such as the students or activists in the regions where autonomy movements are strong, or people who are not greatly impressed by the PCE's declarations of intent regarding their own particular problems.

## The Party in Spain

The question may now be asked whether this power structure, which has remained relatively coherent and effective, is in fact able to operate on a mass of people possessing some ability to act. Before attempting to sketch a somewhat tentative picture of the Party's forces and composition, it is as well to examine its methods of action and communication, looking first at the extent to which it has managed to establish itself at the level of local committees, cells and other organisational units of membership, and then to consider its systems of finance, propaganda and ideological training.

After 1945, the Spanish communists for a long time maintained a rear base somewhat out of proportion with the modest size of its clandestine organisation in Spain itself. Until 1951 in particular, the Party was too much inclined to reproduce abroad, particularly in France and in Mexico, the whole paraphernalia of local and regional structures it could no longer maintain in Spain. At this period, the PCE was not so much an illegal clandestine party as an organisation of émigrés, enjoying semi-official approval in the countries willing to play host to it.

Even though things are not quite the same today, partly because of the repressive measures taken, since 1950, against communist refugees in

Western Europe, and partly because of the more dynamic line taken under Carrillo's influence, the Spanish Communist Party nevertheless still controls a considerable organisation in France, Mexico and Eastern Europe. This exiled organisation sustains the PCE's 'public' life. It is of this life that *Mundo obrero*, in its accounts of meetings, its minor internal news items, as well as its obituary column, speaks, even though the paper does not specify in which country the events it describes have taken place. It is also among the émigrés that the Party's regular activities go on — such things for instance as the training of officers and rank-and-file activists, fund raising or the organisation of petitions. In addition to this, it has been the Party in exile that has, for some years now, shouldered the task of organising and recruiting among the new wave of Spanish migrant workers — a category which was virtually non-existent in 1955 but which is nowadays much more important in France, Germany and Belgium than that of political refugees.

Nevertheless, it is undeniable that the present-day leaders, unlike their predecessors, do not consider the émigré organisation the core of the Party, with the underground Party apparatus as a sort of glorious but — when it comes to everyday practical work — secondary appendage, which is, moreover, a source of internal crises. So anxious in fact is the PCE not to let itself be overwhelmed by the émigrés, that nowadays it even turns over to some local parties, such as the French Communist Party, the work of organising them,[17] so that those who remain directly under the PCE can devote themselves more single-mindedly to tasks directly connected with the struggle in Spain.

In this way, the clandestine apparatus has become the crucial factor on which the authority of the exiled leaders is brought to bear. As we have seen, the keystones of the organisation of the Party in Spain itself are the regional and provincial Party organs,[18] run by full-time officials succeeding one another as their predecessors are relieved of office or, more frequently, as a result of the periodic arrests and wholesale round-ups carried out by the police. According to an article published in 1968,[19] these local organs seem to control fairly permanently some thirty of the fifty provinces of Spain. The author of the article says that the best-established organs at the time of writing were in the Basque country, run by the Basque Communist Party; in Catalonia under the PSUC; and above all in Madrid, Seville and Asturias, under the aegis of the PCE proper. The organisation was also fairly sound in all eight Andalusian provinces, where, the article went on, the communists have displaced the anarchists, as well as in Galicia, especially in the region of La Coruña and El Ferrol. On the other hand, it was rather thin on the ground in the Canaries and in Castile, except for Madrid — a special case. The same applied to the Valencia and Aragon regions, despite occasional successes soon undone by repression. The degree to which the Party has established itself is probably much the same today, except in the Basque country and in Catalonia, where its organisation has been weakened by the recent troubles following the expulsion of García and by the setting-up of the PCE (*Internacional*).

The nuclei of militants on whom the regional or provincial leaderships depend for concrete action, such as organising demonstrations, distributing propaganda material and recruiting new members, take various forms according to area, environment, circumstances and the aims pursued. The factory cells and sections remain in principle the Party's basic organisms; but, as is hardly surprising, they are not very well established except in industrial towns with long-standing working-class traditions, where there was a communist presence before the Civil War. Thus factory cells appear to have remained in existence, virtually without a break, in the metallurgical industries round Bilbao — at Sestao, Baracaldo and Santurce — in the engineering industries in the Basque country, particularly in the Eibar arms and cycle factories at Basauri, as well as in the Asturias coal basin, which for fifty years has been the PCE's firmest bastion. It is also generally reckoned that the communists have managed to obtain a fairly firm foothold in the new plants of the industrial zone round Madrid, particularly at Villaverde and Barajas, as well as in some factories in Seville, Jérez, Cadiz and Malaga. Their presence has also been reported in the El Ferrol dockyards in Galicia, as well as some factories in La Coruña and Vigo. Outside these regions, both in the highly industrialised areas of Catalonia, where the PSUC is bourgeois rather than proletarian in character, and in the provinces where there are no great concentrations of labour and which therefore do not offer favourable conditions for the establishment of homogeneous nuclei of communist workers, the factory cell generally gives way to other forms of organisation, based on the residential quarter, the village, a social or professional group, or even a prison.

In fact, outside the great industrial conurbations of the north-east and the outskirts of Madrid, communist penetration has always been particularly strong among political prisoners. One can even argue that between 1939 and 1950, the hard core of the clandestine organisation was concentrated in the prisons of Burgos, Alcalá de Henares and Carabanchel for men, and at the Ventas jail for women. There are two reasons for this: first, the disproportionate concentration of communists; and second, the PCE's failure to prepare an underground party machine in 1939. While on this subject, one should point out the courage and discipline of the

Spanish communist activists, who managed to organise themselves even in the concentration camps of Germany, notably in Mauthausen. [20]

This type of organisation was very well developed in the prisons of Alcalá de Henares and Burgos, the latter becoming known as 'Burgosgrad'. The Party had a branch committee in each, supported by a secretariat for aid to prisoners and another for education, as well as by a variety of *ad hoc* committees. [21] The branch committees controlled brigade committees, under which came cells in each brigade. [22] There was also a parallel organisation of the United Socialist Youth. All this enabled the communists to publish their own prison editions of *Mundo obrero, Juventud* and *Nuestra bandera*. In Burgos, they started two new reviews — the culture magazine *Spartakus* and the humorous *Cigüeña*.

In these ways, they sought to support political detainees, including non-communists, both materially and morally, even going as far as operating systematic patrols whose job it was to make sure that prisoners did not commit suicide. In addition, they ran a substantial cultural and educational programme through clandestine courses in which, at one time, as many as 1,800 people were taking part in Burgos alone. It was thanks to efforts like these that the prisons played such an overwhelming part as places for the ideological training of thousands of militants, including a substantial proportion of new recruits, attracted by the communists' efficiency and spirit of solidarity.

Nowadays, the reduction in the numbers of political detainees and the progress the PCE has made in establishing itself outside prisons have reduced the importance of prison life in the clandestine organisation. Nevertheless, it remains important, both for its own sake and by virtue of the opportunities offered by places of detention for making new contacts and spreading the communist gospel. The tactic of concentrating on education therefore remains crucial, particularly because of the attraction of the modern language courses offered, Russian being particularly popular. Such courses were available until quite recently in prisons such as Carabanchel.

It is difficult to obtain any very exact idea of the nature and condition of the underground organisation, except that among workers in the great industrial centres and among political detainees. However, the leadership itself admits that the Party's hold on rural areas at the village cell and local committee level is very weak. [23] Communist groups are virtually non-existent in Castile and in country areas in the northern and eastern parts of Spain. The few that do exist are made up of small numbers of farm labourers in western Andalusia and the provinces of Cordoba, Seville, Cadiz, Malaga and Badajoz. Even there, however, it would be really more accurate to speak of a few isolated activists having contacts with like-minded men in other villages, rather than true village cells, or any great degree of activity.

The Party's foothold is a little firmer among the urban middle class, the intellectuals and the liberal professions, thanks to a number of cells made up mostly of artists, particularly painters, as well as writers, university lecturers and doctors. But their turnover is fairly high and their membership almost entirely concentrated in Madrid, Barcelona and the Basque country. The Party, moreover, has not always been very good at making use of the services of this type of supporter, whom it has actually been trying to divert into the citizens' or neighbourhood councils, modelled on the workers' councils.

There are also the women's organisations, such as the Democratic Women's Movement, which appears to have made hardly any impact in Asturias and Madrid; and the students' organisations, headed by the faculty or university committees. It was the latter on which the hopes of the Madrid provincial committee were pinned in the 1961–62 period. But today they occupy only second place compared with the pro-Chinese groups and those which draw their inspiration from the Popular Liberation Front. The Communist Youth Union, though it has a more substantial membership than the organisations listed above, is, like them, confined almost exclusively to working-class circles already influenced by the PCE itself, notably young migrant workers.

## Finance

The human resources provided by the rank-and-file membership are of course indispensable for any sort of action, but they are in themselves insufficient. They must also invariably be backed by financial resources, on which the maintenance of permanent cadres and the conduct of propaganda depends. This is a field which is even less explored than most other aspects of the PCE; it is hardly surprising to find that information available on this subject is scarce and must be treated with a degree of caution.

However, it is known that the Party had quite considerable funds in the years immediately following the Civil War. Some of these came from the sale of precious metals removed to France by lorry on various occasions, more particularly in the months immediately before the fall of Catalonia. [24] Another source of funds was a legacy of 2,500 million francs, entrusted by Dr Negrín to the French Communist Party for the purchase of arms and the maintenance of republican propaganda activity. However, the Spanish communists seem to have been able to recover only a tiny fraction of this money. According to Castro Delgado, all they managed to obtain was a 'compensation' of 5,000,000 francs out of the 100 millions the French Communist Party kept in the Comintern treasury for its own use. [25]

Apart from the sums it thus has at its direct disposal, the PCE is generally said to have made use of a considerable part of the funds of the *Servicio de emigración para republicanos españoles*, thanks to the hold it had on that organisation, which was set up by the republican government in the early days of its exile. [26] But that was only a temporary expedient, as the service stopped disbursing money to refugees in the spring of 1940.

Later, Spanish guerrillas in the south-east of France collected some funds, arms and material, from which the PCE benefited. During the years when it enjoyed quasi-legitimate status in France, the PCE received aid from the French Communist Party, much of it in the form of the use of premises and various facilities. It even found itself the indirect beneficiary of a subsidy from an American foundation, the Unitarian Service Committee, which donated some equipment to the hospital at Toulouse and paid the cost of the medical treatment of Spanish communists who had escaped from German concentration camps.

Moreover, from this time on, the PCE again enjoyed a regular revenue in the form of membership fees from tens of thousands of Party members in France, Mexico and North Africa, as well as the profits from the sale of its papers in these countries. Between 1945 and 1950 it was thus in the relatively comfortable financial situation of a political party of middling importance, enjoying moreover the support of the mighty French Communist Party.

Steps taken in France against the Spanish communists in 1950 and 1951 placed the PCE in a less comfortable position in every respect, especially its finances. True, the Czechoslovak and Soviet Communist Parties very largely relieved the French Communist Party of the burden of providing the PCE's leadership apparatus with the aid it needed when it withdrew from Paris to Prague; but the very need for this aid placed the Spanish communists in a position of close dependence on their protectors, especially since the collection of Party dues was yielding less money by reason of the Party's disarray in the countries from which it drew the bulk of its regular income, especially France. At the same time, the press of the Spanish Communist Party ceased to bring in a profit, following the loss of its principal market among Spanish refugees in France. It did not go fully underground until this time, but now it did so in most West European countries, where its publications had been openly and widely distributed in the immediate post-war years.

Today, although it still receives assistance from some fraternal parties in the form of radio time, publishing facilities and bursaries for students, the use of premises and homes for its leaders and officials, and a variety of facilities for major meetings and so on, the PCE appears to have recovered a measure of financial independence. In Spain itself, it seems to have re-established some channels for the collection of funds in the form of Party dues, fund-raising activities[27] and the sale of papers and books. More important still, it has gradually mended the links of the financial structure it established among Spanish émigrés in Mexico, France and some other Western countries, from which it still draws the bulk of its independent means. There is some hard information on this subject which throws a certain amount of light not only on the financial resources of the PCE, but also on the relative weight of its establishments abroad and in Spain itself.

The relevant figures are abstracted from the published balance sheet of the campaign, 'Thirty Million Pesetas for the Spanish Communist Party', launched in February 1968 and concluded in the late summer of 1969.[28] They show that militants and sympathisers in Spain contributed less than a quarter of the sum collected; more than three-quarters was provided by émigrés, mostly in capitalist, and to a lesser extent in socialist, countries, and by members of the Party's own Central Commitee and Secretariat. The 45,000,000 pesetas collected in the course of that campaign can be broken down as follows:

*Collected in capitalist countries*: 27,275,360 pesetas (61 per cent)

| | |
|---|---|
| France | 16,921,610 |
| Mexico | 2,000,000 |
| Belgium | 1,960,480 |
| Switzerland | 1,790,996 |
| Germany | 1,662,001 |

*Collected in socialist countries*: 6,430,696 pesetas (14 per cent)

| | |
|---|---|
| Cuba | 3,089,730 |
| USSR | 1,851,365 |
| East Germany | 1,021,727 |
| Czechoslovakia | 236,866 |

*Contributed by members of the Central Committee and Secretariat*: 401,962 pesetas (1 per cent).

*Collected in Spain*: 10,879,680 pesetas (24 per cent)

| | |
|---|---|
| Catalonia | 4,281,424 (collected by the PSUC) |
| Madrid | 3,490,146 |
| Asturias | 919,876 |
| Andalusia | 636,562 |
| Levante | 483,384 |
| Basque country | 469,308 |
| Aragon | 226,884 |
| Galicia | 153,860 |
| Old Castile, León | 93,052 |
| Estremadura | 65,555 |
| New Castile | 22,965 |
| Balearic Islands | 22,905 |
| Canaries | 13,209 |

*Total*: 44,987,968 pesetas (approx £ 270,000) (100 per cent)

The difference the money collected in this campaign made — it was equivalent to over 3,000,000 francs — should not, however, be overestimated. The PCE is not a very rich party and fund-raising drives of this type remain the exception rather than the rule. In recent years it would appear that the annual income the Party could count on from membership fees and from collections in Spain and abroad has not exceeded 15,000,000 pesetas or thereabouts. [29] This sum therefore could barely have sufficed to meet the rather meagre salaries of a score or so full-time cadres and officials of the Secretariat, after discharging the Party's obligations to the families of political prisoners.

The transfer of funds to Spain did at one time meet with difficulties, but these appear to have been partly overcome. On the other hand, there are still considerable obstacles to the distribution of periodicals and books. But in this regard, too, things have been considerably better in the past ten years or so, thanks to the development of international tourism and the comings and goings of migrant workers. The time has passed when Party militants had to cross the frontier on foot at night, especially since many Spanish republicans have now acquired French nationality and are not, therefore, easy to spot when they enter Spain with a motley crowd of tourists and foreigners. [30]

## Methods of propaganda

The difficulties encountered in distributing underground literature, as well as books and journals published abroad, remain the chief obstacle to propaganda and the ideological education of the PCE's militants. It may well be that this is why more PCE propaganda is broadcast than printed, thanks to the broadcasting facilities the Party enjoys.

The main channel at its disposal is the short-wave station 'Radio Independent Spain'. Its four programmes a day were for a long time broadcast from Prague [31] over very powerful transmitters. This station, which seems to be the foreign transmitter with the largest audience in Spain, is the successor of Radio Pirenáica, which started up in south-western France immediately after the liberation. [32]

This transmitter secured for the communists a considerable advantage over other anti-Franco groups. The 'orthodox' communists also benefited from the support of the many programmes in Spanish broadcast by the Soviet and East European radios. Between them, these pretty well covered the short-wave band, often reaching listeners who had no idea of the precise political affiliation of the station to which they were listening.

Printed propaganda is less well adapted to underground use, for reasons connected with distribution and the concealment of the origin of literature distributed by the Party. It is therefore, addressed largely to hard-core militants or to declared sympathisers rather than to people merely looking for sources of information not under the Franco regime's control. Periodicals in this category are of two kinds: papers and reviews printed, or at least edited, abroad; and truly clandestine publications printed, duplicated, typed or even hand-written in Spain.

The Party's official organ is the fortnightly *Mundo obrero*, for a long time printed in East Germany and reproduced in Spain from stencils smuggled across the French frontier. [33] According to communist sources, it has a print of some 50,000, [34] a considerable proportion of which is sold to émigrés in France, Mexico and Eastern Europe. The PCE's theoretical journal is the bimonthly *Nuestra bandera*, probably edited in Belgium, the print of which is said to reach 23,000 copies, also sold largely among émigrés. To the same category belong ideological and cultural perodicals like the quarterly *Realidad*, which is not officially of PCE provenance, though almost every article in it is signed by a prominent Party figure. Launched in 1964, this review, aimed at students and intellectuals, circulates mostly in France and to a lesser extent in Spain and Italy.

The mouthpiece of the Communist Youth Union, the monthly *Horizonte*, is also published abroad, as are the monthly journals of the Catalan PSUC and of the Basque Communist Party, *Treball* and *Euzkadi obrera* respectively. These two parties also publish the reviews *Alkarrilketa* and *Nous horitzons*, the former printed in France and the latter in Mexico.

However, *Nous horitzons* does not explicitly acknowledge its affiliation. The same applies to the little review *Nova Galicia*, published in France under the aegis of the Galician Communist Party. There are also two publications which appear at irregular intervals abroad under the titles *Lucha obrera* and *La Voz del campo*, aimed respectively at supporters of the Workers' Trade Union (OSO) Opposition and at farm workers. For the record, it may be worth mentioning here some periodicals, published by Spanish refugees in Mexico and Cuba, which have virtually no circulation either in Spain or in Eastern Europe. They include the theoretical review *El Comunista* and the journals *España popular* [35] and *España republicana.* [36]

Gaps in our knowledge, and the consequent difficulty of obtaining a comprehensive idea of publications which appear irregularly or have appeared once only, make it impossible to present a survey of the underground press published in Spain itself. For instance, how can one make a count of hand-written editions of *Mundo obrero*, got up in prison, or mimeographed leaflets typed by *ad hoc* groups with no organic Party contacts, such as the young workers in Barcelona who round about 1955 published a bulletin called *Estrella roja*? [37]

But not all clandestine publications are so well hidden or so ephemeral. Some have managed to keep up fairly regular publication dates despite the steady pressures on them, as well as to attain relatively big circulation figures at local or regional level. Cases in point are the provincial editions of *Mundo obrero* and *Horizonte*, which are, or have been, published in Madrid, Asturias and Santander, as well as in the Levante region, Andalusia, Galicia and the Canaries. [38]

Also worth a mention are the duplicated bulletins published fairly regularly by some of the regional committees of the PCE and PSUC, such as *Acción* in Asturias, *Hora de Madrid*, and the Barcelona sheet *Unitat*; or those issued by student organisations under the title *Vanguardia* in Madrid, *Universitat* in Barcelona, and *Crítica* in Zaragoza. The review *Revolución y cultura* is published without attribution to the Party by communist intellectuals in Madrid.

The intervals between the publication of these journals, the number of their pages and their style of presentation vary a great deal; even their titles change from time to time. At one end of the scale are the best-established ones like *Vanguardia* of Madrid, which appears three or four times a year, [39] has two to ten roneoed pages and is sometimes rolled off in several thousand copies. At the other extreme one finds typed tracts produced by local cells or committees in no more than a dozen or so copies.

In addition to periodicals printed abroad and those which are genuinely clandestine, the PCE also publishes either directly or through intermediary organisations, series of books and pamphlets. These are produced mainly in France and Cuba, the USSR, Eastern Europe or, more rarely, in Spain itself. Best presented is the 'Ebro collection', published in France by Editions de la Librairie du Globe, whose list includes some thirty titles issued since 1965. The French Communist Party, Editions sociales, the Progreso publishing house in Moscow, Editora politica of Havana, as well as publishing houses in Eastern Europe, put out a considerable number of titles in Spanish, aimed at PCE members and sympathisers, and opponents of the Franco regime in general. The subject matter ranges from the political speeches and writings of Santiago Carrillo, Enrique Lister and Santiago Alvarez, to reports of meetings, histories of the Party or of the Civil War, books on strikes and the clandestine struggle, bibliographies of Party members, or even novels which cannot be published in Spain, such as *La huelga*, the author of which is the Duchess of Medina Sidonia. [40]

Officially the PCE has no direct links with the publishing houses that put out these collections and series of books, in which its name appears only within the text as the subject matter of each book warrants. On the other hand, the Party does acknowledge responsibility as the publisher of booklets designed principally for the ideological and political education of its members, such as the *Cuadernos de educación política* or those published by *Mundo obrero* and *Nuestra bandera*. It has also managed to print underground editions of longer books, such as Carrillo's *Después de Franco ¿Qué?* of which there is an edition especially for the Spanish market, in addition to those published in French and Spanish by Editions sociales. [41]

As a general rule, the quality and presentation of the literature published under the auspices of the Spanish communists, or aimed at them, have greatly improved in recent years. In particular, the reviews *Nuestra bandera* and *Realidad* will bear comparison with, for example, their French contemporaries, and can be classed among the best political reviews published in Spanish — perhaps simply because nothing better is available. The list of the Ebro collection is also attractively presented and the intrinsic quality of the books is also generally high. On the other hand, it remains true that the Party's main organ, *Mundo obrero,* would be the better for a less heavy make-up; it could also with profit abandon the 'official gazette' style and try to look a little more like a political fortnightly similar to those in Western countries. The ideological education booklets aimed at Party members are also rather too reminiscent of the dogmatic tone now abandoned by *Nuestra bandera* and *Realidad.*

However, the wider propagation of the PCE's views in Spain is limited more by the difficulties of spreading printed propaganda than by any intrinsic defect of the literature itself. Yet, the Party has made some progress in this field. The time is past when émigré Party workers hung about the doorways of low dives in Latin American ports, hoping to make contact with Spanish sailors who might be willing to take home a few tracts or papers. [42] Nowadays copies of *Mundo obrero* and *Horizonte* cross the frontier by the hundred, and sometimes by the thousand, every fortnight and every month in the luggage of workers returning from abroad; occasionally they are brought in by tourists, and sometimes, according to *The Times,* [43] in the luggageholds of planes belonging to the Spanish national airline *Iberia.* In the same way several thousand copies of Carrillo's books *Después de Franco ¿Qué?* and of *Nuevos enfoques a problemas de hoy*[44] have been distributed inside the country. The Party press holds up as an example a militant who, it says, distributed seventy-five copies of *Después de Franco ¿Qué?* [45]

But the risks run by the sympathisers and fledgling Party members who are generally asked to take these publications from France into Spain remain considerable. They are occasionally arrested at the frontier and subsequently given stiff sentences. Activities of this kind are probably among the most dangerous undertaken by underground workers, because they leave tangible evidence which can lead to their being reported to the police, and because they need equipment that is difficult to conceal, even for the rough-and-ready work that is produced. A sympathiser caught distributing a few copies of *Mundo obrero* risks a two-and-a-half-year prison sentence and a fine of 1,000 pesetas, [46] and sentences for activists, who tend to get arrested in relays following one of the periodical discoveries of clandestine 'propaganda workshops', average five or six years' imprisonment.

### Party education

All this means that written documents are scarce, and this shortage makes it difficult to improve the theoretical standards of Spanish communists. Standards have always been low among the middle cadres and even among the leaders. Discussing this at the 1956 augmented plenum, the Secretary-General admitted the weakness, which he described as 'underestimation of theory' and 'ideological feebleness'. [47] During the Civil War, only those Party officials able to withdraw from action for a while to attend the Lenin Academy in Moscow were relatively well trained in this respect.

113

One such was Jesús Hernández, who took his course in 1933; others included some of those who had fled Spain after the Asturias rising between 1934 and 1936. [48] Some years later about a dozen refugees, including Amaya Ibarruri, daughter of La Pasionaria, [49] attended courses at the Comintern cadre school; and twenty-eight others, including Modesto, Lister and V. González, attended the Frunze Military Academy. [50] The great mass of refugees however, do not appear to have done much to profit from the prolonged enforced idleness of exile, by devoting themselves to academic work or theoretical studies.

Today, one can at least find a few students sponsored by the Party at the Charles University in Prague and at the infrequent study sessions for Party officials held in France or Eastern Europe. In Spain, however, both cadres and rank-and-file are for all practical purposes left to their own devices. Nor are the lecture courses the Party does manage to hold in Spain or abroad by any means well attended. According to S. Alvarez, the seminars held in Madrid in 1967 and 1968 drew only a few dozen young people. [51] The only exceptions to this state of affairs are the refugees in Mexico — perhaps because they include a sizeable proportion of middle-class and professional people. [52]

A new factor — the result of the tentative relaxation of control over the media begun in Spain in 1962 under Manuel Fraga Iribarne — added somewhat to the intellectual fare on offer to Spaniards interested in Marxism. Authors suspected of Marxism were removed from the index [53] and their books extensively published in Madrid and Barcelona. Today, works not only by Marx and Engels but also by authors as varied as Della Volpe, Garaudy, Lukács or Guevara are generally freely on sale in bookshops, although with interruptions, since confiscations and prohibitions are still commonplace.

The mitigation of the censorship has also affected the press, though to a lesser extent. The daily papers remain extremely hostile to the communists, but some of the reviews, particularly *Cuadernos para el diálogo*, have shown themselves somewhat more favourable to Marxist, and even communist, writers, to whom they have on occasion given space in their columns. [54]

But one wonders whether this development is really to the liking of the PCE. Political education material provided in this way is not under its control, whereas previously it had a virtual monopoly of what little Marxist-oriented literature did circulate in Spain. The Party thus finds itself faced with a form of competition it is finding difficult to counter. It certainly could not have been indifferent to the fact that *Cuadernos para el diálogo* should publish an article on Che Guevara [55] and an editorial

114

celebrating the 150th anniversary of the birth of Marx,[56] preceded by a three-page contribution by Daniel Cohn-Bendit.[57]

## Membership: numbers and provenance

Information on the organisation, methods of action, means of propaganda and educational activities of the PCE is hard to come by and unreliable. Facts about the Party's strength, its methods of recruitment and the social, political and geographical provenance of its members are even scarcer.

What information is supplied by the Party on this point is vague and not very trustworthy. The sole point of reference consists of some figures given by the Secretary-General in April 1964. According to these, the Party had between 35,000 and 40,000 organised members at the time.[58] Articles published earlier refer to 'tens of thousands of organised communists in Spain'[59] or, more modestly, to 'thousands of communists, veterans and young people'.[60]

It is difficult to tell how accurate these claims are, and what exactly the expression 'organised communists' means. The Party membership figures can hardly be known exactly even to the Secretariat itself, in view of the fluctuating character of clandestine groups, the absence of membership cards and the tenuous membership fee. The figure of 35,000 to 40,000 organised members given by Carrillo is most probably stretched to include in a very loose fashion all categories of communists who have any sort of contact with the Party at all. It is likely to include not only PCE members as such, but also members of the Catalan PSU and of the Basque Communist Party as well as those of the Communist Youth Union. It must also be taken to embrace the membership both in Spain and in emigration.

The latter is most important; its numbers can, moreover, be recorded by the Party more accurately than those of Party members at home. The figure of 10,000 organised members in emigration, given by Carrillo in 1970,[61] therefore seems reasonably trustworthy. It may even seem modest, if one considers the number of republican refugees who have settled in France, Mexico, Eastern Europe and the USSR, as well as the great mass of migrant workers who have come to live in Western Europe in the past dozen years or so. In France alone, Spanish republican refugees and their families numbered between 130,000 and 165,000 in 1967, without including those who had become naturalised Frenchmen.[62] The East European people's democracies and the USSR are generally believed to shelter some 7,000 more of these refugees.[63] Moreover, the proportion of

115

communists, relatively low in France where exiles of socialist, anarchist or moderate republican views predominate, is exceptionally high in the socialist countries and Mexico, where the PCE was allowed to send its members after the Civil War. Nor should the recruitment opportunities offered by the million migrant Spanish workers in France, Germany, Switzerland and Belgium be underestimated.

The Party should therefore have little difficulty in maintaining, and perhaps even exceeding, a strength of some 15,000 members abroad — perhaps 10,000 of them in France and around 1,000 in the USSR [64] — despite the rate at which death is steadily reducing the refugee population. In giving his figures, Carrillo was in fact probably referring only to those directly enrolled in the PCE and not to all communist exiles, a considerable number of whom belong to local communist parties. The latter constitute a reserve the Party can 'mobilise' in case of need outside Spain; in the short term they would be a liability rather than an asset because of the advanced average age of the veteran members and the political inexperience of the migrant workers who have been left outside its organisation.

The numerical strength of the membership of the PCE and its associated organisations in Spain is even more uncertain. There is little doubt that the former Secretary for Organisation, García, was stretching the truth somewhat when he put the organised membership at 'some tens of thousands'. [65] It would almost certainly be more exact to speak — as he himself does earlier in the same article — of 'thousands' of members of the clandestine organisation.

According to Benjamin Welles, the real figure is somewhere between 2,000 and 5,000, although he also gives some fanciful estimates, dating from 1965, which put the PCE membership as high as 350,000. [66] The figure of 5,000 members is the one preferred by the American Central Intelligence Agency [67] and the Yearbook on International Communist Affairs which, however, does not make it clear whether it is referring purely to communists in Spain itself or to émigrés as well. [68] The latter estimate appears to correspond more or less to the true numerical strength of the underground membership in 1968. Although way below the figures put about by the Party, a membership of 5,000, or a little more, properly organised, is a considerable one, given the underground situation in which all Spanish political groupings other than the Falange must operate. It is about the same as the membership of the Italian Communist Party in 1943 [69] in the last phases of its clandestine period, and probably puts the PCE ahead of all other opposition political or trade union organisations functioning in Spain, at least as far as membership is concerned.

Of course, this estimate may today be higher than the facts justify, because of the recent splits within the PCE, the PSUC and the Basque Communist Party. It is, on the other hand, also possible that the figure of 5,000 members should be adjusted somewhat upward, to take into account the members of the Communist Youth Union and of the parallel women's and trade union organisations, as well as all those who work, or have worked, for the Party without formally belonging to it — mainly for security reasons.

A few indirect and fragmentary indicators, based either on inferences from known facts or from first-hand accounts, make it possible to put forward some hypotheses on the geographical distribution and sociological composition of the Party membership, or rather of people connected with the Party in various ways. We have already seen that the main communist centres in Spain are in the Madrid region, Asturias, Catalonia, Andalusia and the Basque country. If one wants more precise information, the best one can do is to look at that furnished by the geographical breakdown of the sums gathered in the 1968—69 collection drive — the so-called 'Thirty Million Pesetas Campaign'.

Assuming that the sums collected in various provinces correspond roughly to the area distribution of the Party's strength, it would seem that 53 per cent of the 6,600,000 pesetas collected throughout the country — excluding Catalonia [70] — came from Madrid, 14 per cent from Asturias, 9·5 per cent from Andalusia, 7·5 per cent from the Levante region and 7 per cent from the Basque country, all the other regions of the country accounting for only 9 per cent of the total. [71] The relative preponderance of intellectuals and professional people among Party members in the capital goes some way towards explaining why such large sums were collected in Madrid. However, we can safely assume that Madrid and district account for the lion's share of Party members inside Spain, perhaps somewhere between one third and a half. Asturias and Andalusia, with Seville also well to the fore, must account for another considerable portion, probably slightly higher than the percentage of the sums collected during the drive may suggest, in view of the almost wholly working-class character of the communist population of these areas. The Basque membership, too, probably accounts for a higher percentage of the total than would appear from relying too closely on contributions to the collection drive from the region, because the collection took place at a moment when the Party in the Basque country was in a state of grave crisis. Summing up, it would seem fairly safe to assume that around a third of the PCE's membership in Spain itself is in Madrid, another third in the industrial and mining areas of the north, and the remainder in other areas, with a rather stronger concentration in Seville, Cadiz, Valencia and Aragon. [72]

Concrete evidence to confirm these hypothetical calculations is scarce. All we have to go by are some unverifiable indicators, suggesting the degree to which the Party has established itself in its main centre, Madrid. These derive from statements made in opposition circles in the capital towards the end of 1968. There were at that time said to be some 1,200 to 1,500 organised communists in and around the city; these comprised 500 to 1,000 workers, most of them concentrated in the dozen or so big factories in which there are fairly extensive networks of cells, some 100 to 150 students, and some hundreds of intellectuals, middle-class people and members of the liberal professions.

The PCE has published nothing since 1968 about the social origins or other characteristics of its members. However, a recent article does give some information on the place occupied in the Party by women. [73] The number of women in the Party has always been small — because of 'sectarian opposition' — to use the author's terminology. He goes on to say that certain shortcomings in this field remain to be remedied, but that the situation has improved considerably, so that there is now a 'veritable flood of women and girls who have joined the Party and the Communist Youth'. He says that girls account for some 30 per cent of the membership of the Communist Youth Union and the student movement, and that in some cases girls have been elected officers of Communist Youth groups. However, it seems that the Communist Youth Union is best established abroad, particularly in France, Switzerland and Belgium, rather than in Spain, where members of all ages tend to belong to the Party proper. In Spain only the communist students of Madrid seem to include a significant number of girls. Elsewhere, although more numerous than in the past, they account for a very small part of the membership, particularly among working-class supporters.

The article also supplies some fragmentary information, again impossible to verify, about the age of the Party membership. It lays particular stress on the effort made in the sixties to infuse young blood into the ranks of the cadres. Within Spain, we are told, the average age of cadres is thirty-six and of rank-and-file members as low as twenty-five to thirty in certain provinces. Despite the efforts of the Communist Youth Union, the same probably cannot be said of the émigrés, among whom Civil War refugees still account for an appreciable proportion of the membership.

Information on the social and occupational background of Spanish communists is totally lacking. However, one can make some conjectures by drawing inferences from past information or referring to more recent impressions. Students probably represent only a very small fraction of the membership — perhaps two to three per cent. This is due partly to the crisis which broke out in 1964 with the expulsion of Claudín and the departure of Semprún, [74] and partly to the emergence of Maoist factions. In Spain itself, members of working-class origin are certainly in the majority and must account for at least two-thirds, if not three-quarters, of the membership. The remainder is made up of farm workers, intellectuals and members of the middle classes. The proportions of the various social classes of members must be much the same among the émigrés, except for Latin America, where republican refugees of bourgeois and intellectual origin are particularly numerous.


## Recruitment

The recruiting procedures currently in use have helped to maintain the predominantly working-class character of the Party. Because of police repression, the communists have tended to let potential members approach them, rather than seeking out recruits. Their recruitment has thus been mainly in circles where the communist tradition is still alive: among working-class families in Asturias, in the outskirts of Madrid, in the Basque country, or in the great factories where a skeleton organisation has always survived. On the other hand, they have fewer contacts with the middle classes. Middle-class communists, quite numerous in 1937 and 1938, emigrated almost to a man at the end of the Civil War. Most notably, they have become almost totally extinct among teachers. They were very well represented in the profession until 1939; but it was drastically 'purged' after the Nationalist victory. Hence, a substantial proportion of new members in Spain is made up of the sons and daughters of communist workers, as well as men from the large factories, where the communists have never ceased to make their presence felt — if only by getting arrested. [75]

But family tradition and social and professional background are not the only factors that affect recruitment. The services the Party renders to its members, like the hazards of the repression, are a sort of seed which often eventually ripens into formal membership. For example, many people, arrested and sentenced for having lent a typewriter which was used to produce a communist tract, or for being found in possession of a copy of *Mundo obrero*, eventually join the Party, [76] if only as a reaction against the sentences imposed on them, or out of solidarity with those who have placed them in this position. Outside the ranks of working-class circles with a strong communist tradition, the prestige the PCE has acquired by the quality of its organisation and the courage of its members during and since the Civil War has also contributed to attracting members from other organisations and social strata.

This for instance is how recruitment takes place in prison, or in workers' councils and works arbitration committees particularly during strikes and periods of intensive agitation. It is the Party's prestige, perhaps as much as any ideological conviction, that has attracted into its ranks middle-class and sometimes even aristocratic students and intellectuals, such as Jorge Semprún in 1942 or, much more recently, Daniel Lacalle, son of Franco's Air Minister. [77] And it is this phenomenon that explains why a number of Falangists on the left of that movement, a number of Catholics, many of them former members of the Popular Liberation Front — as well as some former socialists and anarchists, such as Jorge Conill, now in Burgos jail — came to join the Communist Party.

However, prestige appears to be a less reliable guide than family tradition or professional background when it comes to duration of membership. The membership turnover among intellectuals and students, who are perhaps most susceptible to the prestige element, is considerably faster than among workers from communist or socialist backgrounds; and this difference in length of membership is even more marked than in parties enjoying legal status. All this means that the Communist Party is able to count on the support not only of tens of thousands of sympathisers who are not formally Party members, as its propaganda, probably with justification, claims; nor only on the hundreds of veteran militants tested in the fire of battle but not at this moment belonging to its organisation; it must also reckon with all those who have spent only a few months or years in its ranks and have become disillusioned with it.

## 'Leaders' and 'elder statesmen' of the Party

A typical profile of an active Communist Party member living in Spain would be of a family man some forty years of age, relatively comfortably off, living in a subsidised flat and working as a skilled man in a great foundry or engineering plant, where he is known as a keen trade unionist. Another, less common, type is the intellectual — painter, writer, lawyer, university lecturer or even professor — who lives in Madrid, Barcelona or San Sebastian, whose tangible political acts consist of an occasional Marxist article or book, or participation in a 'progressive' exhibition or event.

These two types of activists in Spain do not account for the whole of the Party's manpower resources, which also include students, farmworkers and white-collar workers, including civil servants. Abroad, there are the exiles, on average rather elderly, largely working-class in Europe and rather more middle-class in Latin America. There are also the children of these people, often receiving higher education, who are nowadays the backbone of the Communist Youth Union. But this cross-section of the membership would be incomplete if it omitted the very special and outstanding group made up of the 'leaders' and 'elder statesmen' of the Party.

It is in fact important to distinguish between these two categories among contemporary Spanish communist personalities. For the 'leaders' are the men with power, whereas the 'elder statesmen' have had it taken from them — with great deference — or have never enjoyed it at all. Nevertheless, they have at least had a moral influence on some members and many sympathisers; some of them have personal prestige far greater than any 'leader' can boast.

The 'leader' group includes in the first instance the team of the Party Secretariat, headed by Santiago Carrillo. For many years the other key figure of this group, second only to Carrillo himself, was the secretary responsible for the underground party apparatus, Eduardo García, who was expelled early in 1969.

Today, with the eclipse of García, the two central figures in the Secretariat are Santiago Carrillo and Santiago Alvarez. Carrillo, a former printer, son of the trade unionist and moderate socialist Deputy Wenceslao Carrillo, became a communist sympathiser in 1936 and joined the 'Casadists' [78] in 1939. He was born in Asturias in 1916. In 1934 he was said to have held Trotskyite views. [79] Becoming Secretary of the Socialist Youth Union, he promoted its merger with the Communist Youth Union in April 1936. On joining the Communist Party on 6 November of the same year, he immediately became one of the foremost of the younger generation of communist leaders. A member of the junta for the defence of Madrid, and elected to the Central Committee in 1937, he left the capital on 27 March 1939, among the last to do so. He lived in exile in Latin America until 1945, re-establishing contacts between the communist elements scattered throughout that region, until in 1942 he was instructed to get in touch with the organisation in Spain.

He returned to France after the war and put a stop to the guerrilla incursions into the Valle d'Aran. While retaining the post of Secretary of the United Socialist Youth until its official demise in 1961, he was climbing the highest rungs on the Party ladder, until he joined the Political Bureau. From 1947 onwards, he began to appear at the side of such revered figures as Dolores Ibarruri and Jacques Duclos on important public occasions. From March 1946 to early 1947, he was Minister without

Portfolio in President Giral's republican government-in-exile. In 1949, Carrillo moved from Paris to Prague, where he was re-elected to the Political Bureau at the 1954 Congress. At the 1956 augmented plenum, he emerged as the man who destalinised the PCE and gradually forced the leaders of an earlier generation — men like Mije and Uribe — to retreat. This change of course in Carrillo's favour was made formal at the 1960 Congress, at which he took over the post of Secretary-General from La Pasionaria. During the next well-known period of his life the new Secretary-General put in hand his programme of national reconciliation and non-violent action. He revived the mirage of a general strike, eliminating the group of his opponents headed by Claudín, and finally, after the invasion of Czechoslovakia and the talks in Moscow early in 1970 between López Bravo and the Soviet Deputy Minister Kovalyev, set the PCE apart from the Soviet Communist Party.

Santiago Alvarez appears to be the other key figure at the core of the PCE leadership. Responsible for international relations, Alvarez often represents the Party at major international communist gatherings. Of Galician origin, he became Political Commissar of the Fifth Regiment during the Civil War and returned to Spain after the Second World War. Arrested some time before 1950 together with Zapiraín, he was released some years later and now lives outside Spain.

It is also possible that some of the newest arrivals on the Executive Committee, such as Aurelio López and Mauricio Pérez, now share in the exercise of power in the Party [80] with some of the older leaders like Ignacio Gallego and Gregorio López Raimundo. The other members of the Committee do not have the same access to the levers of power. Some, like Sánchez Montero and Fernández Inguanzo, are cadres working inside Spain, and contact with them is very difficult — especially when they are in prison. Others, like Manuel Delicado, Dolores Ibarruri and Antonio Mije, who have been on the Central Committee since 1932 and the Political Bureau since 1936, belong to that group of respected 'elder statesmen' who were relegated to the sidelines in the fifties. Enrique Lister, the Executive Committee member responsible for international relations, last survivor of the 1939 communist officer class, found himself in much the same position, despite his less advanced age, until his recent expulsion.

The group of 1936 veterans is also the best known of the category of 'elder statesmen'. Since the death of José Díaz, the outstanding member of this group has without doubt been Dolores Ibarruri Gómez. La Pasionaria was born on 9 December 1895, in Biscay Province, into a family of miners. After an early start in the Socialist Youth Union, she joined the PSOE in 1917, following in the footsteps of her husband, a worker at the

Sestao shipyards. She subsequently went over to the original *Partido comunista español*, set up by the Young Socialists, and to the PCE.

Admitted to the Central Committee in 1930, she was made to perform an act of self-criticism in 1932 for having initially supported the line taken by José Bullejos before his expulsion from the General Secretariat. [81] But this incident did not halt her progress, accelerated by the prestige obtained from frequent spells in prison, which began even before the Asturias rising. She took part in the last Congress of the Communist International in July and August 1935 and was on that occasion elected a member of the Presidium of the Comintern. Elected Deputy for Oviedo on 16 February 1936, she became Vice-President of the Cortes. During the Civil War she came to be looked on as the acknowledged standard-bearer of the PCE, and indeed of the Republic.

Dolores Ibarruri sought asylum in Moscow in 1939 and between 1941 and 1944 lived in Ufa, where she succeeded José Díaz as Secretary-General of the Party on his death in 1942. Next year her signature was among those on the document dissolving the Comintern. After going to live in Paris in 1945, she returned to settle in Moscow from 1948 to 1949 and was made Vice-President of the Women's International Democratic Federation (WIDF). During the whole of this period, including the nineteenth Congress of the CPSU, Dolores Ibarruri was among the most fervent worshippers at the altar of Stalin.

Re-elected Secretary-General of the Party in November 1954, she gave way to Santiago Carrillo at the next Congress, in 1960, and was given the honorific title of Party President. Decorated with the Order of Lenin in 1966, she still turns up at most major events of the international communist movement. The first reported show of at least some independence of attitude on her part *vis à vis* the Russians came in August 1968, when she was said to have expressed 'regret' at the intervention in Czechoslovakia. Since then, she has barely been heard of, except on the occasion of a visit to Romania.

The remaining survivors of the old PCE leadership are greatly inferior in prestige to Dolores Ibarruri, or even to Enrique Lister. What remains of their influence does not generally range beyond the circle of a few dozen veteran émigré militants. Such is the case with Mije and Delicado, as well as Francisco Antón Sáenz and Irene Falcón Tobosco, who belonged to another generation but have attached themselves in a subordinate capacity to the old ruling group, Sáenz as a protégé of La Pasionaria and Irene Falcón as her secretary.

In addition to the old leaders, the top group of Party figures includes a second stratum, consisting of senior officers, civil servants, university dons, artists and writers who emigrated after the nationalist victory, and of a far smaller number of intellectuals who joined the Communist Party later, in the underground phase. Unlike the people just described, all of whom were old Party hands of working-class background — except Irene Falcón, who may be classed as an intellectual — this last group share a generally bourgeois family background. Almost all of them joined the Party during, or shortly before, the Civil War. The Stalin era left its mark on them; while it lasted, many of them received financial assistance from the communist parties and governments of the USSR and the people's democracies. Today they live scattered throughout Mexico, Cuba, Argentina, France, Italy and the Eastern bloc countries. They have never had any real influence. Their names head lists of signatures under declarations and petitions reprinted in *Mundo obrero*, and many of them have seats on the Central Committee, frequently as alternate members. Unlike the young intellectuals and students who joined long after them, they never speak up to criticise the policies of the leadership. The great majority of these figures are of very advanced age and their numbers are diminishing.

Thus, almost the entire little cohort of communist professional army officers has disappeared with the death of Colonel R. Gil and Generals Matz, Herrera, Cordon and Hidalgo de Cisneros. Despite the death in Moscow of the sculptor Alberto Sánchez in 1968, the number of surviving émigré communist artists and writers is somewhat greater, the poet Rafael Alberti being the most distinguished among them. Others in this category include Alberti's wife, the actress and novelist María Teresa de León, and the novelist and journalist Jesús Izcaray. Mention should also be made in this context of a number of novelists, playwrights, poets, painters and film makers now living in Spain. A small group of refugee communist university teachers remains fairly prosperous: it includes such men as the economist Juan Gómez; Wenceslao Roces, one-time professor of law at the University of Salamanca and a member of the Central Committee, now resident in Mexico; the philosopher Sánchez-Vásquez; and a team of economists consisting of Enrique Andrés, Anastasio Mansillo and Ramón Peña. All three at first taught in Moscow. Mansillo and Peña went on to Havana, where they rejoined the philosopher Rafael Martínez, who also left the Soviet Union to settle in Cuba.


### The dissident communists

The last section of the Spanish communist Who's Who consists of dissident organisations, the leaders of which come from a mould rather different from that of the mass of PCE members. Ever since the beginning of the thirties, isolated or dissident communists have always been relatively common in Spain. One need only recall the period of the Second Republic, with Maurín's Workers' and Peasants' Bloc; and POUM, which was crushed by the Stalin-style repression of 1937. Later, in the underground phase, came the splits in the Party apparatus in Spain. These proliferated particularly between 1940 and 1942, involving such people as Quiñones and the breakaway group led by Hernández. The PSUC broke up into a 'Catalanist' faction under Comorera, a Titoist one led by Del Barrio and a right-wing one under Serra Pamies. Today the dissidents are even more numerous and varied. They are also more insignificant, since one can now list over a dozen micro-organisations distinct from the PCE or set up in opposition to it, all of which have come into existence since 1963. [82]

All these organisations have the peculiarly communist characteristic of coming into being and recruiting their members in three fairly distinct areas, that is among intellectuals, students, and advocates of regional autonomy. The intellectuals' and students' propensity to form breakaway groups hardly requires comment. In Spain, as elsewhere, these people have a function of criticism, which they practise extensively, especially in left-wing organisations held together by ideology and even more so in clandestine groups the activities of which are mostly verbal. The Trotskyite and Marxist-Leninist groups which have cropped up in recent years were born, as it were spontaneously, among the students of Madrid and Barcelona and some of the coteries of émigré intellectuals in Colombia, Switzerland, Belgium and France.

The chronic squabbling of the Catalans, on the other hand, is a phenomenon peculiar to Spain. It is a reflection within the communist movement of the more generalised tensions between the autonomy-seeking provinces, notably Catalonia, and 'Castilian centralism'. The PCE, too, is suspected of being infected with this disease. The PCE has succeeded no better than any other party with nation-wide aspirations in obtaining a firm foothold in this province, where political organisations which are more Catalan than Spanish have held the upper hand ever since the beginning of the present century. It is this regionalist feeling which explains why the POUM was so successful in Catalonia and Aragon between 1935 and 1937. It came into being in these two provinces at the initiative of Catalan intellectuals who had broken with the Communist Party and did not meet locally the obstacles encountered by socialist and communist organisations consisting almost exclusively of, and run by, non-Catalans.

It is this same reaction which today contributes to the internal divisions and weakness of the United Socialist Party of Catalonia which, despite its

125

name, is generally regarded as being nothing more than an appendage of the PCE. It is hardly surprising that, at least until the expulsion of García, the only splinter group in recent years which managed to take a fairly appreciable number of rank-and-file non-intellectual members out of the Party with it should have been based in Catalonia. The PCE (*Internacional*) did just that between 1967 and 1969.

It should, however, be made clear that the PCE (*Internacional*), because of the generally petty bourgeois nature of Catalan communist membership, is not essentially a working-class body. But the dissident groups established outside Catalonia are even less so, save in a few isolated and generally short-lived instances. [83] Based essentially on a few hundred students in Madrid and a few score in Seville and Bilbao, they have barely touched the white-collar and professional classes, among whom the PCE (*Internacional*) alone has managed to make some impression in Catalonia, and more recently in the Basque country. [84]

The total following of these various organisations may be in the 2,000 to 2,500 range, both émigrés and people living in Spain. Most belong to the PCE (*Internacional*), which has greatly reinforced the ranks of communist dissidents.

On the ideological and tactical level these organisations embrace four main political trends — ignoring for the moment the infinite variations of each. The first is Trotskyism, represented by the tiny Revolutionary Workers' Party (Trotskyite) or POR (T). This party, which follows the ideas of J. Posadas, was founded in Madrid in December 1966 on the initiative of José María Borras. In 1969 it had a mere few dozen members, mainly in Madrid and Barcelona. [85] Despite its very small numbers, and thanks to the virtual disappearance of elements flirting with Trotskyism in the POUM, virtually all of whom have fled abroad, the POR (T) has the field more or less to itself in its own particular ideological area. The Revolutionary Action Front, also of a Trotskyite flavour and set up in 1965 by Francisco Crespo Méndez, seems in effect to have had only a nominal and short-lived existence. [86]

Two other shades of opinion are represented by a number of Marxist-Leninist organisations, which have been further split since 1968, after a series of earlier fissions and reconciliations between the so-called 'military' line of the original PCE (ML) and the more 'peaceable' one represented by the *Movimiento comunista (ML) de España*. Both have close links with equivalent movements in France and Belgium, whose ideological views they echo.

The fourth trend, embodied by the PCE (*Internacional*), is probably the worst thorn in the flesh of the orthodox communists, both because it has

126

been responsible for the defection of a considerable proportion of the PSUC membership, and because it bears the strong imprint of the near-Trotskyite ideas which have found a ready echo in Catalonia and are today so ineffectually advocated by the POR (T). Unconcerned by the contradiction between its principles and its actual social composition — it is in fact more intellectual and petty bourgeois than the PCE proper — the PCE (*Internacional*) has concentrated the fire of its criticism on the social composition of the organisation it has abandoned. Its outlook is summed up by the statement that 'petty bourgeois habits and attitudes which have struck particularly deep roots among the comrades in the leadership who are not of working-class origin' are at the root of the PCE's tactical deviations and that, as a result, 'correct political positions' have been abandoned. [87] To remedy this situation it proposes a new bolshevisation of the Party by introducing the class war into the Party itself and 'proletarianising' the non-working-class members through a sort of internal cultural revolution.

Judging by the presentation of the literature they put out, the material resources of these organisations are very uneven. Those of the POR (T) — the Spanish affiliate of the Fourth International — seem to be virtually nil, being insufficient to provide it even with the use of a duplicating machine for its fortnightly, *Lucha obrera*, a twenty-page affair rolled off by hand. Nor do the two organs of the PCE (*Internacional*) look much more impressive. *Mundo obrero* (*Internacional*) and *El Quehacer proletario* — the latter put out by the Party's Madrid committee — are crudely mimeographed and run to between fifteen and twenty pages.

The Maoists, on the other hand, seem to command rather ampler financial resources, if the appearance and volume of their publications are anything to go by. *El Comunista*, organ of the *Movimiento comunista*, consists of eleven to thirteen offset pages between printed covers with artwork. This relative opulence is even more noticeable in the case of the PCE (ML), the main mouthpiece of which, *Vanguardia obrera*, compares well with the orthodox *Mundo obrero* as regards format, number of pages and quality of printing. The theoretical journal of the PCE (ML), *Revolución española*, compares unfavourably with *Nuestra bandera* but is of acceptable quality, with a printed cover and anything from 100 to 250 pages.

Furthermore, the PCE (ML) benefits from the support of the Spanish programmes of Tirana and Peking radios, [68] as well as of its Belgian opposite number, which provides it with a rear base.

The formal structures of these parties are largely modelled on the PCE, with some simplifications and terminological variations; for instance not all of them have a political bureau. The contrast between the model and the actual structure on the ground is even more marked than is the case with the orthodox party, especially as regards the real machinery of leadership and the non-existence in fact of the supreme bodies claimed to exist in theory.

It also seems likely that the real apparatus of these organisations is more fragile than that of the PCE, which, despite all the hazards of repression and despite the world crisis of communism, has managed to survive underground for more than thirty years. This fragility is due to the doctrinaire quarrels which continually divide the dissident parties and thus periodically provide them with fresh rivals. It derives, too, from the fact that their leaders and members have less experience of underground work. Thus, although fewer in numbers than those of the PCE, they are more frequently arrested, and arrest is invariably followed by the destruction of the local groups they have put together with so much trouble.

Because of the disarray of its competitors — both communist and socialist clandestine dissident opposition groupings — the PCE remains the best organised underground political force in the whole of Spain, despite all its difficulties and internal divisions.

But the fact that it still has at its disposal a sizeable organisation tells one little about its real importance as a force opposing the Franco state. A real take-over of power based on the direct use of force being out of the question, it would seem that the power of a political group such as the PCE depends less on the quality of its organisation than on the opportunities for action it is given by the regime in power, and also on what sort of reaction — positive or negative — such a body elicits from the population. Quality of organisation can even become a factor which helps to rob an organisation of power, particularly if it is an illegal one, and it becomes an end in itself for a membership obsessed by an over-perfect, emotional and egocentric image of its micro-society. An analysis of the true organisational structure of the Spanish communist movement would be almost gratuitous and misleading without an examination of the subjective impression the population has of it.

### Notes

[1] On the sub-provincial level, the Spanish communist press distinguishes between local committees, sector or 'rayon' committees and zone committees or *comités comarcales*. ('Por un Partido comunista de masas' *Nuestra bandera* 54, 2nd quarter 1967, p. 127.) However, this is a formal design,

which somewhat exaggerates the extent and complexity of the Party's organisation in Spain. In practice, the distinction between these three types of committee tends to be blurred.

[2] The seven Congresses so far held by the PCE took place in March 1922 in Madrid; in the summer of 1923, also in Madrid; in 1929 in Paris; in March 1932 in Seville; from 1 to 5 November 1954 in Prague; and from 28 to 31 January 1960, also in Prague; the last Congress to be held – in 1965 – took place amid total secrecy, in a place which has not been identified.

[3] Five plenums were held between 1956 and 1963: in August 1956, September 1957, October 1958, October 1961 and November 1963.

[4] *Mundo obrero* 36 (2), 1 December 1965, pp. 1–2.

[5] We have been able to draw up a list of twenty members of the Executive Committee as it was at the beginning of 1971. It consisted of the following: Santiago Alvarez, Santiago Carrillo, Juan Diz, Horacio Fernández Inguanzo (in jail), Ignacio Gallego, Juan Gómez, Dolores Ibarruri, Aurelio López, A. Lorenzo, Gregorio López Raimundo, Francisco Marín, Ramón Mendezona, Antonio Mije, Mauricio Pérez and Simón Sánchez Montero. Five new members of the Executive Committee were appointed in September 1970: Ester Blanco, Juan Calanda, José María González Jérez, V. Martín García and Ricardo Orneta.

[6] National Front for Aid to Prisoners.

[7] Sometimes described as 'groups', although this expression is occasionally also used to describe the regular cells.

[8] S. Carrillo, 'La situación del partido ...' in *Informes y resoluciones del pleno* ... , pp. 199–200.

[9] S. Carrillo, 'Après Franco ... quoi?', p. 181.

[10] S. Carrillo, *Discurso ante una asamblea de militantes del Partido*, French Communist Party, Paris 1964, p. 46.

[11] Ibid., pp. 43–4.

[12] S. Carrillo, 'La democracia en el Partido leninista' *Mundo obrero* 40 (7), 5 April 1970, p. 6.

[13] 'Communist Campaign in Spain' *The Times,* 1 May 1968, p. 5.

[14] Member of the Central Committee since 1954, and successively of the Political Bureau and Executive Committee since 1956. Imprisoned from 1945 to 1952, and again from 1954 to 1966, Sánchez Montero is said to have been in charge of the Madrid region in the period between his two spells in prison.

[15] Fernández was recently sentenced to twenty years' imprisonment. He was accused of being the senior Party officer for the coal-mining region of Asturias.

[16]   Member of the PSUC Central Committee since 1956, Núñez was accused of being the leader of the Party in Barcelona. He left Spain in 1944 or 1945, returned in 1948 and lived in hiding from 1948 to 1956.

[17]   Because of their knowledge of the language, these people have been organised into French Party cells, or cells appropriate to their 'language group'.

[18]   Known by initials such as ALE, ALS, ALO, ALN, etc.

[19]   E. García, Le Parti communiste consolide ses rangs, *Nouvelle revue internationale* 8 (120), August 1968, pp. 171–3.

[20]   On this subject, see M. Razola, and M. Constante, *Triangle bleu, Les Républicains espagnols à Mauthausen, 1940–1945*, Gallimard, Paris 1969.

[21]   Information about communist organisation inside prisons is drawn from M. Rodriguez Chaos, *24 años en la cárcel*, pp. 192–208.

[22]   The word 'brigade' is borrowed from the terminology of prison administration.

[23]   E. García: article referred to above (see note 19) pp. 172–3.

[24]   El Campesino, *La vie et la mort en URSS*, pp. 177–180.

[25]   E. Castro Delgado, *J'ai perdu la foi à Moscou*, p. 86.

[26]   S. de Madariaga, *Spain*, p. 584.

[27]   For which PCE representatives in Spain itself are provided with books of block tickets signed by Dolores Ibarruri and Santiago Carrillo. (Cf. 'Cobraba boletos firmados por Dolores Ibarruri y Santiago Carrillo' *Ya*, 10 December 1969, p. 35.)

[28]   'Más de 40 millones recaudados en la campaña de los 30 millones' *Mundo obrero* 39 (15), 2 September 1969, p. 4.

[29]   The principal collections made abroad have been those in aid of prisoners. In 1968–69 these collections brought in 2,570,000 pesetas, some 1,714,000 pesetas of which was collected in France on the occasion of the *L'Humanité* festivals.

[30]   Those caught by the police are mostly people found in possession of some clandestine publication for their own use, without having been asked by the Party to carry it.

[31]   The leaders of the PCE now insist that this transmitter is no longer in Prague or indeed in Eastern Europe.

[32]   Earlier, between 1940 and 1947, the PCE broadcast a daily programme beamed to Spain from Cuba, where it bought time on a commercial channel.

[33]   Contrary to the assertions of an article to which we have referred before (see note 13 above), the communists insist that *Mundo obrero* is no longer edited in East Berlin. Perhaps it is now put together in a West European country. From 1956 to 1961, *Mundo obrero* was printed in

France. Its circulation was then several tens of thousands of copies, some 65 per cent of which were read by non-communists (El gran acto de *Mundo obrero* en el Palais de Chaillot de París' *Mundo obrero* 54, 20 February 1947, p. 2). In 1947 the number of copies sold in the Paris area alone was 3,600 ('Cómo la Organización de París aumenta la difusión de *Mundo obrero*'. *Mundo obrero* 89, 23 October 1947, p. 2).

[34] This information about the circulation of the communist press is drawn from E. García, 'Le Parti communiste consolide ses rangs' (article cited above, note 19) p. 181; and 'Encuentro internacional de periodistas' *Mundo obrero* 36 (19), 6 November 1969, p. 8.

[35] *España popular*, published in Mexico, became a semi-official mouthpiece of the Party between 1940 and 1945. Before *Mundo obrero* restarted publication in France, *España popular* enjoyed a modest circulation in France, North Africa and even in Spain.

[36] Marginal support for Spanish communist propaganda was also given in the bulletin *La Verdad*, published in Spanish by the French Communist Party, and in similar material issued by the CGT. In a different vein, there was also the Spanish-language edition of *Nouvelle revue internationale*. The French Communist Party and CGT bulletins were banned by the French Ministry of the Interior in a decree dated 5 April 1965.

[37] S. Carrillo, 'La situación del partido ...' in *Informes y resoluciones del pleno ...* , p. 199.

[38] Provincial bulletins issued by the Communist Youth also have titles distinct from its central organ, *Horizonte*. The Madrid one, for example, is called *Joven guardia*.

[39] We have been able to assemble a run of issues of this bulletin, consisting of the April, November and December numbers for 1967 and those of January, March and April 1968.

[40] Under the pseudonym Alvarez de Toledo — see general bibliography.

[41] See general bibliography.

[42] S. Carrillo, *Cuba 68*, Editions de la Librairie du Globe, Paris 1968, p. 12.

[43] 'Communist Campaign in Spain' (article cited in note 13 above).

[44] See general bibliography.

[45] Verdaguer, 'Después de Franco ¿Qué?' *Mundo obrero* 36 (2), 1 December 1965, p. 8.

[46] 'Inicua condena por distribuir *Mundo obrero*' *Mundo obrero* 38 (8), 1 March 1968, p. 2.

[47] S. Carrillo, 'La situación en el Partido ...' in *Informes y Resoluciones del pleno ...* , pp. 171–3.

[48] B. Lazitch, 'Les écoles de cadres du Comintern', in J. Freymond (ed.), *Contributions à l'histoire du Comintern*, Librairie Droz, Geneva 1965, p. 145.

[49] W. Leonhard, *Children of the Revolution*, Henry Regnery Co., Chicago 1968, pp. 54—5.

[50] El Campesino, op. cit., pp. 26—8.

[51] S. Alvarez, 'Sobre la educación teórica' *Nuestra bandera* 59, 3rd quarter 1968, pp. 54—5.

[52] The crisis triggered by the Czechoslovak affair, however, produced some critical thinking, even at grass roots level; this is bound to have had a good effect on theoretical education.

[53] After the Civil War works like *Das Kapital* became practically unobtainable in Spain.

[54] Thus Simón Sánchez Montero published an article in this review before he was arrested.

[55] 'El Che no ha muerto' *Cuadernos para el diálogo* 62, November 1968, p. 22.

[56] '150 aniversario de Carlos Marx' *Cuadernos para el diálogo* 63, December 1968 pp. 3—4.

[57] D. Cohn-Bendit and others, '¿Para qué sociólogos?' *Cuadernos para el diálogo* 56, May 1968, pp. 25—7.

[58] S. Carrillo, *Discurso ante una asamblea de militantes del Partido*, p. 38.

[59] E. García, 'Le Parti communiste consolide ses rangs' (article cited above), p. 183.

[60] S. Carrillo, *Nuevos enfoques a problemas de hoy*, p. 188.

[61] 'M. Santiago Carrillo estime que le mouvement communiste ne peut plus avoir son centre à Moscou' *Le Monde*, 4 november 1970, p.4.

[62] G. Hermet, *Les Espagnols en France*, Les Editions ouvrières, Paris 1967 p. 37.

[63] T. C. Rivero, 'Españoles trás el telón de acero' *Ya*, 22 December 1968.

[64] 'M. Santiago Carrillo estime ...' (article quoted above), p. 4.

[65] See footnote 59 to this chapter. Carrillo himself said recently that the number of members organised in Spain was now greater than the émigré membership: S. Carrillo, 'La democracia en el Partido leninista' (article referred to above), p. 6.

[66] B. Welles, *Spain, The Gentle Anarchy*, F. A. Praeger, New York 1965, p. 206.

[67] According to a confidential report mentioned in the Spanish press in 1970.

[68] 'Spain' in *Yearbook on International Communist Affairs 1966*, p. 114.

[69] L. Pintor, 'Il Partito di tipo nuovo' *Il Manifesto* 4, September 1969, p. 22. According to Pintor the Italian Party's underground membership in 1943 was 5,000.

[70] We have omitted the sums collected by the PSUC since we did not know whether they had been collected entirely within the region.

[71] 'Más de 40 millones recaudados ...' (article quoted above).

[72] The same method, based on a geographical analysis of the 1968—69 collection drive, also made it possible to make some estimate of the relative importance of the various Spanish communist colonies abroad. It would seem that the money collected in France — and thus also presumably the number of Party members living there — represents about half the total outside Spain. The remainder is divided roughly equally between other West European countries, Latin America and the socialist countries.

[73] E. García, 'Le Parti communiste consolide ses rangs' (article quoted above), p. 174.

[74] Semprún is thought to have been one of the Party officials responsible for work among students. Since 1964 communist students in Madrid, even those who remain faithful to the PCE, have been constantly at loggerheads with the Party leadership.

[75] See: 'Respuestas ...' *Nuestra bandera* 55, 3rd quarter 1967, pp. 69—76.

[76] In his book on the clandestine opposition in Spain, Vilar cites several cases of this type. See in particular pp. 373—5 of S. Vilar, *Protagonistas de la España democrática. La oposición a la dictadura 1939—1969.*

[77] Arrested in 1969, Lacalle was sentenced to eight years' imprisonment for belonging to the Party. Released before completing his sentence, he was one of the pall-bearers at the funeral of the underground worker Justo López de la Fuente, who died in jail in April 1967.

[78] The term applied to the followers of Colonel Casado, leader of the junta that negotiated with General Franco during the capitulation of Madrid.

[79] According to P. Broué and E. Témime, op cit., p. 57.

[80] It is worth noting that the effective leaders of the Party are working class almost to a man. If not workers themselves — like Gallego or Alvarez and even Ibarruri, Mije, Delicado and Lister — they at least have working-class fathers, like Carrillo. This working-class preponderance at the highest level, however, contrasts with the somewhat less proletarian character of the intermediate grades of the PCE hierarchy. Thus the Central Committee elected in November 1954 included not only thirty-five industrial workers and seven farm labourers, but also nineteen intellectuals ('Elec-

ción del comité central' *Mundo obrero* 23 (24), 15 November 1954, p.l). Women are still under-represented. In 1954 they accounted for only two of the sixty-one members of the Central Committee; nor did their numbers increase in 1965, when a Central Committee of eighty-eight members was elected. However, a second woman, known by the pseudonym Ester Blanco, joined Dolores Ibarruri on the Executive Committee in September 1970.

[81] According to E. Comín Colomer, *Historia del Partido comunista de España*, pp. 465 and 494—5.

[82] Details of these organisations are given at the end of Chapter 2. We are dealing here only with organisations which have broken away from the PCE and claim to be exclusively Marxist-Leninist or Trotskyite in character. We have not concerned ourselves with revolutionary groups of more eclectic ideological orientations, such as the ETA or *Acción comunista*.

[83] Small working-class Marxist-Leninist groups were at one time established at Baracaldo and in the mines of Biscay Province as well as in Seville. All were broken up in 1968 and 1969.

[84] The support given by Lister to certain communist groups is at the time of writing of too recent duration for its effect on the PCE's working-class supporters to have become measurable. In any case, unlike García, Lister has been trying to tilt the scales against Carrillo within the local committees rather than to set up rival organisations.

[85] The Barcelona group broke up in 1969.

[86] See 'Denuncia de un provocador' *Vanguardia obrera* 3 (22), March 1967, p. 7.

[87] '¿Existe el Partido de la clase obrera?' *Mundo obrero (Internacional)*, December 1968, p. 6.

[88] Tirana radio puts out four half-hour programmes a day in Spanish and Peking radio one, lasting an hour. The Maoists are the only Spanish opposition group apart from the PCE to have radio propaganda backing.

# 4 The Image of Communism in Spain

Do the traumas of the Civil War still colour the ideas Spaniards have about communism and communists? One should begin by realising that prior to 1936 there was no considered idea of the Communist Party among Spaniards outside the communists themselves and the few groups of militant workers. The USSR, the 1917 October Revolution and the Bolsheviks were certainly not unknown, but in the eyes of the masses eager for political and social change — as in those of the middle classes, who were terrified of such a prospect — the likely agents of the revolutionary alternative were the anarchists and socialists, whose numbers were counted by hundreds of thousands, and not the few thousand communists in the country. Nevertheless, it was known that during the first months of the Republic the PCE had launched what virtually amounted to revolutionary strikes in its stronghold, Seville, and that in the Seville area it had rallied to its side a considerable section of anarchist trade unionists. It was also known that, after the Asturias rising, the communists had helped to create the Popular Front, which won the elections of February 1936. Some working-class militants also knew from experience that at least in the short term the communists were less revolutionary than the anarchists, and less so even than Largo Caballero's majority socialist faction after the latter had abandoned the PSOE's reformist programme.

The very sharply contrasting accounts Spaniards have been given of the communists thus go back largely to the Civil War, and are conditioned in each man's mind by his personal experiences and the propaganda of the two warring camps; and since the Civil War by the anti-communist indoctrination campaign of the regime and the Church. We shall not deal here at length with the image of the PCE as the 'party of order' — even of counter-revolutionary order — which first cropped up in the republican camp between 1936 and 1939. Although very widespread at the time, today it hardly exists any more, except among a few thousand republican exiles, among whom it is still a subject of passionate debate. In Spain itself, this image lingers on among elderly men who spent the Civil War in the government-controlled zone, and who have not tried too hard to forget their attitudes of those years.

The images which have developed in the nationalist camp, both during the war and afterwards in Franco Spain, are a rather better aid to an understanding of current political attitudes. Here, the two mutually exclusive portraits of the communist prototype — that of the malevolent 'Red' on the one hand, and of the 'communist hero' in the vanguard of the battle against dictatorship on the other — retain their full force and hold on most of the population.

But if the trauma of the Civil War exerts an unmistakable influence, it is none the less vital not to get bogged down in static concepts of the stereotypes which shape the ideas Spaniards entertain about communism and its representatives. There is a change taking place in this respect — one which has so far affected only a minority of intellectuals, young Catholics and migrant workers, but which is likely to spread in the fairly near future as the Civil War generation disappears, as more restrictions on the media are lifted, and the government's anti-communist propaganda becomes less crude.

### The Party of order — exiles among the exiled

The moderating role played by the Spanish Communist Party between 1934 and 1939 is well known. In the economic and social fields, the communists during the Civil War consistently opposed any impulsive or hasty nationalisation of industry or trade as well as the immediate collectivisation of agriculture. On the political plane, they relied from 1937 onwards on the middle-of-the-road socialists and moderate republicans, repudiating their short-lived alliance with Largo Caballero and the more revolutionary elements in the Socialist Party. They thus effectively put an end to the latter's and the anarchists' hopes of a trade union government which would have broken with the parliamentary tradition of the Spanish Second Republic. In military affairs, they were among the main architects of the new professional army, gradually built up as the people's militia units attached to the other left-wing organisations were disbanded. In a word, the communists upheld the primacy of the 'bourgeois' republican system for the sake of efficient government in the face of the immediate threat posed by the nationalist rebellion. Without renouncing the ultimate aim of revolution, they were prepared to postpone it *sine die*, until after a military victory and a democratic-liberal stage which, according to them, was bound to precede a socialist regime.

The reasons for these attitudes have been the subject of a wide-ranging debate which, at least among the republican émigrés, has helped to build up a picture of communism as a counter-revolutionary and Stalinist force.

136

Those who see the PCE in this light accuse it of having been a mere tool of the USSR, which in turn helped the Republic just as long as it thought it capable of promoting its own political ends, and stopped doing so the moment the idea of a rapprochement with Germany arose as a prelude to the German—Soviet Pact. Its critics also accuse the PCE of having resorted to moderation only to promote the policies of Stalin, who until the end of 1938 was anxious to enlist British and French support against the threat of the Berlin—Rome Axis.

In the eyes of the anarchists, who account for a considerable proportion of republican refugees settled in France and Eastern Europe,[1] the Communists were responsible for halting in its tracks the economic and social revolution they had begun at the start of 1937, as well as for the final defeat.[2] It was in fact the forces under communist control that enabled the moderate socialists and republicans to halt the experiments in near-total socialism which had been tried in Catalonia, Aragon, the Levante region and parts of New Castile. The anarchists argue that the communists contributed to Franco's victory with this 'counter-revolution', which broke the people's will to resist. But it was that will, they say, which was the only effective obstacle barring the rebel officers' advance. Like the followers of the POUM, the anarchists entertain grievances with emotional overtones against the 'Stalinists' — to use the term they nowadays apply to the communists of the Civil War period — whom they look upon as assassins, or, at the very least, as the torturers of their comrades who fell victim to the repression which followed the 1937 Barcelona uprising. They also find it hard to forget the fate of all the men who perished in the non-communist units of the republican army. These were often in the most exposed positions and were worst provided with Russian war material.[3]

Most socialists take a different, though equally hostile, view of the communists. It would be ungrateful of them to reproach the communists for helping the reformist wing of their party to put down the attempted anarchist revolution, and they have fewer emotive personal scores to settle with the PCE, which treated them with more consideration than it showed the anarchists. But they are the bitterest critics of the communist infiltration into the republican army and government apparatus and of the way the communists made use of the power they had thus acquired to promote Soviet interests.[4] Nor is it surprising that the socialists should nurse bitter memories of the way the communists took over the United Socialist Youth Union and the greater part of the General Workers' Union, of which they had managed to obtain almost total control by the end of the Civil War.

The communists are also criticised for the petty bourgeois character of their membership at this time. But if it is true that in March 1937 10 per cent of the Communist Party membership was middle-class and professional, and that 30 per cent of its members were small and middle peasants,[5] it was by no means the only left-wing organisation in this situation. It was in fact mostly in areas where the anarchists were strong, such as Catalonia and Malaga, that the PCE had a strong petty bourgeois following, which was something of a backlash against anarchist domination. But the reverse often happened in areas where the communists were well established, especially in Madrid, where there developed a variety of anti-communism peculiar to the middle classes, who were otherwise inclined to sympathise with the PCE — perhaps for the lack of anything better — in other republican-held areas.[6] An anarchist writer has remarked in this context that 'everyone who resented the dominance established by the Stalinists — left-wing socialists, republicans, or even uncommitted people — sought refuge in the Confederation (the CNT) . . . . In a sense the same thing was happening in Madrid as in Barcelona, but the other way round'.[7]

As a result of all this, in republican circles the communists have always been exiles among the exiled, and not only their past mistakes and misdeeds, but also their role as efficient organisers, have in a way been held against them. However, no matter what opinions about communism may in the past have been prevalent in the republican camp, they are relevant today mainly for the record. They might conceivably also foreshadow the reactions which might appear as a result of the recent emergence of almost identical feelings among leftist militants in the workers' councils, factory committees and Christian-radical, Marxist-Leninist, Trotskyite or quasi-anarchist underground groups.

However, the image of the PCE as a party of order and the habitat of the middle class and the small farmer has been completely wiped from the minds of these very people as a result of thirty years of propaganda about 'Red' communism, the destroyer of the social fabric and of peace in the land.

### The 'Reds': 'Christ versus Lenin'

The word 'propaganda' should here be understood in its wider sense, to include the output of government and Falangist services as well as Church *propaganda*, the latter being virtually indistinguishable in tone and content from the former for an extended period, during which its spirit of 'crusade' identified it with the anti-communism of the Franco leadership and its spokesmen. A case in point is the statement made in the Vatican by Cardinal Pizzardo some months before the Civil War. He told a delegation of Basque nationalists that the choice facing the voters in the 1936 legislative elections was 'between Christ and Lenin'.[8] The outbreak of the war brought a proliferation of even more simplistic statements from the Church hierarchy, some of which put even the most extreme utterances of the official nationalist propaganda in the shade. Not content with open support for the rebels, the bishops concentrated on denouncing the 'monstrous' plot they said the communists and their overt or covert sympathisers had hatched against the nation. On 6 August 1936, the Primate of all Spain, Monsignor Gomá, and the Bishops of Pamplona and Vitoria, Monsignor Olachea and Monsignor Múgica, issued a pastoral letter warning Basques against 'this modern monster, Marxism, or communism; this seven-headed Hydra, this amalgam of every heresy'.[9] A few weeks later, echoing the Nazi slogans of the time, Cardinal Gomá stigmatised 'Jews and masons, outside the law and against the law, or on the side of the law when their moment has come, [who] shackle the nation's soul with their absurd doctrines — Tartar or Mongol tales brought up-to-date and hammered into a political and social system in shady clubs manipulated by Semitic internationalism . . .'.[10] A pastoral letter signed by Monsignor Pla y Deniel, Archbishop of Salamanca and future Primate of Spain, at the same time asserted that 'the communists and anarchists are the sons of Cain, murderers of their own brothers, hating those who cultivate virtue, whom they murder and martyr for that very reason . . .'. And on 1 July 1937 a joint letter from the Spanish episcopate described the Civil War as 'an armed plebiscite' in answer to the menace of 'communist revolution'. Earlier that year, on 19 March, in his Encyclical *Divini Redemptoris,* Pope Pius XI devoted a chapter to the 'Horrors of Communism in Spain'.

The Church's contribution to anti—communist propaganda continued unabated after the war, especially at school, in the youth movements, and in the 're-education' of the children of dead, imprisoned and exiled republicans.

But there are other factors to consider besides direct propaganda by the regime and the Church. For thirty years, and certainly up to 1962, no Marxist or even Marxist-inclined book or article has been available to any young Spaniard, and because of the censorship the young have been subjected to a totally one-sided ideological domination.

The impression of communism thus put about was largely coloured by the Manichean ideas on which it was based. Reading the speeches of General Franco, for instance, one finds that communism is by no means the only political evil that could befall Spain, for he condemns Western-style liberalism in one and the same breath. However, since the defeat of Germany and Italy, Western liberalism has been criticised much less often, and in much milder language, than communism. And when the Head of State advocates overtaking both capitalism and communism by choosing a third path, he nowadays confines himself to stressing the injustice of the Western system. However, in referring to Russia as recently as 1962, he was still talking of the 'Cheka and the slavery of the concentration camps'.[11]

It would appear that General Franco is particularly hostile towards the Spanish communists, whom he regards as inveterate instigators of revolution. His other opponents, even the socialists, tend to be treated as belonging to the intrinsically less evil category of democrats. According to one of his biographers,[12] he was, for eight years before the Civil War, an assiduous reader of the *Bulletin de l'Entente internationale anticommuniste*; and he has certainly used his prerogative of mercy very sparingly when it comes to communists, as witness the Grimau affair. On the other hand, according to the same biographer, he is generally less severe with other types of opponents, such as socialists.[13]

In his eyes, communists are not only members of the coalition of 'eternal enemies of peace in our country';[14] they are the very heart of the plot against Spain, manipulating people who are unaware that they are nothing but puppets. When, on 7 February 1969, Admiral Carrero Blanco, Vice-President of the Government and the man considered to be the Caudillo's *éminence grise* was justifying the proclamation of a state of emergency in his speech to the Cortes, he only recalled in passing the immediate reasons for the measure — agitation at the university and a wave of strikes and separatist plots. Instead, he was at pains to emphasise that 'the most serious aspect of the matter is what lurks behind this subversion'. And he went on to add that endemic agitation tended to obscure the fact that 'the communists are today trying to bring about what they could not do thirty years ago with the complicity of an abject regime and of the armed brigades of international communism'.[15]

The press continually echoes this line, or even sets the tone for it. Thus before Admiral Carrero Blanco had spoken, on the day after the proclamation of the emergency, an editorial in the only paper to appear in Madrid on Mondays was talking about a supposed 'plan for subversion' to which 'communist organisations' had allegedly been putting the finishing touches. On the strength of this 'disclosure', and without regard to the fact that most of the people being arrested under the state of emergency were members of the new social democrat and Christian socialist workers' opposition groups rather than communists, the paper's leader writer went on: 'Marxist infiltration is incompatible with the welfare of Spain . . . When communism shows its hand and tries to impose its methods, there is nothing for it but to call: Enough'.[16]

The police, too, have tended consistently to put the blame on the communists for almost any display of opposition. In its announcements, the national police headquarters as a rule lumps together as 'communists' all small leftist groups and sometimes even ETA associations or progressive Catholic clubs. Early in 1969, in Barcelona, where she was taking part in a left-wing Christian gathering, Mme Emmanuel Mounier said she had been described during an interrogation as 'a liaison agent between Cohn-Bendit and the communists'.[17]

Nor is it surprising that the authorities are willing to resort to any method to discredit the communists in the eyes of potential sympathisers, and especially other opponents of the regime. The news agencies controlled by the Ministry of Information are particularly given to harping on Spanish communism's continuing subservience to Moscow and to putting out half-truths which almost completely gloss over the deterioration of relations between the PCE and the CPSU. The Soviet intervention in Czechoslovakia furnished them with material particularly well suited to the technique of significant omission. Thus, on 12 September 1968, the national news agency EFE issued an item asserting that the PCE 'has reaffirmed the subordination of the Spanish Communist organisation to the Soviet Communist Party', and 'has ventured to voice only the most timid criticism of the invasion of Czechoslovakia by Warsaw Treaty troops'.[18] Ever since that time, government media have said virtually nothing about the Spanish communists' highly critical attitude, except to underline the internal dissensions they have caused in the Party.

The media also do their best to tarnish the reputation of the communist leaders by presenting them, in the infrequent paragraphs they devote to them, as 'professional émigrés' living a life of luxury on Russian remittances. Commenting on the award of the Order of Lenin to Dolores Ibarruri the Madrid papers remarked with heavy sarcasm that Spanish émigrés in the USSR now called her 'la Pensionaria'.[19]

Even more persistent is the effort to stir up quarrels between underground opposition groups by circulating forged leaflets which suggest that the communists are concerned only with the interests of their own party, ignoring those of their tactical allies and of the working class as a whole. An instance of this occurred during a strike in Asturias, when a leaflet dated 30 December 1968, purporting to have been issued by the Langreo

Communist Party branch, attacked the local leader of the USO (a clandestine trade union movement with Christian leanings), whom it accused of 'staying at work, like the coward he is, while he wretchedly incites honest mineworkers [ to strike]'. This was followed up by a second duplicated sheet, falsely claiming to be of USO origin, which called on the strikers not to let themselves be 'ensnared by those evil communists, who have no souls and whose only aim is to ruin our families'.

Another official propaganda theme is the 'duplicity' of the communists. There is, for instance, the allegation that Julian Grimau, 'while giving orders for acts of violence' had simultaneously 'advocated peaceable contacts with other groups, in accordance with the tactic of advancing step by step, which yielded the communists such excellent results in the conquest of power in Red Spain a quarter of a century ago'. [20] On suitable occasions, the press makes a point of showing how no man of 'good faith' can remain a communist for long. Thus a new film on Yesenin was used as an opportunity to point out that the Russian poet had 'committed suicide because he could take no more — just like Mayakovsky and other writers of the period who had all in various ways favoured communism at one time'. [21]

The Manichean view of communism allows various secondary elements to be brought in as well. The media never fail to stress that the communists are anti-religious and even guilty of sacrilege. There is no point in dwelling at length on the innumerable statements to this effect published during and after the Civil War. Yet even today, the communist policy of 'the hand outstretched to the Catholics' is never mentioned, except in an effort to represent it as a mere manoeuvre. Evidence of this determination to perpetuate the image of out-and-out communist anti-clericalism is found in a leaflet, attributed to the 'pro-Chinese' faction and distributed in the suburbs of Madrid at the beginning of 1969, in which Fr. Mariano Gamo, at that time parish priest of Moratalaz, is described as a 'ravisher of women'.[22]

The aim of this propaganda is to implant the idea that cold-blooded cruelty and a propensity to terrorism are attributes peculiar to communists. For instance, the Catholic daily *Ya* reported an incident which it said had occurred 'in Stalin's Russia at the height of the Stakhanovite fever'. When a Soviet workman fell into a Bessemer converter in front of a political commissar, the paper related, the latter had not betrayed the slightest emotion. [23] The same paper, reporting the attacks made on 5 July 1969 on the Spanish Tourist Bureau and Cultural Service in Paris, alleged in its headline that 'the communists claim responsibility for the anti-Spanish attacks in Paris' [24] — when anyone who is even moderately well-informed knows that the PCE gave up this type of action more than fifteen years ago. Nor is there any hint in the body of the report that the two groups which claimed responsibility for these actions [25] not only have no connection whatever with the Spanish Communist Party but are hostile to it.

Latterly another new theme has been added, intended to bring the communist image up to date while keeping it wholly negative. Seizing on a number of incidents relating to the tiny extreme left groups some of which claim to be communist, the regime's propagandists have produced a composite image of a pimply 'daddy's boy', 'an individual of dubious morals' or someone with an unhinged mind inciting young students to debauchery. Thus the Spanish papers treated their readers for months on end to tales about 'groups of agitators from the so-called workers' councils, communists and other clandestine groups' who were in fact 'well-dressed young people in collars and ties, plus a number of bearded, long-haired individuals'.[26] They also alleged that 'the head of a group who introduced young people to drug-taking' was 'a communist student agitator' and a 'Muscovite communist' to boot. [27] They claimed, too, that the student E. Ruano Casanova, a member of the Communist Revolutionary Party, who committed suicide on 29 January 1969 by jumping out of the window before the eyes of the police was 'a poor type . . . a typical psychopath . . . an unwitting tool of subversives'. [28]

Another press story asserted that the nine members of the PCE (*Internacional*) arrested in Barcelona on 9 June 1969 had robbed a bank and a cashier and had extorted money from people by blackmail. [29]

It is easy to analyse the way this image of the communist as a stock 'Red', for ever plotting against Spain's internal peace, is put together. One can do so on the basis of the wealth of material published over the past thirty-five years by the official press and information services. But it is more difficult to determine the degree to which this image has 'taken' among the population, without surveys and opinion polls of a type which cannot be undertaken in Spain at the present time.

A certain proportion of Spaniards naturally did accept this description especially in the first ten or fifteen years after the Civil War. For, in the first place, it cannot be denied that the communist presence had become all-pervading in the republican zone, especially in Madrid and the Levante, and in the army itself. The portraits of Marx which covered the Alcalá Gate in Madrid and the walls of the Hotel Colón in Barcelona remain associated in the minds of Spaniards who lived through this period with the tragic memories of the Civil War. And it is likely that many who were forced to join the Party retain some bitterness towards the communists

143

who put pressure on them to do so against their will. It is no less likely that the great mass of the population in the territory under the control of the lawful government, even those who were most loyal to the Republic, took a very poor view of the orders to resist to the very last which the PCE, and virtually the PCE alone, went on issuing in the final weeks of the war, when all hope of victory had gone.

Those who lived in the nationalist areas and who were enlisted willingly or under compulsion in the struggle against the republicans cannot forget to this day that the communists were their most tenacious and dangerous enemies and that Soviet arms and advisers played a decisive part in prolonging the war. Immediately after the Civil War, moreover, anti-communist feeling was kept up by pro-German propaganda calling for an 'anti-Bolshevik crusade' and even more by the very real though not very effective, menace of the armed guerrilla movement operated by the communists in Spain from 1944 to 1951.

The response to the regime's propaganda has of course always varied considerably according to social category and geographical area. It goes without saying that as far as the Catholics and the urban and rural middle classes of Castile and Andalusia were concerned, it was preaching to the converted, these people having sided with the nationalists from the start. The same goes for the mass of small shopkeepers and farmers in the period 1937—38, who were alarmed by the revolutionary economic changes made in the republican zone, which included Catalonia, a region traditionally hostile to Castilian centralism.

It is equally clear that the working classes, sustained for three years by the hope of radical changes and then hit by a repression from which few families of workers escaped completely, offered a far less receptive, if not almost wholly recalcitrant, target for this type of propaganda. But even here, one may suppose that former anarchist and socialist supporters, who far outnumbered those of the PCE, did not entirely reject the picture of a 'communist plot' of which they, too, had been the victims. The Basques, too, despite their devoted loyalty to the Republic, have probably always been more anti-communist than anti-Franco.

The students and intellectuals were no less receptive to the anti-Marxist propaganda of the regime and the Church. Already largely linked by family loyalties to their bourgeois and conservative roots, they were moreover, under the influence of teachers chosen for their nationalist attitudes during the Civil War, [30] after the departure into exile of almost every single left-wing or even liberal university teacher. [31] In these circumstances, it is not surprising that even some of those who have since drawn nearer to Marxism should, like Manuel Sacristán, [32] have belonged briefly to the most fascist wing of the Falange. And to this day, the anti-communism of some of the new Christian and socialist extreme left groups is perhaps not unrelated to the reflexes picked up at university during the forties and fifties. That at least is how the communists explain it.

Despite its exaggerations and travesties of the truth, or perhaps because of them, the regime's anti-communist propaganda had thus had an undeniable effect. By associating communism closely with the painful memories of the Civil War, it has been able to imprint on the minds of the majority of Spaniards an almost totally negative image of it, and of communists. Does the same still hold good today? Do the masses of Spaniards still visualise the 'Reds' of the present Communist Party as potential, and always threatening, fomenters of fresh disorders?

However, the succession of the generations is not the only factor to be considered in this context. One must also take into account the evolution of the PCE, and above all the way the Spanish press has been depicting it. There seems little doubt that the Spanish Communist Party, which for a long time followed the attitudes of its Soviet elder brother so closely, nowadays displays a certain degree of independence. It is no less true that the communists of the PCE must now be seen as moderates. If not exactly 'allies of Franco', as the Maoists and other leftists depict them, they are moderate in their aims and methods of action, the non-violent character of which contrasts with those of the ETA and the various near-anarchist groups. But these facts can be of no importance in Spain except in so far as they are effectively brought home to the mass of the population, and not just to the small minority of politically well-informed people.

A change is beginning to be discernible in the press and official statements in this respect, but it is a limited and ambiguous one. True, the papers are putting more and more stress on terrorist actions by the ETA and on kidnappings and other outrages committed by libertarian groups, while they accuse the communists most often of fomenting strikes and street demonstrations. These are, moreover, generally represented as failures, which makes them seem a relatively reassuring phenomenon. It is equally true that the relaxation of literary censorship has considerably improved the opportunities for imparting reasonably objective information about the Marxist ideology and communism. [33] Moreover, since the beginning of 1970, some papers have begun to refer to the quarrels which have taken place within the extreme left due to the moderation of the PCE. For instance, they have reported that among the miners of Asturias 'the most extreme would place Santiago Carrillo almost on the right'. [34] The paper Ya, [35] using material provided by the War Ministry's Department of History, has carried its efforts at objectivity to the point of recalling that 'the republicans were undone by the extremist base of the Popular Front' and that 'a bid for unification was made by relying on the Communist Party, which in the course of the war transformed itself into an aristocratic and almost right-wing group both by virtue of its [ Spanish] domestic policies and the number of members of the nation's élite within its ranks'. But the paper goes on to undo immediately the almost laudatory tone of this statement by adding that, despite its moderation, the Communist Party had at the same time become 'more and more the prisoner of its servile dependence on a foreign power which looked on the Spanish Civil War as a remote theatre of operation' and that, moreover, 'outside its ranks it had as few supporters in the republican zone as it did in the nationalist one'.[36]

However, only the day after this paper — much read by the new urban middle classes — had conceded for the first time the Church's decisive responsibility for 'lumping together the many elements of a complex hostile force under the unjust but very effective epithet of Reds', [37] it tempered the effect of this admission, which in its columns must be rated almost sensational, with a three-page article about the burning of churches and other acts of revolutionary violence immediately before the Civil War. 'anyone who is less than forty years old today', *Ya* explained, 'would otherwise not know about these things'. [38]

Generally speaking, government statements and the press still fail to distinguish between the various types of communists and socialists, almost always presenting them under the general label of 'sympathisers with the communist ideology'. [39] Thus an official statement issued by the Government Presidency and read in the Cortes on 22 April 1969 speaks of the 'communist-separatist segment of the ETA'. [40] The police still seize cheap editions of Marxist books, while expensive editions not generally accessible to the general public are tolerated. An abridged version of *Das Kapital*, priced at 30 pesetas, was impounded in December 1968, but one costing 1,000 pesetas remained in the bookshops.

On the other hand the government and the press have been stressing that the re-establishment of economic, cultural and consular relations with the people's democracies, and even the start made towards a normalisation of relations with the USSR, do not imply that things will get better for the Spanish communists. For them, it has made little difference that the Caudillo has changed his tune since the speech he made on 17 June 1941, in which he insisted that 'the terrible nightmare of our generation, the destruction of Russian communism, is absolutely inescapable'; for in December 1963 he declared that 'since socialism and communism have now spread over an incomparably greater area, we must reconcile our-

146

selves to recognising their political influence in the world', and that 'time will eventually transform these systems, ridding them of their many errors, correcting their failures and causing them to borrow all that has been good and efficient in the evolution of the free peoples'. [41]

The press has followed the Caudillo's lead. It publishes at fairly frequent intervals reports from the Eastern countries which contain a minimum of criticism and even some praise, and it gives prominence to visits by Spanish scientists and artists to the USSR and to Soviet exhibitions and performances in Spain. At the beginning of 1970 a photograph of the crossed Soviet and Spanish flags, displayed on the occasion of an exhibition of medical goods, was published in a prominent place in several of the daily papers. The tone of articles about the USSR has often been quite warm — even at moments as awkward as the period following the entry of the Warsaw Treaty forces into Czechoslovakia. Only a few weeks after that event, the Spanish papers covered with evident approval a visit by two eminent Spanish doctors to Moscow and Leningrad.

Editors as a rule make a point of emphasising the goodwill and serious intent of the Russians, who 'with great delicacy avoided discussing political questions'. [42] 'The girl dancers of the Ukrainian ballet appearing in Madrid', they report, 'wear mini-skirts that do not go to extremes'. [43] The affair of the Bank of Spain's gold, which has remained in Moscow since 1936, has become a 'legend' which 'casts a shadow . . . across the prospects facing two nations which in some strange and mysterious way have understood one another through the ages'. [44] A few weeks later, the reader was told that, contrary to certain allegations, 'Soviet war equipment throughout the Civil War was as good as, if not better than, German and Italian material'. [45]

Yet Spanish communists cannot expect any more favourable treatment. A few months before publishing the picture of the Soviet and Spanish flags together on the occasion of an exhibition, *Ya* also published a picture of a Red flag bearing the hammer and sickle found in the offices of the Rector of Barcelona University after a student demonstration. But the object of this particular picture was quite different: it was intended not to underline the friendship between two nations, but to show the reader that 'proof of communist complicity is so evident that one cannot consider the sacking of the Rector's office and the attack on the Rector himself as simple acts of student high spirits'. [46] In the same way, when commenting on the reservations expressed by the PCE about the conversations which had taken place at Moscow airport between the Spanish Foreign Minister, López Bravo, and a Soviet Deputy Minister, the press did so not to show the Spanish Communist Party's independence of the USSR but, on the contrary, to suggest that it remained Spain's domestic enemy number one, opposed to the normalisation of Spanish-Soviet relations and to expunging the memory of the quarrels of the Civil War. [47]

### The communist as a hero: communists as seen by themselves and by their sympathisers

The picture communists have of themselves is no less monolithic than the image of the 'Red' put about by the official propaganda service and the legal press. It, too, has undertones which could be called Manichean, although its orientation and its emotive connotations are diametrically opposed to the official versions. This communist image takes on different forms and shadings among Party members proper on the one hand and among sympathisers who stand apart from the Party, either by choice or against their will, on the other.

The former, like probably all communists in countries where they are not in power, and indeed the Russian communists themselves during the first fifteen years of the Soviet regime, see the Party as a community that is almost totally ideal, with its own material base, moral code, heroes, rites, vocabulary and axioms, accepted by all. Anything one says in this respect about the Spanish-communists is to a large extent also applicable to those of France, for instance, with the difference that for the past thirty-five years the Spanish communists have had to put up with persecution of the kind their French comrades have only known for five years: between 1939 and 1944. This situation has helped to reinforce certain positive aspects of what anthropologists would call their sub-culture, especially their devotion to the Party, their high regard for courage, and their emphasis on realism, moderation and caution in clandestine work. But difficult conditions have also lent strength to certain negative attitudes, such as those which have allowed a particularly extreme form of the personality cult to survive. There has also been a marked sense of superiority to other clandestine opposition forces, which has persisted until quite recently, if not indeed to this day. Another negative phenomenon has been a distorted and crudely oversimplified view of the political, economic and social realities of contemporary Spain.

For the Spanish communists, and especially for the militants most exposed to the dangers of the everyday battle as for the exiles of all ages, the Party is more than just the alternative society a French or Italian communist might opt for. For him, it is the only refuge available, the indispensable rear base for the harassed political fighter, a sort of extended family in which memories and hopes are shared and to which he is tied both emotionally and materially. In a letter to his wife from prison, Julián Grimau uses just this word — family — when he refers to the Party, saying that it was sending him too many parcels, considering the financial difficulties it was in. [48] Fifteen or twenty years ago, this family was even more extended, at least as far as the top-level leaders were concerned, since it included the ultimate asylum of the USSR, known to initiates as 'the house'. As depicted by the communist press, this family thinks of itself as being working class, although open to other social categories. Out of 172 allusions to the various social strata, in random numbers of *Mundo obrero* between 1961 and 1964, seventy refer to the working class, thirty-three to peasants, thirty-three to intellectuals, seventeen to the middle class or bourgeoisie, and nineteen to the ruling classes, the clergy and the military. [49]

The ethics of this community dictate that the Party should set particularly stringent standards of bravery for its members, who are constantly reminded of the heroism of the communist victims of persecution. This courage — which is undeniable — is magnified and upheld as an example in terms which owe more than a little to the 'lives of the saints' of religious literature. Cells are very often called after these heroes — men like Narciso Julián, Cristino García, Justo López de Fuente, Horacio Fernández Inguanzo, Julián Grimau, Constantina Pérez and of course, La Pasionaria; [50] and books and papers published by the PCE abound with highly edifying references to these people, tales of their resistance to torture or noble behaviour in face of death, and anecdotes of sudden 'conversions' brought about by the compelling words spoken by one or the other of them. One such story is of a young man whose father, a communist militant, saw the error of his indifference to politics and his excessive preoccupation with football and the cinema. Julián Grimau, so another story goes, 'spoke to this young man two or three times as to a friend. Soon afterwards, the boy asked his father to be sure to pass on to him the copies of *Mundo obrero* and Party literature he was getting; eventually, he joined the Communist Youth Union'. [51]

Equal emphasis is put on the fact that the heroes of the Party never deny their communism. Thus Julián Grimau tells his judges: 'I have already told you that I have been a communist, that I am a communist and that I shall die a communist'. [52] Matilda Landa, when offered her freedom provided she recants her political faith, answers that she is a communist and would a thousand times rather die than sell herself'. [53]

The courage of the communist hero is always shown as being permeated with simple modesty and generally devoid of hate, even for his executioner. When he was arrested in 1939, we are told, José Cazorla told the police: 'I shall tell you nothing. I have done all I could for the Republic and the workers' cause and I shall go on doing so to my dying day'. [54] An obscure Party member, arrested for being found in possession of a copy of *Mundo obrero*, does not weaken under torture 'because he is a man — a communist'. [55] Simón Sánchez Montero, arrested in 1959, the story goes, resisted ill-treatment for several weeks; he answered one of his jailers, who asked him whether he did not feel 'deadly hatred' for him and his fellows: 'No. Our struggle draws its strength from love of the people, of the Spanish working class'. Moved by this magnanimity, says the report, the policeman realised that 'there must be something great, something mighty here, to make men behave like this'.[56] Nor do these edifying stories fail to point out how many Party leaders of the highest rank — members of the Central and even the Executive Committees — there are among these heroes and martyrs of Spanish communism.

The idealised picture the Spanish communists have of themselves is thus of a band of brave men, inspired by heroic examples recounted in publications intended for their own consumption. Discipline, perhaps the supreme virtue in most fraternal parties, is perhaps less cherished by them. But their press exhorts them also to consider themselves heroes who are prudent, practising moderation in their contacts with non-communists and avoiding excess even in their words. Like their French and Italian comrades, Spanish communists are no longer encouraged to behave as protagonists of an imminent Marxist revolution. Evidence of this is the minor place given in PCE literature to words carrying revolutionary overtones. An analysis of 106 documents distributed between 1945 and 1963 shows that even the term Marxist appears very rarely in them — Marx is quoted only four times, Engels twice and Lenin three times. [57] Likewise, a study of a sample batch of numbers of *Mundo obrero* shows that the key words 'revolution' and 'revolutionary' occur only twenty times in ten issues, while such anodyne words as 'liberty' and 'strike' turn up thirty-three and thirty-four times respectively. [58]

All this did not prevent a cult of personality and a totally uncritical pro-Sovietism from developing in the years before the Twentieth Congress of the CPSU, at least as perniciously as in most other Stalinist parties. No need to dwell here at length on the chanting of 'Salve Rusia' by the Young Communists in 1938 [59] or on the eulogies of the 'wise and noble Stalin', [60] 'great leader and teacher of progressive and advanced mankind', [61] or even on the flattery lavished on La Pasionaria, to whom 'no mistake can be attributed because she is never wrong'. The effect of all this, it seemed, was that Party members, 'proud of belonging to the great

Communist Party and disciples of their Pepe [ José Díaz] and their Dolo-res', [62] were less concerned about the blows of their torturers than about 'insults aimed at the leaders of [ their] Party'. [63]

Most members nowadays are less pro-Soviet, but still preserve an almost absolute certainty of being the sole repositories of the solution to all their country's problems and of belonging to the only effective — and one might almost add legitimate — political organisation in the land. Their attitude to the Franco regime is summed up in their unflaggingly repeated prophecies — so far always belied by events — of its impending doom. On 29 January 1945, Uribe announced that 'the Spanish people is about to rise again against Falangism'; [64] a handbill distributed on 16 June 1962 — seventeen years later — asserted that 'the dictatorship [ is] in an advanced state of decay'; and early in 1965 Santiago Carrillo declared: 'We are now witnessing Franco's very last moments'. [65]

The terms employed by the communists to describe this perennially tottering regime are no less damning than those used by official propaganda to describe the communists themselves. When *Mundo obrero* discusses it, its talk is all of violence, terrorism, brutality, repression, excesses, crimes, murders and outrages, of the Civil War mentality, insecurity, bank-ruptcy of authority, anachronism, impotence, incompetence, extreme ex-haustion, fear of change, deliberate mystification, the Mark of Cain, phan-tom institutions — and so on and so forth.[66] The Caudillo is given even rougher treatment. He is depicted as the incarnation of evil, who 'hits out indiscriminately at all social strata, without regard to which camp they be-long' (1956). He has 'decided to cling to power and plunge Spain into a nuclear conflict' (1961), for 'he does not care whether the army loses its prestige and honour, he does not care about the honour of Spain or about the very existence of the state, as long as he can stay on' (1962).[67] However, since 1964 the most extreme forms of anti-Franco abuse have been toned down, possibly following the criticisms voiced by Claudín at the time.

Towards the other left-wing opposition groups the Spanish communists display a kind of paternal — one might almost say imperial — condescen-sion which reflects their awareness, whether justified or not, of being the most coherent and most substantial force among them, as well as of having suffered the most from persecution. However, for some years now they have shown a more open-minded attitude to co-operation, on what would seem to be a footing of equality, with the new Christian workers' movement. They have, on the other hand, remained as unaccommodating as ever when it comes to the anarchists and socialists, against whom the reflex of mistrust carried over from the years of the Civil War still comes into play.

151

It is an indisputable fact that the communists are among those who have suffered most from persecution, despite the accusations of moderation made against them from the extreme left. Thus, seventy-two of the 199 people indicted before the Public Order Tribunal between December 1969 and January 1970 were accused of being communists — though whether this meant belonging to the PCE or to one of the dissident organisations we do not know. [68] And of the ninety-five people sentenced in the same period for endangering the internal security of the state, eighteen were accused of having belonged to the PCE, compared with thirty-one alleged members of workers' councils, twenty-four who were said to have belonged to the Basque Nationalist Party and the ETA, six socialists and fourteen members of underground student organisations.

One must in this context beg leave to question the psychological insight of the communist leaders when they point to the number of arrests of Party members in a particular area as proof of its strength there. [69] No less dubious is their habit of claiming credit for the PCE for acts of opposition of uncertain origin on the strength of an indiscriminate mixture of police and other official reports — even where such reports appear only in the fictitious tales composed for the edification of Communist Party members and sympathisers. [70]

The communists continue to display towards those of their socialist comrades who have remained faithful to their old party, the PSOE, the same haughty disdain tinged with false pity; nor are they any more civil to the republicans and anarchists. However the days are gone when Dolores Ibarruri, while criticising the idea of using lawful methods within the vertical trade unions — since then largely adopted by the PCE — could assert that 'the traitors to the anti-Franco struggle' were to be found among 'the anarchist and socialist leaders'. [71] She went on to say that the government-in-exile of Alvaro Albornoz did not represent 'heroic and fighting Spain' but consisted of zealots of 'the US State Department [who] give decorations to Titoite spies treacherously sent to our country to destroy the people's resistance'. [72] Even much more recent statements by Santiago Carrillo on this subject are still very unflattering. Though perhaps not without a grain of truth, they are not easy to reconcile with communist overtures for united action made to the socialists and anarchists. The PCE Secretary-General appears no more worried than before that he might alienate possible goodwill when he declares, for instance, that the republican parties consist only of 'a few pieces of flotsam in exile', and that apart from the few small groups it had managed to rebuild in Biscay and Asturias, all the Socialist Party had in the other provinces was 'a handful of veterans [who] live under the delusion that they are nursing a sacred flame by regularly meeting in certain cafés. Everyone knows that in these places one can come across socialists who occasionally get a copy of their party's paper, which they discuss, or who write to Toulouse when their Executive asks them for support in the form of a letter'. In view of this it is a little surprising that the communists should set such store by 'achieving as much as possible jointly with the socialist comrades'. [73]

As for the anarchists, PCE members are encouraged to regard them as potential recruits, on the grounds that the anarchist organisation, the CNT, 'is not a workers' party but a trade union organisation'. According to this concept, 'neither the CNT nor any other trade union body can expect political uniformity of its members. One can belong to the CNT and belong to the communist or any other political party without ceasing to be an excellent trade unionist'. [74]

At another level, the light in which sympathisers of all sorts who are not PCE members regard the communists is most varied and difficult to define. However, there is little doubt that the Party retains considerable prestige in a variety of quarters which have resisted the regime's anti-communist indoctrination.

The small communist concentrations which have remained continuously in being in the great factories of the north and in Madrid enjoy a degree of respect among the working-class population, including new immigrants from the country, whose class consciousness is by no means always inferior to that of industrial workers of older standing. This is witnessed by the bitterness of some strikes in factories whose work force includes a considerable proportion of men recently arrived from the countryside. [75] In this context, however, the word 'respect' is more appropriate than 'active sympathy' to describe the attitude of the working-class masses towards the communists. They think of the communist as a man who belongs to an organisation that is still powerful, who is bold and brave, who has the benefit, not available to his comrades, of contacts and support outside the factory. There is no denying that he enjoys special prestige among them, but this prestige will gain him, at best, only reluctant co-operation. He belongs to a group of people 'who know a thing or two', who 'knows what to say and what to do' — according to a fictitious survey of a working-class parish in Biscay Province; [76] but he is isolated from his work mates, who are afraid of sharing his fate in case there is another wave of police repression.

According to information collected by an observer who spent a considerable time on the great estates of Cordoba, the same applies to the agricultural proletariat. On the one hand, the day labourers share the fundamental views of those who 'know what's what', and these are very likely to be communists, because of the virtual disappearance of the anarchists from this area. On the other hand, they contemplate 'almost with horror how, as experience shows, such men seem to march steadily to their doom, very likely dragging along with them those they have been able to talk into joining them in spreading the word'. According to the same source, these people feel that 'the worker who has ideas and puts them into words risks not merely coming up against the authorities, but also the disapproval of his mates, who, although they are in favour of "ideas", don't want to "stick their necks out" and suffer the consequences'. [77]

Finally, the communists' prestige makes its most effective and convincing impact inside the prisons, not only among convicts who are working-class militants and do not share the hesitations of their brothers outside, but also among students, intellectuals and middle-class people in jail for political reasons. In fact, communists still account for a considerable proportion of political prisoners: in 1963, Carabanchel jail had forty-eight politicals, of whom twenty-nine were communists. [78]

The harsh treatment meted out to communists by the courts and prison authorities speaks in their favour and makes them into models for their fellow prisoners, including the many Christian militants still in search of a political orientation. Accustomed, moreover, for many years to the prison environment in which some of them have spent the greater part of their lives, the communists are better at organising themselves in these conditions than the newcomers, and at skilfully playing on the hardships imposed on them to build up debts of solidarity between inmates and to ensure the spread of their ideas.

It is therefore hardly surprising that some of the political prisoners should join the PCE either before or after their release, or entertain at least an active sympathy for it. Many, like the Catalan militant quoted by Vilar, would probably remember that 'the people with whom we had most in common in there were the communists — they are regulars in jail'; and that 'the three or four of us who were Catholics were faced with this anomaly: the people with whom we came into collision ideologically were in fact our best friends — men with whom we lived in intimate communion. Paradoxically, it was the prison governor, who belonged to Opus Dei, who demanded our collaboration in the name of our common religion'. The man came to this conclusion: 'If I had to vote today, things being what they are in Spain, I should most certainly vote for the PCE'. [79] There is also the young intellectual who acknowledged 'an inescapable obligation to state that when I look about me to see who is fighting for the people, for their liberty and welfare, I find it is only, or mostly, the members of the Communist Party who are doing so — and suffering the most grievous persecution for it'. [80] A Madrid man of letters, a member of the Spanish Academy, has said of the PCE that he felt unworthy of joining such a 'company of heroes'.

## Left-wing anti-communism

The examples we have cited to illustrate the image of the 'communist as a hero' are generally speaking one or two years old. Do they still hold good, after the ravages the PCE has been suffering for some time, after the growing rifts within it, the reappraisal of its links with the USSR since the invasion of Czechoslovakia, and after the appearance on the scene of new candidates for the laurels of 'political heroism' in the shape of the Basque nationalists of the ETA? Some people, especially those of the student far left, have been speaking — not without some exaggeration, of the bankruptcy of the Spanish Communist Party. According to them, the image of the orthodox communist militant is no longer that of a brave, dynamic and efficient revolutionary, but of a reformist and revisionist, whose real function is 'conciliatory and in actual fact petty bourgeois', [81] and according to whom 'all that needs to be done is to get rid, if possible politely, of four or five "ultras" in the government, including Franco, who have a bad image because of their obviously fascist ways'. [82] This view, which first cropped up among the Maoists, is now shared by a considerable number of dissident communists in Catalonia, the Basque country and Andalusia, as well as in emigration. It is also gaining ground among a growing section of Party members who are still loyal to the PCE, but no longer know where to find their own kind among the proliferation of organisations which have mushroomed since 1964, and even more since 1968. Some progressive Catholics, too, consider that the tactics of the Communist Party have helped to weaken the workers' councils and to 'demoralise' some of the left-wing groups, who are shocked by its 'reformist' attitudes. [83]

But, lacking adequate information, the great mass of the Spanish people know nothing of these debates, or of the distinction between 'revolutionary' and 'petty bourgeois' communists. For them the communist remains a 'Red' perhaps a little less to be feared today then he was once upon a time. He tends to turn up as a hero about whom one hardly ever knows whether he is a 'Carrillist', a Maoist of this or that variety, a Trotskyite, an internationalist, pro- or anti-Soviet, or whatever. Only politically aware students and the members of the workers' councils or clandestine trade unions are really fully aware of the differences that might exist between these types of communist — that is when they are real enough to go beyond mere clashes of personality or between sects.

## The Catholics and communism

A more important factor in the transformation of the image of communism in Spain is the attitude of Catholics and communists to one another. The Civil War found these two groups at extreme opposites: on the one hand, the anti-clericalism of the republican prisoners had been made more bitter by the pressures put on them by the prison chaplains; and on the other, there was the horror evoked by 'atheistic Marxism'. However, Catholics and communists have now arrived at much less antagonistic attitudes, at least as far as the politically and ideologically most open-minded elements among them are concerned.

On the communist side, the policy of national reconciliation has since 1958 inclined the Party strongly in favour of a rapprochement with the Catholics — at least with those they consider people one can talk to. In 1956, Dolores Ibarruri went as far as to admit the possibility that priests might join the Party. There are also signs that anti-clericalism at grass roots level has mellowed. Thus, in the mining parish of Somonostro, a bastion of veteran PCE members or their descendants, the men have given up the habit of going to the cafès during religious ceremonies such as weddings and funerals. Nowadays, they actually go inside the church. Families, including those who are notoriously communist, ask the parish priest to administer the sacraments to the dying and to provide Church funerals. This is so universally true that no secular funeral has taken place for over twenty years. The church even serves as a meeting point when men who were once local PCE leaders are buried.

The present leadership strongly encourages this trend, which has gathered speed as personal contacts have been established in the workers' councils and during strikes, particularly in Biscay, Madrid and Asturias — this despite resistance in some militant circles. One has only to recall the tribute paid by Alvarez to 'Catholic militants who have fought shoulder-to-shoulder with us, and whose attitude to the working class is one of loyalty'. He has also referred to 'the informal alliance of communists and Catholics — the cornerstone of our entire democratic mass movement'. [84] Similarly, Santiago Carrillo nowadays points out to Party members that religion 'is no longer an opium; objectively, it is the yeast of progress'. [85]

On the Catholic side, joint campaigns have also played a decisive part in

156

allaying Christian prejudices towards the communists, at least as far as the lay members of the Catholic Action and its Workers' Fraternities and the younger priests in the industrial parishes are concerned. The 'opening towards Marxism' operated by groups of intellectuals, students and professional people, doctors in particular, who belong to, or have belonged to, Catholic organisations has also contributed to the reappraisal of the anti-communist clichés spread by official propaganda. This is how some of the circles, dubbed by their detractors 'Communists of the Infant Jesus', [86] have come into being. One of these was the 'Circle of John XXIII' at Cordoba, since disbanded. In some cases this change of mind has gone so far that it has induced working-class militants and Catholic intellectuals to join the Party. A recent book mentions the names of a worker and former member of the JOC and a doctor who formerly belonged to the Catholic Action, both of Barcelona, who allegedly joined the Communist Party. [87] And these are not isolated instances: in 1965 a faction of the Popular Liberation Front joined the PCE *en masse*; another turned itself into an independent movement known by the name of its underground paper *Acción comunista*. Some left-wing Catholics have taken up even more extreme positions, which have led them to replace their earlier prejudice against the communists with a new form of hostility not unlike that of the Maoists and anarchists. This is the case of the former army chaplain José Bailo Ramonde, arrested in Madrid on 17 January 1969 for being a member of the *Partido comunista revolucionario*.[88]

True, only minorities have undergone such radical transformations. But a slower change has become discernible among the great mass of the clergy and among the faithful who are under the sway of younger priests and are influenced by the most liberal religious publications. Few priests, however, would go as far as J. Bailo or the Aragonese priest Domingo Laín, a missionary who joined the Colombian guerrillas early in 1970 under the influence of Camilo Torres, for to do so would be to run counter to the tactics of non-violence advocated by the PCE. [89] However, the earlier tendency identifying socialism and communism with godlessness is rapidly going out of fashion with the younger priests, and even with some of their elders. A survey conducted in 1969 showed that 62 per cent of the 6,886 priests questioned in twenty-two Andalusian, Castilian and Aragonese dioceses had either wholly or partially rejected the Spanish Church's — until then conservative — views in both political and social matters; 39 per cent thought it was an evangelical and pastoral duty to act in favour of social justice or to assist strikers; 55 per cent in one way or another advocated the separation of Church and State. [90] It should be noted in this context that the Andalusian, Castilian and Aragonese priests questioned are considered among the least progressive elements of the Spanish clergy: the priests of the Basque country and Catalonia are much more outspoken.

The cautious, but nevertheless real, political 'opening' operated by some of the religious orders and Church publications, and even some bishops, can hardly fail to influence the better informed section of the faithful. For more than ten years Father José María González de Ruiz has urged a dialogue between Christians and Marxists, declaring that it must be 'more than a polite drawing room debate between intellectuals'; it must first and foremost be a collaboration, [91] and he went on to say that 'an unreasoning rejection of Marxism is a sin against one's neighbour'. [92] He and a number of Spanish Jesuits have taken part in international meetings also attended by PCE representatives such as Santiago Alvarez, Manuel Azcárate and Federico Antón. Some Catholic publications, moreover, like *Signo, Voz del trabajo* and *Juventud obrera* — the first two of which are now banned [93] — have repeatedly emphasised the community of views and the fraternity which existed between Christians and communists. The monthly journal *Cuadernos para el diálogo,* the semi-official mouthpiece of the Spanish Christian Democratic left, has even gone so far as to publish an article on strikes by a member of the PCE Central Committee shortly before his arrest. The daily *Ya*, the paper of the episcopacy, has not gone to such lengths; nevertheless, in 1969 it gave publicity to a statement by the ILO demanding an inquiry into the ill-treatment of political prisoners. [94]

Despite blunders like the statement condemning political strikes, [95] or their prolonged connivance at some of the more questionable aspects of the practices of prison chaplains, [96] the more liberal among the bishops have begun to modify — even though in terms which are still ambiguous — the condemnations of communism and communists voiced by their predecessors. Thus Monsignor Cirarda, Bishop of Santander, in a fairly widely publicised article, stated that it was wrong to apply the term 'communist' to everybody who wanted to promote social advance and uncover hidden injustice'. [97] Coming from one of the most eminent members of the liberal minority among the bishops, should this statement be interpreted as a compliment, a first step towards rehabilitation or an expression of regret? Regardless of what Monsignor Cirarda may have had in mind when he spoke in this vein of the communists, there can be very little doubt that the public image of communism in Spain is beginning to change, especially among the extreme left minority groups and in certain circles of the Catholic clergy and laity. However, can the same be said of the mass of the population, among whom people who have gone through the Civil

War as adolescents or adults account for one-third, but who nevertheless have too little information to allow them to form clear political attitudes?

## Communism as seen through the opinion polls

Although the information being offered to the Spanish public is both scant and one-sided, we should be wrong to overlook the likely effects of certain new developments. As regards the masses, we must take into account the large number of workers and their dependants who have returned from France and other European countries. Many have come into contact with French, Belgian or Swiss communists as well as communist fellow Spaniards, most of whom would be members of the 'orthodox' PCE. [98] According to a survey conducted in ¯1967 among Spanish immigrants in Saint-Denis, it would even appear that many of them read the communist or CGTU press more or less regularly while in France. Although this survey should be treated with caution, since its author does not make it clear how he selected those questioned, the survey does give some idea of the range of this readership. It shows, in particular, that among the fifty immigrants questioned six said they sometimes read *L'Humanité* and two *La Vie Ouvrière*. In the same group, as many as thirteen occasionally read *Le Parisien Libéré*, ten *France-Soir*, seven *ABC* and six *España-París*. [99]

As regards the middle classes, who account for the majority of the readership of the Spanish press, it is fairly safe to assume that the image of 'the communist conspirator against the internal peace of Spain' is beginning to give way as the symbol of the ultimate political peril to the 'terrorist' Basque demanding autonomy, and the Maoist student. Despite the attempts of official propaganda to depict all extremists indiscriminately as communists, those members of the public who are used to reading between the lines and analysing their paper's contents cannot fail to be aware of the differences between the various kinds of opposition to the regime, especially since they are kept fairly well informed of the political debates and ideological quarrels which take place abroad, above all in France and Italy. Furthermore, the attacks on the 'bourgeoisification' and moderation of the PCE, news of which is now being given publicity in the press in order to highlight the disarray among the communists, tend in fact in the long run to improve the image of communism in the eyes of a large part of the public, for they show that the 'Carrillist' party has become less hegemonistic and extremist.

159

However, evidence which would allow these hypotheses to be tested is signally lacking. Surveys of a political nature remain almost unknown in Spain, and when they do take place they deal only with very general or anodyne topics. But in the absence of anything better, let us examine two opinion polls, conducted in the autumn of 1968, and again of 1969, by the Spanish Institute of Public Opinion, which give some quantified information about Spanish political attitudes.

The first of the two polls shows that despite the massive re-emergence of strikes as a social phenomenon, and the growth of student strife — the sole forms of opposition that show above the surface in Spain — a majority of Spaniards favour the restoration of freedom of expression, for communists as for everyone else. Those favouring such a development accounted for 53 per cent of the sample, which consisted of 1,953 people aged over eighteen from all parts of the country and all walks of life. Among men the proportion was as high as 59 per cent; among members of middle management 72 per cent, and among students 85 per cent. The percentage was lower among women and the lower socio-professional and educational groups, but mostly as a result of unwillingness to answer. This largely reflects the people's distrust of questioners representing any institution associated with the state. The same survey showed that 31 per cent of those questioned either wanted the parties to be restored or political associations created which would take their place. Only 20 per cent were opposed or indifferent to these ideas, while 49 per cent refused to answer the question. [100] It should be noted, moreover, that among the 12 per cent who explicitly wanted genuine political parties to be restored — i.e. about a quarter of those willing to answer this particular question — a considerable proportion may have been thinking of left-wing parties or specifically of the Communist Party, which would stand little chance of being allowed to function within the framework of the political associations foreshadowed by the Government.

The second poll, which was concerned with the attitudes of the Spanish public towards the USSR as well as Soviet and Czechoslovak communism, [101] was the first ever to be conducted in Spain on these topics. Although it gives no specific indication regarding the hostility or otherwise of those questioned to communism in the Spanish context, it may in fact throw some light on this matter.

To nobody's surprise, no fewer than 89 per cent of the sample disapproved of the Soviet troops' entry into Czechoslovakia. Those who approved — 3 per cent of the total — included rather more middle-grade technicians (6 per cent) and people aged seventy or over (8 per cent) — in which categories there are perhaps more people 'inseparably attached' to

160

the USSR. Rather more meaningful were the answers to a question about the knowledge Spaniards had of earlier Soviet interventions comparable to the invasion of Czechoslovakia. They show in effect that memories of Soviet influence in Spain during the Civil War are waning, since fewer than one person in one hundred questioned referred to this episode. Should we therefore conclude that the image of communism among Spaniards is no longer closely associated with memories of the Civil War?

More interesting still are the answers which draw a line between Russian and Czechoslovak communism. These indicate to what extent those questioned are aware of the existence of various alternative forms of communism, some of which might be more humane than the Soviet variety. On this point, the survey showed that 54 per cent of the sample considered the Russian regime bad and 8 per cent good, compared with 33 and 15 per cent respectively for and against the Prague Spring, [102] which has the sympathy of the PCE.

The survey also shows that Spaniards do not seem to fear very greatly that a communist regime might be imposed on them by force, since the majority of those who replied to a question on peaceful coexistence with the communist countries thought coexistence was possible. [103] Generally speaking, no matter what the question, answers most favourable, or least unfavourable, to communism were most numerous among the young, [104] students, [105] big city dwellers, [106] and in individual provinces, [107] as well as the top social, professional, cultural and income brackets. [108] They were fewest among agricultural workers and day labourers, [109] perhaps because they distrusted the pollsters.

Tenuous though these indices may be, they do seem to show that Spaniards are less afraid of the communists than they used to be and that those who are hostile to communism now regard it in a less sinister light. However, it remains to be seen who will benefit from this change in attitude, which has given communism a better image in Spain. Will the part which has fallen to the PCE in the present phase of the Franco regime allow it to preserve enough cohesion and realism to benefit, before it is too late, from the public's less prejudiced attitude towards it, always assuming that this change proves sufficiently marked to allow the Party's formal reintegration into the national body politic?

## Notes

[1] Because the two refugee aid organisations created in 1939 and controlled by the communists, socialists and republicans secured passages for

many of their own people to Latin America, but to all intents and purposes abandoned the anarchists, who were unable to leave France.

[2] The anarchist viewpoint is developed by C.M. Lorenzo, *Les anarchistes espagnols et le pouvoir*; and by P. Broué and E. Témime, op. cit.

[3] Nor do anarchists find it easy to forgive the communists for having tried to ban their press and their organisations in the early summer of 1937. Colonel Casado's putsch in March 1939 was largely an act of vengeance against the communists.

[4] As evidence of the loathing some socialists feel for the communists, it is worth quoting the words of Trudi Araquistráin, wife of one of the members of Largo Caballero's circle, who said: 'It makes me sick to think that La Pasionaria has escaped — that she wasn't shot in Madrid' reported by L. Fischer, '*Men and Politics*', p. 560.

[5] J. Díaz, *Por la unidad hacia la victoria*, p. 51.

[6] Could the findings of a recent survey of the attitudes of Spaniards aged over eighteen towards the USSR and Russian communism be an indication of the persistence of this phenomenon? The survey showed in effect that Madrid and Aragon are the most anti-Soviet areas in Spain. Some 32 per cent of the Madrid sample thought that peaceful coexistence was impossible, compared with 25 per cent in the country as a whole and 24 per cent in Catalonia ('Opiniones sobre problemas nacionales e internacionales, otoño 1968' *Revista española de la opinión pública* 17, July-September 1969.

[7] C. M. Lorenzo, op.cit., p. 214.

[8] Quoted by M. Tuñón de Lara, *El hecho religioso en España*, Librería española Paris 1968, p. 125.

[9] Ibid., pp. 134–5. However, Monsignor Mateo Múgica was one of the three bishops who did not sign the collective statement of 1 July 1937, the other two being Cardinal Vidal y Barraquer, Archbishop of Tarragona, and the Vicar General of Orihuela.

[10] I. Góma y Tomás, *Por Dios y por España*, Rafael Casulleras, Barcelona 1940, pp. 312–13.

[11] *Sistema institucional, sucesión y movimiento. Pensamiento de Franco y leyes fundamentales*, Ediciones del Movimiento, Madrid 1966, pp. 79–80 (speech made on 18 September 1962 at Cinera, León).

[12] B. Crozier, *Franco*, p. 92.

[13] Crozier reports the following conversation, which he says took place after the arrest of the film-maker Bardem in 1956. Told that some fifty protest telegrams from foreign intellectuals had been received, General Franco asked his Minister of the Interior: 'Is he a Communist?' The Minister said Bardem was a social democrat; whereupon the General replied:

'To me, that's the same as a Christian democrat. Let him go'. (From an article by J. Barry, 'The Defiant Ones', *New York Post*, 8 January 1959, p. 50).

[14] *Sistema institucional . . . ,* (speech by General Franco, tabling the Organic Law in the Cortes on 22 November 1966).

[15] 'Pleno de las Cortes españolas' *Ya*, 8 February 1969, p. 11.

[16] Editorial by A. J. González Múñoz in *Hoja del lunes* of 27 January 1969 (quoted in 'Spain: arrests hit intellectuals, lawyers, doctors, trade unionists and even clergy' *Le Figaro*, 28 January, p. 4).

[17] 'Spain: After her interrogation, Mme Mounier states her case' *Le Monde*, 1 February 1969, p. 6.

[18] 'Sumisión del comunismo español a Moscú' *ABC* 13 September 1968, p. 32.

[19] See *Ya*, 10 December 1965, p. 10: *ABC*, 10 December 1965, p. 97.

[20] *Crime or punishment*, Madrid 1963, p. 12.

[21] V. Horia, 'Sergio Esenin, otro poeta decepcionado por el comunismo' *Ya*, 27 March 1970.

[22] 'Una provocación más contra nuestro partido, *Vanguardia obrera* 5 (41), February 1969, p. 7.

[23] R. Jorganes, 'Espíritu y materia' *Ya*, 4 February 1968.

[24] L. Blanco Vila, 'Los comunistas se atribuyen los atentados anti-españoles de París' *Ya*, 6 July 1969, p. 6.

[25] *Partido comunista marxista-leninista español* and *Partido comunista español*.

[26] 'Los brotes de desórdenes en Madrid fueron pequeños' *Ya,* 15 May 1968, p. 5.

[27] 'Iniciaba a los jóvenes en el consumo de drogas': *Ya*, 15 December 1968, p. 15.

[28] Quoted under the headline 'Agitation continues at Madrid University', *Le Monde*, 24 January 1969, p. 24. The newspaper *Ya* added that 'among the docunents seized at the accused man's home is a kind of diary which reveals his suicidal obsessions'. ('Muere un estudiante al arrojarse desde un séptimo piso' *Ya*, 21 January 1969, pp. 5—6.)

[29] 'Detención de varios afiliados al Partido comunista español en Barcelona' *Ya*, 13 June 1969, p. 25.

[30] Rather than for their teaching qualifications, which were often dubious.

[31] Out of the 550 university professors in Spain in 1936, 156, including seven rectors, left the country in 1938—39 (J. B. Climent, 'España en el exilio' *Cuadernos americanos* 126 (1), January—February 1963, pp. 104—5).

[32] Who has translated more of the works of Marx published in Spain since 1965 than anyone else.

[33] The list of books published in Spain in 1968 includes seven works by Marx, three by Engels, three by 'Che' Guevara and eleven studies by Marxist authors. There is no book in the list by Lenin or Mao Tse-tung ('Indice de autores de las obras publicadas en el Repertorio bibliográfico de "El libro español" durante el año 1968' in *Libros nuevos*, 15 December 1968, pp. 593—637).

[34] J. García Candau, 'Mañana, día decisivo para las huelgas asturianas' *Ya*, 11 January 1970, p. 10.

[35] Of the Madrid papers, *Ya* has the second biggest circulation, following the monarchist *ABC*.

[36] R. de la Cierva, 'Revisión histórica y objetiva de la guerra española', *Ya*, 31 March 1970, p. 8.

[37] Ibid.

[38] 'La tragedia española al través de una sesión de Cortes dramática e histórica' *Ya*, 1 April 1970, p. 7.

[39] 'Participación en una huelga de carácter sedicioso' *Ya*, 26 December 1969, p. 37.

[40] 'El estado de excepción explicado a las Cortes' *Ya*, 23 April 1969, p. 12.

[41] *Sistema institucional ...* , pp. 269—270 and 275—6.

[42] N.R., 'El doctor Obrador a su vuelta de Rusia' *Informaciones*, 13 September 1968, p. 32.

[43] J. G. P., 'Bailarinas ucranianas en Madrid' *Ya*, 1 October 1969 (illustrated supplement).

[44] J. García Candau, 'El gobierno español recibirá un informe sobre el oro de Moscú' *Ya*, 4 February 1970, pp. 3—4.

[45] R. de la Cierva: article quoted above, p. 7.

[46] 'Rotundo no' *Ya*, 19 January 1969, pp. 20—1.

[47] See, for example: 'Los comunistas españoles contra las relaciones hispano-soviéticas' *Ya*, 10 March 1970, p. 7.

[48] *'Julián Grimau'*, Editions sociales, Paris 1963, p. 109.

[49] E. Martín López, 'Análisis de contenido de la declaración del Partido comunista en España (Junio 1964)' *Revista de trabajo* 8 (4), 1964, p. 203.

[50] Other cells are named after international communist figures such as Ho Chi Minh or 'Che' Guevara, or have evocative labels such as Red Volunteers, Red Star, Action, First of March, Vanguard, October, Alert, The Castellón Tricolour, Olive Green, New Horizons, the *Comuneros*, Guadarrama, Sons of the People, Hope, The Captains of Jaca, Proletarian Dawn, etc.

[51] *Julián Grimau*, p. 43.

[52] Ibid., p. 119.

[53] M. Núñez, *Cárcel de Ventas*, Editions de la librairie du Globe, Paris 1967, p. 25.

[54] M. Rodriguez Chaos, *24 años en la cárcel*, p. 76.

[55] Ibid., p. 145.

[56] 'La ejemplar conducta de Simón Sánchez Montero' *Mundo obrero* 29 (18), 15 September 1959, p. 4.

[57] M. Adam, *Etude sur les thèmes de l'opposition communiste en Espagne de 1945 à 1963*, Paris 1956, pp. 140–50.

[58] E. Martín López: article quoted above, pp. 193–5.

[59] N. Pla, 'Juventud: lo pro-soviético y lo anti-soviético' *Nuestra bandera* 59, 3rd quarter, 1968, p. 30.

[60] 'Llamamiento del partido Communista de España con motivo del Primero de Mayo' *Mundo obrero* 21 (11), 1 May 1952, p. 1.

[61] 'Saludo de la camarada Dolores Ibarruri, secretario general del PC de E al XIX Congreso del PC (e) de la URSS' *Mundo obrero* 21 (23), 1 November 1952, p. 3.

[62] A. Benaya, *Un ejemplo de trabajo* [Ediciones *Nuestra bandera*], no date or place, p. 11.

[63] 'El comportamiento heróico de López Raimundo frente a los torturadores franquistas' *Mundo obrero* 21 (10), 15 April 1952, p. 2.

[64] V. Uribe, 'Todos unidos por la reconquista de la República' *España popular*, no date or place, p. 2.

[65] S. Carrillo, ¡Libertad! *Nuestra bandera* 60, December 1968 – January 1969, p. 6.

[66] Expressions taken from ten numbers of *Mundo obrero* published between 1961 and 1964 (E. Martín Lopez, Article quoted above, p. 191).

[67] M. Adam, op. cit., p. 142.

[68] Fifty-six of them were accused of having connections with Basque nationalist organisations; forty-one with workers' councils; eleven persons were charged with membership of illegal students' unions; and nineteen of the accused were charged with other political offences.

[69] E. García, the former Secretary for Organisation, for instance, writes: 'In the Valencia and Aragon regions, where we had difficulties two years ago, we have made considerable progress . . . . Proof of this is that the police made 300 arrests in Valencia and about 100 in Zaragoza ('Le Parti communiste consolide ses rangs' *Nouvelle revue internationale* 8 (120), August 1968, p. 173).

[70] Describing a leaflet drive in a village in Castile in or around 1960, Jesús Izcaray writes in one of his novels: 'The appearance of leaflets

calling for a strike suggested that there was a more or less well-organised communist group at Nobleda'. At no point is the reader invited to consider that the leaflets could have been of any but communist origin. (*Las ruinas de la muralla*, Editions de la Librairie du Globe, Paris 1965, p. 145).

71  D. Ibarruri, 'Carta de la camarada Dolores Ibarruri a la redacción de *Mundo obrero' Mundo obrero* 196, 17 November 1949, p. 1. Also worth noting is a book by M. Rodríguez Chaos, dealing with the years immediately after the Civil War but not published until 1968, in which he writes about three communist and two socialist leaders emerging from their prison cells: 'When Girón, Messón and Ascanio [the communists] were fetched for interrogation, all three had the same thought: they would be killed. When Henche and Arivalo [the socialists] were ordered out of their cells to be questioned, the rumour immediately spread among the other socialist prisoners that they were having a talk with the leaders of the vertical trade unions, who were offering them senior posts in their fascist syndicate'. (M. Rodríguez Chaos, op. cit., p. 64)

72  D. Ibarruri, 'Interpelación' *Mundo obrero* 208, 9 February 1950, p.1.

73  D. Carrillo, *Après Franco... quoi?* Les Editions sociales, Paris 1965, pp. 78–9 and 82.

74  S. Carrillo, 'La situación en el Partido....' in *Informes y resoluciones del pleno....*, p. 209.

75  The longest strike in Spain took place in a rolling mill outside Bilbao which employed a particularly high proportion of workers newly come from country to town.

76  J. L. Martín Vigil, *Los curas comunistas*, Richard Grandio, Oviedo 1968, p. 44.

77  J. Martínez Alier, *La estabilidad del latifundismo*, Ruedo ibérico, Paris 1968, pp. 132–3.

78  *Julián Grimau,* p. 112.

79  S. Vilar, *Protagonistas de la España democrática. La oposición a la dictadura comunista, 1939–1969*, p. 321.

80  L. Ramírez, *Nuestros primeros veinticinco años*, Ruedo ibérico, no place 1964, p. 202.

81  'El pacto para la libertad' *Voz obrera* 3 (9), February–March 1970, p. 6.

82  'Débats áctuels du mouvement ouvrier' *Le Semeur* 1, 1967–1968, p. 127.

83  C. Prieto, 'La tactique du Parti communiste a contribué à l'affaiblissement des commissions ouvrieres' *Le Monde*, 18 February 1970, p. 5.

84  S. Alvarez, 'L'alliance des catholiques et des communistes' *Nouvelle revue internationale* 9, September 1968, pp. 126–7 and 129.

[85]   S. Carrillo, *Nuevos enfoques a problemas de hoy*, p. 132.

[86]   Quoted by S. Vilar, op. cit., p. 348.

[87]   Ibid., pp. 251 and 274.

[88]   'Muere un estudiante . . .' (article quoted in note 28 above).

[89]   The PCE (ML), however, favours the use of armed force and remains hostile to the Church, from which, it declares, 'nothing can be expected' ('Carta sin respuesta' *Mundo obrero (ML)* 2 (11), June 1966, p. 4). Despite this, some Spanish priests living in France or Switzerland have been attending meetings of Marxist-Leninist groups.

[90]   'El verdadero rostro del clero español' *Vida nueva* 722, 21 March 1970, pp. 419 and 421. Also worth noting is a survey carried out in 1968–69 among Spanish Jesuits, from which it seems that 75 per cent of the priests questioned considered it their duty to comment publicly on political and social conflicts (Question no. 65, p. 177).

[91]   J. M. González Ruíz, *El cristianismo no es un humanismo*, Ediciones Península, Madrid 1966, p. 220.

[92]   Quoted by R. Castellanos, 'Camilo Torres y el diálogo entre revolucianarios' *Cuadernos americanos* 158 (3), May–June 1968, p. 70.

[93]   Precisely because of these editorials.

[94]   'Los detenidos por razones sindicales y la OIT' *Ya*, 21 September 1969, p. 15. In 1963, on the other hand, no Spanish paper mentioned the appeal of Pope John XXIII to General Franco on behalf of Julián Grimau three days before the latter's execution.

[95]   'Texto integro del documento episcopal sobre sindicatos' *Ya*, 14 September 1968, p. 6.

[96]   In 1963 the Bishop of Burgos was still allowing communist prisoners to be compelled to attend mass and to kneel (M. Rodríguez Chaos, op. cit., p. 245; and S. Vilar, op. cit., p. 259).

[97]   'El mote de "comunista" *Ya*, 5 December 1968, p. 15.

[98]   Spanish students abroad have more contact with Maoist and Trotskyite groups.

[99]   F. Aguilo, *Emigration et syndicalisme*, Les Editions ouvrières, Paris 1968, p. 30.

[100]   'Opiniones sobre cuestiones nacionales' *Revista española de la opinión pública* 18, October–December 1969, pp. 280–1 and 299–300.

[101]   'Opiniones sobre problemas nacionales e internacionales (Otoño 1968)' *Revista española de la opinión pública* 17, July–September 1969, pp. 165–237.

[102]   The proportion of 'don't knows' was 26 per cent to the first question and 38 per cent to the second. The most strongly anti-communist answers, both with regard to the USSR and Czechoslovakia, were given by farmers

owning large and medium holdings, 55 per cent of whom gave a totally negative response to the first question and 45 per cent to the second.

[103] 39 per cent thought coexistence possible, 27 per cent impossible, and 34 per cent did not answer (out of 1,876 persons questioned).

[104] Thus 48 per cent of young people aged between eighteen and twenty-nine thought coexistence possible, against 35 per cent of people aged between forty and forty-nine, and 23 per cent aged seventy or more.

[105] 63 per cent of the students questioned considered peaceful coexistence possible; only 17 per cent of them, against an overall average of 34 per cent of the sample as a whole, thought Russian communism fundamentally evil. The corresponding figures for Czechoslovak communism were 9 and 16 per cent.

[106] 45 per cent of people living in cities of 100,000 inhabitants or more believed peaceful coexistence to be possible as against 31 per cent of residents of villages with fewer than 2,000 inhabitants.

[107] Asturias, Galicia and Catalonia are, generally speaking, the regions where anti-communist attitudes are least marked. Aragon is the most anti-communist area, followed by Castile, Madrid and Andalusia.

[108] Thus 53 per cent of middle management personnel and 50 per cent of the heads of large firms admitted the possibility of peaceful coexistence, against 39 per cent of the entire sample; 50 per cent of the heads of large firms and 33 per cent of members of the liberal professions thought that the socialist regimes were very likely to undergo a process of liberalisation some time in the future, against only 14 per cent of the sample as a whole and 3 per cent of the day labourers questioned.

[109] In regard to these categories, it is more useful to look at the percentage of 'don't knows', which grows in inverse ratio to the degree of skill of manual workers.

# 5  The Political Role of Communism in Spain

The Spanish communists have a long and varied history; they have organisations that are still alive today, albeit split and sometimes mutually hostile; they even retain a relatively important place in the mental make-up of their compatriots, even though different people think of them in very different ways. But do they still fulfil any real function in a political system dominated by an authoritarian and conservative regime with numerous and effective means of repression and propaganda at its disposal?

Are their efforts to formulate programmes and tactics for the take-over of power purely marginal − or even futile? Do they achieve anything except to contribute to the permanence of a political élite in a society which has become virtually impervious to debate on public affairs? Is it perhaps no more than a sort of prop for governments brandishing the communist bogey? Is it permissible, even for the sake of argument, to allot any political role at all to organisations totally rejected by the system, and which in their turn reject any idea of participating in the existing government machinery in Spain?

## The functions of a clandestine party

Applying a functional yardstick to the part played by underground revolutionary opposition groups in right-wing authoritarian regimes gives rise to an immediate paradox. In the language of sociology, the concept of function is defined as 'the contribution made by a component part of a civilisation to a particular socio-cultural pattern'. [1]  Thus, if we read 'party' for 'component part of a civilisation'; and 'regime' or 'political system' for the looser concept of 'socio-cultural pattern' it becomes clear from the outset that the notion of function applies only very loosely to the Spanish Communist Party − or for that matter to any other communist group in any capitalist country, whether it leads an overt or covert existence, and no matter what its institutional superstructure may be like. The Spanish communists have no intention of contributing to the perpetuation of the Franco regime, any more than the French communists intend to perpetu-

169

ate the post-Gaullist regime, or their Italian comrades intend to prolong the life of the Christian Democrat-dominated system which has prevailed in Italy since 1945.

Thus a purely voluntarist concept of function would seem to apply fully only to parties which do not basically contest the political systems in which they operate. But the fact remains that political parties and organisations of all kinds perform more than voluntary roles and pursue other goals besides those they openly aspire to. In particular, it would appear that organisations radically challenging the system in which they operate do more than merely exercise a potentially destructive 'spoiling' function in the system. Basing his arguments on T. Lowi's classification,[2] Georges Lavau has demonstrated that the French Communist Party, while doing little by way of formulating programmes and acting as a political alternative, has in effect contributed considerably to giving the existing French regime an aura of legitimacy. By accepting most of the principles, standards and practices on which the regime is based, the French Communist Party has in its own way contributed to making the regime work and keeping it in being. And it has another function too — what G. Lavau describes as being 'the people's tribune' — the task of 'organising and defending[3] the plebeian social categories (i.e. those who are excluded, or feel themselves excluded, from the political system's process of participation)'.[4]

The Spanish Communist Party, unlike its French equivalent, cannot organise the proletarian masses on a vast scale. Nor is it able to use their votes to argue their case tellingly before authority; especially since the latter refuses to take part in any dialogue — even an implied one —with it. Is it therefore true, as official propaganda maintains, that the PCE has no part whatever to play in the Spanish political system, to which it is in some way foreign, and that its sole function — a very secondary one at that — is in fact the one it performs within the international communist movement? Or could the PCE on the contrary be playing quite specific parts, both overt and covert — roles quite distinct from those characteristic of parties which explicitly support a particular regime, or of those, like the French Communist Party, which participate extensively in the processes of a regime without giving it full recognition?

Viewed in this light, it seems clear that the function of giving legitimacy and stability to regimes in power cannot be openly performed by illegal parties beyond the political pale. But in fact it often happens that such parties perform this function in a latent and involuntary manner, in spite of themselves. They then become little more than symbols made use of by the propaganda apparatus of their adversary, serving to justify the authoritarian and reactionary character of the establishment, which then poses as

170

the only effective barrier against their subversive plots. Such is the role thrust today on the Spanish, Portuguese, Greek and Turkish communists, as well as on most of the communists of Latin America.

On the other hand, it is permissible to ask whether underground organisations like the PCE, with their relatively large human and propaganda resources, could not within certain limits perform the dual function of producing programmes and offering a political alternative. The options they offer are of course somewhat irrelevant in the short term, since there is little chance of their being put into effect in the foreseeable future and since the majority of citizens are not even aware of them. But is the case of legitimate parties like the French Communist Party, with a place of their own out in the open, all that different? Their programmes are carried out no more effectively and are not that much better known outside the circle of dedicated militants. In the last analysis, the communist alternative in France is not all that much more plausible, or felt to be all that much more imminent, than in Spain, despite the difference between the political regimes in the two countries.

Nevertheless, it is quite plain that as things are today the Spanish Communist Party is hardly in a position to exercise to the full its function as 'tribune of the people' — the task of organising and defending the social categories of people who find themselves on the fringes of the political system. True, it does perform this function to some extent by staging strikes and demonstrations, some of them quite important, with growing frequency, as was the case in Barcelona at the time of the Burgos trial in 1970. But the tribune must be recognised as such, both by the broad circles of the people whose patronage he seeks and by the authority he is addressing. To play tribune you must therefore have, if not genuine influence, at least the right of assembly and substantial means of expression, widely and freely distributed. An illegal party, even if it has a by no means negligible clandestine press and a radio transmitter sited outside the country, cannot truly assume such a role. The PCE and the other Spanish communist organisations have tried hard to present themselves as the champions of the broad masses, despite the handicap of their illegal position; but this very fact has forced them to remain in this field in a world of make-believe and of promises unfulfilled. They have not managed to cross the credibility threshold, beyond which they might play a genuine role of 'people's tribune' in their own right.

But underground organisations can perform another function — perhaps the most crucial one they have in monolithic authoritarian states, short of seizing power by force. This function, which one could describe as the education and upkeep of a working-class consciousness, consists of fielding an opposition team and keeping it up to strength. Such a team is a politically motivated élite free from that passive apathy official propaganda holds up as the ideal mode of existence. Such a role does not involve organising the greater part of the marginally involved masses, only keeping alive in their minds an appropriate sense of social identity and, first and foremost, keeping in being at any cost a reserve force of militants able to get to work on the masses whenever opportunities arise for greater freedom of action. In such a case, the communists would really be able to play the part of 'tribune of the people'. The practical value of such activity is undeniable. Its symbolic value is no less great, in the sense that it shows the masses that, thrust as the communists are beyond the pale of legal political action, there is a continuity of political opposition in the country; it shows them too how high a value some people are prepared to put on political commitment.

To what extent do the Spanish communists perform the functions theoretically attributable to underground political organisations confronting authoritarian regimes? Those they most openly lay claim to are the related ones of drawing up programmes and providing a political alternative. Let us analyse these first, on the concrete basis of documents published by the PCE and by the groups hived off from it. We shall then turn to the two other functions of the maintenance of a working-class consciousness and of the indirect endorsement of the existing establishment, which are probably those with the most effect exercised by a revolutionary opposition in Spain. We shall perforce have to study the last two more subjectively.

### The communist programme

For all the undeniable originality they show in certain respects — which explains the revival of interest enjoyed by the Spanish communists today — the Spanish Communist Party's general ideological position does not fundamentally differ from that of other Western communist parties. According to the PCE, 'communism will be a society without a state, in which classes will have disappeared and in which there will therefore be no political struggle; there will be no more political parties — naturally not even a Communist Party'. Communist society will be characterised not only by an abundance of goods, but also by the ultra-modern organisation of the production process, as well as by the absence of any state, politics or coercion, and by full freedom for Man.[5] Like the French and Italian Communist Parties, the PCE foresees in the shorter term its 'determination to do all it can to make the victory of socialism follow a peaceful and

172

parliamentary course, to ensure that the socialist future of Spain, which must come, shall come without bloodshed, without insurrection and without civil war'.[6] It also considers that the change-over to socialism can take place in the framework of 'collaboration between the various socialist-oriented parties'.[7] The Party's leading, but no longer dominant, role will then be to 'put forward the course of action it considers proper, to make objections to the suggestions of other parties or groups, and then to play its part with them in working out a synthesis'.[8]

But it is noteworthy that the PCE continues to dwell more than the other two parties on its interest in the lesson of the Czechoslovak Spring of 1968, to which it refers explicitly as a model. It considers that in Czechoslovakia 'socialism underwent a renaissance through the enlargement of political freedom' and gives pride of place to the undertaking that 'the Spanish way to the victory and building of socialism will be based on the development of political liberty'.[9] It also pays considerable attention to the nationalist movements of Catalonia, the Basque country and Galicia, the importance of which is incomparably greater than that of any regionalist movement in Italy or France.

However, the essential core of the PCE's programme is concerned not with its concept of socialism but with the political arrangements in the stage of transition to it. The existence of the Franco dictatorship means that the questions that arise in this connection cannot present themselves in the minds of Spanish communists in the form in which they appear to their comrades in the legal parties of Western Europe. Like the French and Italian communists, the PCE considers that the only way to arrive at socialism is gradually, in stages. But it also holds it essential to bring about before the establishment of socialism in Spain that democratic bourgeois 'revolution' which the liberal monarchy and the Spanish Second Republic could not pursue to its successful conclusion, and which is today an accomplished fact in most nearby countries. It is certainly in this regard that the PCE's contribution is most original and least orthodox.

In this context, the PCE has declared several times[10] that it would agree to supporting a provisional government which was without any formal constitutional affiliation, even if the communists were not invited to join it. The only conditions for its co-operation would be the re-establishment of political liberties without discrimination — i.e. without any provisions excluding the communists from them — as well as a total amnesty for political prisoners and exiles, and the election by universal suffrage of a constituent Cortes.[11] In a somewhat earlier statement, the PCE endorsed the programme of minimum demands attributed to the '565 intellectuals'. This calls additionally for the restoration of trade union freedoms and the right to strike, as well as immediate pay increases. [12]

The communist attitude to the new regime's constitution is equally straightforward. It could eventually be determined by the Spanish people themselves, pronouncing on proposals made by the Cortes, the PCE says, while proclaiming that 'democratisation in Spain is synonymous with the republic' and that 'the monarchy is the government of the moneyed and landed aristocracy, of the palace *camarillas*, . . . the reign of the sword'. However, should the electorate opt for a monarchy, the communists would bow to its will, 'without giving up the right to work for a republic under the rules of the democratic game'. [13] In fact, the only formula they absolutely reject is that of a regime imposed from above without popular consultation. This explains why Santiago Carrillo made it known even before Juan Carlos' designation as successor to Franco that if this move were put into effect, his Party would call on the people to 'overthrow this monarchy and to set up a republic by direct action'. [14] Since 23 July 1969, the PCE has been describing the Juan Carlos succession as 'an attempt to institutionalise resistance to change' — by which 'Franco has made any kind of monarchy impossible in Spain and put paid to the illusions of some sections of the population who thought a democratic monarchy was possible'. [15]

The structure and aims of a regime of transition to socialism which would conform to the Party's programme are defined in detail in two books by its Secretary-General, published in 1965 and 1967. The first of these books [16] says specifically that the regime will be 'a new anti-feudal and anti-monopoly democracy in which social forms of ownership in the strategic sectors and a multitude of bourgeois-capitalist forms of ownership will coexist'. It goes on:

> The gradual transition to the social ownership of all means of production ... will not come about as a result of individual expropriation measures. It is the development of productive capacity which will give rise naturally to gradual progress beyond the stage of small and medium-scale industry. Methods of compensating the former private owners and, more importantly, of their integration as individuals into the new socialist production system — taking into account their experience and management skills — will ensure that the transition will not be a personal tragedy for anyone except for those who may resist democratic progress by force.

In the second book, [17] Carrillo explains that 'the power that will bring about the transition from capitalism to socialism will be a power consisting of an alliance of the forces of labour and those of the intellect — a democratic multi-party power'. In this respect, the Secretary-General of the PCE explains that the Spanish communists do not think it either useful or practical to set up a single party of 'all socialist and progressive forces'.[18] The reason, he says, is twofold: on the one hand, they do not want to be accused of harbouring hegemonistic ambitions and, on the other, they cannot see any way of reconciling the many different ideological schools of thought, representing a wide range of classes, that exist. Carrillo therefore advocates creating a loose-knit alliance, allowing 'parties and organisations of varying ideological hues to live together in a common framework, each retaining its identity and independence ...'.

Carrillo had emphasised two years earlier that this was no tactical manoeuvre but a complete

> strategic concept ... based on the idea that the building of socialism in the present-day world is not a task for the working class alone but also one for other social groups and strata; [and also] on the idea that nowadays there are other socialist trends besides the Marxist-Leninist contingent which give expression to the concept of scientific socialism personified by the Communist Party. These other groupings can be represented by other political parties, whose contribution is vital to the creation of a society with neither exploited nor exploiters.[19]

The question remains: What are the limits of the pluralism the PCE has in mind? Recalling 'the repugnant experience of what the liquidation of the multi-party system means in the conditions of our country', Carrillo declared in 1965:

> Parties, for all their inherent faults, are elements of democracy in the political life of a country, to the extent that they reflect the diversity of interests and positions of the various social classes and strata. Even parties whose leaders are thoroughly subservient to monopoly capitalism feel compelled to take account of the people's will in some way or other when great movements of opinion arise among the masses and among their members in the country. Moreover, the existence of parties and their political propaganda are a means of getting the broad masses to take an interest in the life of the country and of making them play a part in it — in other words of combating the phenomenon of what might be called mass political absenteeism, which plays into the hands of monopoly capitalism and which the latter therefore favours.[20]

It would seem that non-socialist opposition parties might be tolerated 'in certain circumstances' — according to an article which appeared in

1969 [21] — but only on condition that 'they stay within the bounds of legality and that they do not conceal the nature of their programmes'. *Nuevos enfoques a problemas de hoy* further suggests that their political functions would be somewhat of a formality since 'acts calculated to overthrow the new social order' would on no account be tolerated. [22] The political institutions and political and economic mechanisms best suited to ensure the success of the stage of transition from a feudal and monopoly dictatorship, first to a bourgeois democracy and then to socialism, are described in a wealth of detail seldom found in the publications of other communist parties. [23] According to the Spanish communists, the new power should ideally assume the form of a multi-national, rather than a federal, state and should recognise without reservations the national rights of Catalonia, the Basque country and Galicia. [24] In this state, the three 'nations' would have autonomous status, coexisting with the Spanish provinces proper, which would themselves be organised along democratic and decentralised regional lines. Parliament, in which the autonomous regions would be represented, would be a single-chamber assembly elected by proportional representation. The PCE does not favour a Senate, some of the functions of which would be performed by an Economic and Social Council whose task it would be to draft general and local economic plans [25] and which would consist not of representatives of capital but of the classes and sections of society engaged in production — workers, peasants, technicians, businessmen and non-monopoly industrialists.

On defence, the communists want the army to be stripped of 'all public security duties' and to become 'a force created and maintained by the nation, whose sole purpose it shall be to defend the nation's territorial integrity and independence'. They propose, moreover, that reservists should belong to a people's territorial militia which would be quite distinct from the standing army. But they take care to reassure the officers corps in advance by explaining that they have 'no intention of dismantling the army, and even less of replacing it with the old People's Army' — the force the Party sponsored in 1936–39. They even pledge to improve the financial position of professional servicemen: 'Commanders must receive sufficient pay to live decently in accordance with their position in the hierarchy, so that they can devote themselves to their profession'. [26]

Carrillo justifies retaining the greater part of the military machine by the fact that the present-day army is 'not the army of the Civil War' and that 'the majority of its officer corps is of post-Civil War vintage'. He argues that 'many of the military are aware that the regime is at a dead end and that the army has suffered from its identification with it'. [27]

The communist programme also accords an important place to Church

—State relations. The programme says: 'the barrier of religion, used by the ruling classes as an instrument against all forms of revolutionary politics, divides communists and practising Catholics to an ever-diminishing degree, despite the survival of reactionaries who confuse the altar with Franco's throne'. [28] In this spirit, the PCE advocates the separation of Church and State, not in any spirit of discord or conflict, but 'in the mutual interest of both institutions'. The State, moreover, will seek to maintain an atmosphere of respectful coexistence with the Church 'and even to co-operate with her in some respects'. The programme likewise proclaims its dedication to the principle of religious freedom and says that with this in view, it favours 'enabling families wishing to send their children to Catholic schools or universities to do so, by permitting such establishments to operate'. Carrillo even allows for the possibility of forms of subsidising religion being worked out, and guarantees given that 'the religious orders will not be molested'. In the same vein, he wants Spain to have diplomatic relations with the Vatican and calls for the conclusion of a new Concordat 'which would correspond more closely than the present one both to the spiritual interests of the Church and the interests of the State'. [29]

In international affairs, the PCE stands for the formula of 'positive neutrality'. It naturally considers 'the resumption of diplomatic, commercial and cultural relations with the socialist countries' indispensable — but only after the fall of Francoism, not before. Equally essential would be a 'revision of the 1953 treaties with the United States, so as to get rid of the American bases in Spain'. [30] But in a later statement Carrillo said: 'A democratic state with a government including communists would not necessarily take an anti-American line unless provoked'. Such a state could give the USA guarantees that it would not allow other foreign bases to be set up on its territory and that it would not conclude military alliances with other powers'. In this connection, the Party Secretary-General added that there was no justification for 'the rule that small states must necessarily ally themselves to powerful blocs, or even become integrated with them. Should a particular coalition commit aggression against our country on such a scale that the national defence forces would be inadequate to resist it, Spain, like any other state, could call for the help and support of a — no less powerful — opposing coalition'. [31]

On intra-European relations, the PCE's attitude underwent marked changes between 1962 and 1964. In 1962, it proclaimed its 'total opposition to Spain's membership of the Common Market', which, it said, 'would leave her at the mercy of the great foreign monopolies, prevent the country's independent economic and political development and gravely jeopardise its future'. [32] But in 1964, the PCE leader adjusted this outright condemnation in a number of important respects, calling for 'a treaty with the EEC, which today takes about 60 per cent of our exports'. [33]

Communist literature rarely refers to the problem of Gibraltar, which is treated largely as one of the Franco regime's propaganda hobby-horses. The Party pays rather more attention to Mediterranean questions and to relations with the Arabs. Here the PCE follows the CPSU line of calling for 'the creation of a nuclear-free zone in the Mediterranean' [34] and supports the Moroccan claims to the Spanish Sahara. [35] Its attitude to the enclaves on the northern coast of Morocco is less clear, although it has stated that 'we cannot speak of friendship with the Arab countries so long as we occupy ... Ceuta and Melilla'. [36] Since the Six Day War, the PCE has, moreover, been proclaiming its 'solidarity with the just cause of the Arab peoples', faced with 'Israeli aggression'. [37]

The economic and social programme put forward by the PCE for the transitional stage of anti-feudal and anti-monopolist democracy is couched in terms as moderate and realistic as its political and constitutional programme. There is no question in it of any fundamental change in the ecomomic structure, although it does contain major innovations: a limited land reform, the introduction of democratic control by the workers in major public and private enterprises, and the nationalisation of the key sectors of the economy. Thus a nationalised sector consisting of the banks and other sources of credit, the mines, the power industry and 'the major industrial monopolies' would exist side-by-side with a private sector consisting of the majority of firms that have not been nationalised, being presumably considered 'non-monopolistic'. The agricultural sector would be only partly affected by the land reform.

There are certain ambiguities as regards the nationalised sector. The programme states that the functions of management would be carried out by the state and the workers in partnership, the latter having the right to participate in the planning and organisation of production. It also states that 'nationalisation can take place without prejudice to the interests of shareholders, who could continue to receive a dividend on their shares until the latter are bought in'. [38] But it is none too clear whether all the biggest firms would be nationalised under this formula, with the aim being of depriving them of 'the political hegemony now enjoyed by monopoly capital' and forcing them to 'strive for that predominance through the interplay of party politics in completely new conditions in which the other social classes and strata would also have political weapons'. [39]

However that may be, the programme stipulates specifically that there is no question of doing away with 'capitalist property', but only with the feudal monopolies. What for the sake of convenience we have called the

178

great sea of small and medium enterprises would in this phase of economic democracy remain in the hands of their owners, whose interests would not suffer as a result of these changes. Indeed, they ought to profit by them, since they would be 'functioning within a system which would provide them with guarantees they do not now possess ...'. [40]

## The replacement of the Franco regime

Despite its critics, the PCE's programme forms a genuinely coherent whole. It could even promote the functioning of the Spanish political system — if there were any chance of its being put into effect in the foreseeable future. But there is no such chance, since its implementation presupposes precisely that the system should be what it is not, and also because the policies advocated and practised by the Party with a view to overthrowing the Franco regime are not likely to make a decisive contribution to its downfall.

On this point the PCE has for twenty years more or less consistently maintained the view that the Franco regime can be replaced peaceably by means of a semi-legal struggle combined with reconciliation and an alliance between all the opposition groups. This tactical prudence and insistence on non-violent methods — which only the left has deplored — must be seen as a frank admission of the communists' inability to attack in any but a symbolic manner a regime which has overwhelming means of repression at its disposal.

The militants' confidence in the effectiveness of a political general strike has been greatly diminished by the repeated failures of the attempts in 1958, 1961, 1962 and 1965 to launch strikes, failures which resulted in a grave crisis within the Party in 1963—64. [41] Nevertheless, this form of action still enjoys official support and has even come back into favour since the events in France in May 1968. Carillo considers that the French events to some extent confirm that the capitalist state can be made to disintegrate by means of mass action. [42]

Thus, what the PCE is hoping for is that a non-violent uprising by the mass of the workers, students, peasants and members of the petty bourgeoisie will force a change of regime. Violent action is not excluded altogether, but would play only a secondary role in neutralising any armed forces which had failed to make common cause with the uprising. It is stated in this context that 'faced with an irresistible movement — a political general strike and its sequel, a national strike — the army may withdraw its support from the regime and help the people impose their will'. [43]

179

Consequently, the Party does not consider that its main task is to prepare in secret a conspiracy against the powers that be. What it wants is to make itself known to the masses 'without a mask' in order to prepare them for this decisive action. It admits the dangers these tactics entail for its militants, but insists that the 'Spanish communists are step by step winning legality for themselves',[44] at least indirectly by means of their participation in trade union activity, and in elections, and by joining officially permitted organisations and the workers' councils, for 'to fail to exploit such opportunities... would be to return to the catacombs and, in the final analysis, to give up the fight'.[45]

The success of this method of wearing down the regime prior to the final blow (a national strike involving the majority of the population) implies a minimum of understanding among those called upon to take part in striking that blow, the majority of whom are not members of the Party. Hence the importance the Party attaches to concluding agreements with other opposition forces and to bringing about unity of action at grass roots level. As regards this last point, the Secretary-General considers — with some optimism — that unity has already been achieved, particularly among 'the most dynamic and most aggressive elements, notably communists and socialists'.[46]

But agreements at the top level are yet to be concluded, as the communists themselves admit, despite the many proposals they have made to this end, first within the Juntas of National Unity of 1944 and then as part of the policy of national reconciliation the PCE has followed since 1954. Its latest formula is the 'covenant for freedom', to which all forces are invited to subscribe that have 'unambiguously decided to break with the Franco regime and which concede that the people asserting their sovereignty in conditions of full democratic liberty, are entitled to determine the future of the country'.[47]

A few months before the publication of the covenant, in November 1968, the PCE announced that it was prepared to conclude a minimum compact with any opposition group, including those of the right.[48] Not even the Carlists and the conservative Catholics led by Gil Robles were excluded.[49] Nevertheless, the Party continued to give priority to the alliance with the socialists and left-wing Catholics, and the PCE has repeatedly emphasised that any Catholic joining the Party would not be expected to 'renounce his religious beliefs'[50] in any way. The Party has stressed even more insistently the importance it attaches to the creation of 'a socialist movement ... in which Spanish Catholics will be able to be socialists [while] preserving what they consider to be Christian values'.[51]

To conclude this analysis of documents published by the PCE, let us make it clear that the programmes and tactics advocated by the dissident communist groups differ markedly from those advanced by the 'orthodox' Party. The ideology and attitudes of the Spanish communist dissidents are very similar to those of the parallel French and Italian movements. All that needs to be said is that the Marxist-Leninists largely reject the principle of non-violent and semi-overt action, and instead advocate armed action as their first choice — whereas the PCE looks upon it as a last resort. To this end, they recommend the formation of small armed groups which would wage a guerrilla war. The latter, they say, might well develop into 'a true people's war against Yankee imperialism, since it would be childish to exclude the possibility of an American armed intervention'. [52] However, the instructions actually issued by the various dissident communist splinter groups occasionally belie these principles. Thus one of the Marxist factions recommended its followers to abstain in the 1966 referendum on the organic law — just as the PCE did [53] — while another urged its supporters to return a blank ballot slip. [54] Likewise, most of the leftist organisations have refused to join the workers' councils, which they suspect of 'legalism', although some, such as the *Movimiento comunista*, a breakaway from the PCE (ML), favour the idea of recapturing them from within.

To uphold the class struggle most of these groups also oppose the policy of national reconciliation so dear to the PCE. Here again, some Marxist-Leninists reject the idea of an alliance with the liberal bourgeoisie and consider that only a front of workers and peasants would be acceptable, [55] while others would not jib at a 'people's democracy directed by the working class, based on the worker—peasant alliance but including broad strata of the urban petty bourgeoisie and even the patriotic and democratic sector of the middle bourgeoisie'. [56]

There is in fact only one point on which all the groups are agreed, namely the rejection of the intermediate phase of bourgeois democracy. Trotskyites, Marxist-Leninists and other varieties of dissidents, including Claudín's 'right-wing' faction, all hold that the transition to socialism must take place under the leadership of the proletariat immediately after the downfall of the Franco regime.

Whatever their tenor, all these discussions on the seizure of power and the setting up of one form of democracy or another are as sterile as the communist programmes themselves. The initiative for a change of regime can come only either from within the ranks of the existing political élite, from certain specific social groups or through the intervention of external political forces. None of these contingencies would appear to be based on realistic assumptions. External intervention in Spain, which did not occur

181

immediately after the last war, seems inconceivable today. Moreover, even if certain social groups, notably sections of the working class and the Basque and Catalan autonomy movements are in fact hostile to the regime, few have gone beyond the stage of what Linz calls 'apathetic alienation' or 'haphazard opposition', [57] and they thus represent no real threat to the power-holders.

As for the establishment, many of its members are glad to be associated (or would like to be associated) with an authoritarian, but not totalitarian, regime which has had the sense never to lose touch with them. A sort of 'limited pluralism' has thus developed. This excludes the majority of the population but remains accessible to the 'semi-opposition' groups 'which are neither in a dominant position nor represented at government level ... [but which] aspire to a share in the exercise of power without, however, opposing the regime'. [58] Much the same applies to the more intellectual radical 'pseudo-opposition' such as the left-wing Christian Democrats led by Ruiz Giménez, who have in fact come to terms with the Franco regime reasonably easily.

The communists are unable to make an impact on either of these categories. For them to come to power would require a kind of miracle, an unforeseeable cataclysm of some sort. Above all, the army would have to cease being the regime's principal line of defence. In fact, despite certain incidents [59] the armed forces are still a long way from meeting the expectations of Carrillo, who has claimed to have detected the first signs of a change of heart on the part of the soldiery. True, the regime has long since been on the defensive, but it is defending itself very well, effectively shunting on to the sidelines groups it rejects or feels unable to show favour to, and absorbing any élite groups which might conceivably resist it as they gradually gain in importance. As that long-awaited 'miracle' — the fall of the Franco regime — is further and further delayed, it would appear that the forms of action advocated by the left-wing groups and the PCE have met with hardly any response outside these organisations, or the sections of society in which they operate, any more than have their programmes. The leftists play virtually no part in the country's political life, and they have no chance whatever of destroying the Franco regime by preaching violent action without themselves resorting to it on any scale. [60] By their behaviour they tend in fact to justify the regime. However, their line is successful in keeping up the enthusiasm of their supporters — radical students and young workmen repelled by the prosaic ways of the orthodox communists. On the other hand, the PCE's propaganda and sporadic propaganda activities do not represent an immediate challenge to the regime either. They certainly do not expose it to any real risk, although they are a nuisance to the government, just as strikes, student agitation and the like are a nuisance to the French, Italian and British governments.

## The potential functions of a worker élite

Is it right to say — as we have suggested — that the only truly effective and discernible function [61] of the Spanish communists consists of recruiting, educating and keeping in being a working-class élite and of keeping alive the Spanish workers' class consciousness? In fact without them, and without the Catholic Action organisations, which have more recently begun to play the same part, this élite would probably have disappeared completely, just as the anarchist groups have vanished from most of Spain. And it is likewise almost certain that without the communists and the Catholic militants the Spanish working class would not have shaken off the demoralisation and apathy which beset it during the days that followed the Civil War.

Since the regime is at present not particularly interested in the working masses, this function of the communists is of potential importance only; it is nonetheless the communists' most important function at national level, and even more as far as the sections of society which have been thrust aside from the centre of events since 1939 are concerned. The considerable increase in strikes, which are today at least as numerous and as prolonged as they were before 1936, is clear evidence of this.

The Franco dictatorship is a typical example of an authoritarian and conservative regime[62] in which the process of 'totalitarianisation' has been blocked after the initial destruction of the groups and institutions totally hostile to the established order. This has happened for reasons arising simultaneously from the international situation, the nature and aims of the governing coalition, and the state of Spanish society. It was only during its earlier years that the regime showed any real interest in monopolising the political life of the population as a whole, and even then this preoccupation was shared between the Church and the Falange.

Once it had eliminated its declared adversaries in the country, which it did during the Second World War, the regime chose to base its power not on a 'mobilisation' and ideological indoctrination of the masses, which were in any case hostile to it, but on their political apathy. At least until the beginning of the present decade, it counted exclusively on the support of the traditional ruling classes and interest groups, which were in a sense its founding fathers. It therefore had to cater to their sectional demands, and secure for them actual, or at least potential, participation in the exercise of power.

The smooth running of such a regime presupposes firm exercise of authority, but also that authority will in its turn be as receptive as possible to the demands of the groups that support the regime, both as regards the defence of their interests and their participation in government. This is why the Franco regime is to some extent a pluralist one, with participation limited, however, to the actual or potential members of the ruling coalition. The only party is but one pressure group among several: that is, the army, the Church, business and the great families.

A modicum of opposition must hence be allowed, in the interests of the regime itself, provided that opposition does not contest the foundations of the system and provided that it is not too obtrusive or aggressive. Moreover, this pseudo-opposition can be tolerated only within the élite and among the groups likely to support the government once their demands are met. The true function of such an 'insider' opposition is neither to overthrow the regime, nor to replace more than a minority of the power-holders. Its only task is to enable the authorities to highlight their response to the demands of those categories of citizens they are able to satisfy and whom it is to their advantage to reconcile. Such an opposition also helps the regime by supplying the ruling clique with fresh blood, thus constantly rejuvenating and reinforcing it.

On the other hand, the Franco system cannot allow this pseudo-opposition to organise itself into parties or groupings of an openly political character. If it did, elements genuinely representing the people, who have been forced on to the political sidelines since 1939, would also seek organised representation. A real opposition would thus emerge and would put an end to the political disarray of the masses and promote the development of new élites difficult to absorb in the establishment.

The absence of legal political organisations other than the Falangist movement has done no harm to the 'cohesion without consensus' [63] of the special interest groups. The fact is, that these groups have found in the professional associations, the chambers of commerce, the Falange, unions of every sort, Catholic colleges, Church institutions, the army, the civil service, and so on — instruments quite capable of putting their demands to the authorities. These bodies have also provided them with facilities for rudimentary political training, as well as with means of recruiting new members. The ban on parties virtually denies a political outlet to the masses, and especially to the working class, while it helps the élite associated with the regime to make its voice heard by simplifying and shortening its lines of communication with the state.

The purpose of this preamble on the role of the opposition in Franco Spain is to draw attention to the process which has led to the working class becoming practically the only section of the population to be deprived of any lawful avenue of political training and any chance of recruiting its own élite. It is this situation that is at the root of the 'depoliticisation' of the majority of Spaniards, who seem to prefer 'peace' above all else. In other words, there is virtually no public debate liable to lead to conflict. [64] But this situation has not prevented various political 'sub-cultures' older than the present regime from maintaining their cohesion among certain minorities. They have also kept alive, though in a more covert and fragmented form, among a considerable number of apparently 'depoliticised' people. However, the principal field in which these sub-cultures exist is that of Catholic Church movements operating among the workers, as well as some groups on the left of the Falange and of the official trade union movement which serve as a substitute for political parties. In addition, there are the clandestine political organisations, among whom the communists are probably the most prominent.

The part played by these organisations as agencies of socialisation and for the recruitment of a working class élite is as important as their role of opposition is negligible in terms of political effectiveness, despite the relatively large scale of some of the demonstrations for which they are responsible. The reason is that the political sidetracking of the working class, and the authoritarian state's policy of virtual ideological non-intervention in working-class circles, have given something of a monopoly to groups prepared to shoulder the risks involved in any activities in this field. Like other underground organisations, but generally more efficiently and on a wider scale — and moreover without the prolonged interruptions and occasional cessations of activity to which many of the others are subject — the PCE has undertaken a multitude of tasks. Its first concern has been to guarantee the security, and above all the continued clandestine existence, of the cadres it has already trained. To this end it has to maintain a sizable logistic apparatus and to provide places of refuge for its militants in immediate danger of imprisonment or even execution. There are some informal rules on this subject: communists likely to be sentenced to relatively brief terms of imprisonment — say two to three years — must serve their sentences and not count on a 'safe trip' abroad. On the other hand, those liable to incur long sentences — eight, ten or more years in jail — benefit to the greatest possible extent from the use of an 'underground railway' and are given facilities for a prolonged stay outside Spain. Some are offered permanent employment on these occasions, either within the Party or in one of the East European people's democracies, more often than not in publishing or broadcasting.

The PCE must, moreover, sustain its cadres ideologically and replace them when they have been struck down by age, persecution or, as sometimes happens, when they fall victim to splits within the Party. Hence the need to run an adequate propaganda apparatus, to organise training and further education courses in Spain and abroad, and, last but not least, to maintain the recruitment of new members at a level compatible with the need to furnish an élite from which to recruit the Party's officials.

In this regard, irrespective of directives calling for mass recruitment, the Party considers it less important to gather a vast formation of shock troops for a direct confrontation with the regime than to maintain a structure capable, at the very least, of ensuring the lasting survival of a communist nucleus in Spain. No large-scale propagation of communist views is possible in present circumstances, but it would become quite conceivable in conditions of somewhat greater freedom, provided that elements devoted to the cause remain in being. It is thus comparatively unimportant whether the Party has nearly 50,000 members, as the most generously inclined observers allow, or only 5,000, as a recent CIA report claims. [65] What is supremely important is that this membership, no matter what its numbers, should be so organised as to make possible the Party activities of a nucleus of communists, the training and replacement of its militants, and the emergence of an élite that will discharge organisational, ideological, and if possible political, tasks.

Viewed in this light, local organisations relatively weak in numbers can be quite adequate for this role; perhaps even better than larger but more vulnerable and less coherent groups. An example is the Cadiz provincial committee, rounded up by the police early in 1970. Although it had hardly more than a few hundred active members, divided between Cadiz, Rota, Sanlúcar de Barrameda, Jérez and Seville, and organised in a variety of groups and cells, the committee was at the top of a complex pyramid of well-defined organisations which was virtually a mirror image of the structure of equivalent committees working in legal conditions. In addition to its Secretary-General, it had a secretary for propaganda with three assistants, a finance secretary, a liaison officer, and a secretary for relations with local and works cells. These were organised, above all, in the building industry, and in some of the great wine-producing companies such as Caballero, Osborne and Terry. It also had a branch at Jérez whose job it was to circulate the communist press at regional and occasionally national level. In addition, there were separate organisations of the Communist Youth and Young Workers' Councils. [66] This whole machinery gave the officers and militants of the Party what almost amounted to a sand-table model with which to play a sort of permanent war game, maintaining goodwill under pressure and selecting those best adapted to the work of directing and inspiring the Party.

These small-scale models of the organisation have a further advantage: they can play their part fully without making it necessary to do more than to co-opt new recruits in quarters which remain under working-class influence. This formula provides members with an outlet for their enthusiasm and some encouragement, thus ensuring a degree of continuity of recruitment. It also makes it possible to recruit the sons of old anarchist militants, today almost entirely deprived of their own organisation, and thus helps to accelerate the disappearance of the entire anarchist movement.

We should add that the training and recruitment of a working-class élite does more than merely contribute to the survival of the Party, and of communist influence in Spain, pending the establishment of a new political system. Among the masses, who have been deprived of a political say, it has the secondary effect of demonstrating that opposition to the regime must not be confined exclusively to the harbouring of mental reservations, but must be paid for with sacrifices despite the absence of any prospect of immediate success. In this way communist militancy helps to maintain an exemplary and symbolic 'politicisation' in a working-class society which would otherwise remain in the throes of apathy. Thanks to the communists, that society has come to the fore again as the regime's most dangerous adversary.

The communists are not alone, however, in maintaining a political vigil among the sections of the population neglected by the Franco regime. Statistical comparisons in fact tend to show that the activities of the Catholic Action among the working class have a wider, if not more profound, influence. While the PCE has the support of a few tens of thousands of militants and more-or-less declared sympathisers, the twelve Catholic Church missions to workers and employees alone claim 235,000 members, according to official figures for the period 1962 to 1968. [67] Missions working among the rural population are said to have about 50,000 members. Comparisons with the membership of the Falangist movement's most highly politicised organisations are less meaningful, since the Falangists find their members largely among the middle classes and students from 'good families'. However , even so one must yet again concede that there is no comparison between the number of people politically 'socialised' by what remains of the Falange and those who belong to the Communist Party. Thus, the Falangist left wing, organised mainly in the 'José Antonio circles', alone has 50,000 supporters, while the most typical 'national trade union' organisation, the Old Guard (or *Vieja Guar-*

*dia*) had nearly 38,000 members at the beginning of 1963. [68]

But if the number of those subject to the influence of Catholic workers' movements and Falangist organisations is much greater than that of those supporting the communists, the intensity of the political indoctrination received by the latter is very much greater. The Falangists, of whom there are very few among manual workers, are by reason of their actual or supposed association with the regime, virtually cut off from the mass of the people. For their part, the members of Catholic movements find themselves belonging to lawful bodies which make few demands on them, in which strictly political matters are generally of secondary importance, and precise ideological definitions are eschewed. These organisations constitute a potential field of recruitment for political or trade union organisations with Christian or revolutionary leanings, rather than being associations of active militants. Only a small minority, hardly greater in numbers than the communists, go beyond the stage of formal membership and take an active part in working-class politics, and even these people remain mostly at the level of sub-political underground trade union militancy. In contrast, the communist militants incur grave risks and embrace a well-defined ideology within an organisation that makes much greater demands on them as regards both studies and responsibility.

True, the communists play a much smaller 'cultural' part outside the working class, particularly among students and intellectuals. In these circles, they do not enjoy the virtual monopoly created by the isolation of the broad masses from political activity. Intellectuals, like students, have access to the opening for 'participation' offered by the regime. Many hesitate before making the choice between illegal opposition groups outside the system and the more or less radical pseudo-opposition groups ready within limits to make their peace with the establishment. Thus their political education tends to be eclectic rather than ideologically committed as is the case in the Communist Party. This does not only apply to members of universities under conservative authoritarian regimes such as the one in power in Spain; however, the tendency is more marked in the universities, if only because of the dangers of repression and the temptations held out by the system, which its opponents must utterly renounce.

### Lending legitimacy to the regime — the spectre of communism

The value of the communist opposition to the Franco regime as a symbol is strengthened by persecution, for the very existence of persecution can be used against the communists to justify the existence of a regime which claims to be the only available bastion against Marxist revolutionary subversion.

Moreover, the 'spectre of communism' is not the only one put to such use. Official speeches harp endlessly on the baneful part played by the old parties, and never cease to contrast the present 'peace' with the partisan quarrels of the past. [69] In that past, a number of pamphlets voicing extremist Catholic views made no distinction between 'Hydra-headed Marxism', the 'monster of Judaism' and 'universal freemasonry'. [70] In those days, the Socialist Party was accused of being 'a carrier of an ineradicable and most virulent virus of revolutionary violence'. [71]

However, just as repression has always struck hardest at the communists, the communist menace has always been cited more frequently and more noisily than any other. This is still the case, but now communism shares this privileged position with the Basque separatists. Other opposition groups tend to be shown in a less sinister light.

There is no need to waste time on the actual content of the image of communism put about by the official propaganda machine. On the other hand, one may well ask why the communists are made into a sort of star turn, in preference to other opponents of the regime. And one should equally ask oneself what kind of legitimacy it is the regime is seeking by such methods, whether the latter are effective, and also why the regime attributes such importance to its anti-communist protestations when it has other means of maintaining itself in power.

Much of the answer to the first question is known. All conservative authoritarian regimes delight in exploiting the twin themes of the international communist plot and the subjection of the local communist parties to Moscow. Way back in December 1923, when General Primo de Rivera seized power, he declared: 'I have come in order to fight communism'. Thanks to the efficiency and solidity of their organisation, the communists make especially 'spectacular' adversaries for any anti-Marxist dictatorship. Besides, the very fact that this enemy resists and remains in being makes him always handy for propaganda purposes. There are also other specific reasons why the regime puts such emphasis on the struggle against communism. One arises from the fact that in 1939 the communists were rather unpopular with the majority of Spaniards. By making them into scapegoats, the regime managed to appeal at one and the same time to the right, terrified of the Red Peril, and to the socialist and anarchist left, annoyed at the hold the Communist Party had established over the republican army. The fact that immediately after the Civil War communist prisoners proved even more hostile to 'rehabilitation' within the framework of a 'national trade union' pseudo-revolution than their anarchist and socialist fellows certainly also told against them. This explains why anarchists who joined the Falangist trade unions were sometimes praised as 'Spaniards of good faith' who had been briefly misled by a false ideal, [72] whereas the Falange very soon stopped stressing the points it had 'in common' with the communists' programme.

Not that all communists are treated alike. The regime seldom mentions artists and intellectuals who have ties with the Party so as not to detract from the image of communism as 'low', vulgar and terrorist. Its purpose probably remains unchanged, even where it tolerates — as it now occasionally does — a few allusions to these men in the press. Where this happens, the aim is to show that communists would be capable of salvation if only they showed themselves the least bit willing, if only they were all as law-abiding and loyal as so-and-so, the great painter or writer — it being understood that most of them, alas, do not come up to this ideal.

Thus a well-known poet who is a member of the PCE and as a rule lives in Spain was able to give a press conference for foreign jounalists in 1962. Although he did so on his Party's behalf and in a Madrid hotel, this open declaration of his position did not get him into any trouble. Likewise, Pablo Picasso has never been officially condemned for his political views. Nowadays, the regime even claims him as a national hero, and the same applies to the sculptor Alberto Sánchez, whose work was exhibited in Madrid in 1970 without the press making any secret of his communist convictions. [73]

While the constant reminders of the misdeeds of the partisans are intended to legitimise the system, anti-communist propaganda also has a more specific function: to justify the harshness and permanence of repression and the absence of freedom face to face with an adversary that is represented as being beyond the pale and unworthy of the guarantees society offers to its members. There can be no doubt that it is under the influence of this image of communism that the police, who are particularly receptive to such propaganda, describe as 'Chinese' all communists, and even all Marxist activists, whether Maoist or not. It thus sets them apart from 'true' Spaniards who remain within the national community even though they belong to the opposition — provided it is not communist. In the same spirit, laws and military emergency tribunals carry labels which imply — or explicitly state — their mainly anti-communist purpose. This is the case with the 'Special Act of 1940 on the Suppression of Freemasonry and Communism' [74] and the 1941 'Decree on Terrorism and Banditry'. The Act was resuscitated in 1968 and is now used only against the Basque activists, the communists and anyone described as such. In the same way, people apprehended and indicted before the Special National

Tribunal for Subversive Activities [75] seldom fail to be accused of communism or pro-communist sympathies.

These methods are specifically designed to suggest to the Spanish people that they are the intended victims of Marxist extremists, at whose door the real blame for the continuing restrictions on personal and political freedom should be laid. According to this concept, all the authorities are doing in applying these restrictions is to react to a situation forced on them by the continuing communist menace, it being understood or implied that good Spaniards whose criticisms do not exceed the bounds of constructive moderation would on no account be made to share the fate reserved for communists.

There is no doubt that these arguments remain effective — shop-worn though they may by now be — despite the opening to the East and despite the relative liberalisation of the media. However, for a variety of reasons their influence is waning among the young urban middle class, and it is safe to assume that their impact has always been fairly limited in circles where there is an old-established working-class tradition. But they still exert a strong influence on people with a country background, whether still living in the countryside or newly settled on the outskirts of industrial towns.

Country folk, who are culturally isolated, little influenced by the press and thus not much aware of its changed tone, still live with the wildly exaggerated stereotypes put out immediately after the Civil War. It would even be true to say that primitive anti-communism is today a typical feature of the sub-cultures of certain provinces, with characteristic sayings which have come into being in the past thirty years. In Estremadura, for instance, pejorative terms like 'you have communist hands' or 'this child has communist hands' [76] have appeared, meaning, respectively, 'you are a thief', 'this child breaks everything he lays his hands on' or 'there's no trusting you'. In the same way, a Galician peasant woman, wishing to complain about a shopkeeper whose prices are too high or whom she thinks dishonest might say: 'He's a communist'. [77]

Many members of the middle and upper classes, particularly older people, retain similar verbal and conceptual reflexes, although they express them with more refinement. Very few have in fact managed to rid themselves of the mental stereotypes stamped on them by one-sided literature which alone has been available to them both during their adolescence and adulthood. Throughout this time communism has been systematically pictured as mendacious and no more than a mask for envy and the vilest ambitions.

One more question arises concerning the unwitting role communist organisations of every hue play in helping to justify the existence of the Franco system. It is this: compared with the other means of coercion and patronage [78] at the disposal of the authorities, how important is the support given to them willy-nilly by one of the most stubborn detachments of the opposition?

The might of the Franco regime's repressive machinery is by no means negligible. It is in fact decisive, the threat or use of force being the *ultima ratio* of authoritarian and totalitarian regimes, in which the political pre-eminence of the forces of coercion is not subjected to any restraint. To prove this case, it is not necessary to dwell at length on the overwhelming protection provided by an omnipresent and efficient police, or on the part played by the civil and military emergency laws and tribunals. [79] It is a fact, however, that these days the Franco state employs deterrent, rather than coercive or penal, methods of repression. Political prisoners, who numbered hundreds of thousands immediately after the war, today total no more than a few hundred, [80] despite a fresh wave of arrests in the Basque country. Capital punishment has become infrequent, as shown by the exceptional stir caused by the execution of Julían Grimau and the eventual reprieve of the men condemned to death at Burgos. Torture, too, is less frequent and, according to some of its victims, less savage. [81]

Moreover, the regime's forces of repression are no stronger in numbers, in relation to the size of the population, than in neighbouring European countries, and the army is less well paid than the armies of Spain's neighbours. In fact in 1968, the Spanish defence budget amounted to only 2·2 per cent of the gross national product — less than that of any other European country except Luxembourg. [82] But none of this means that the regime has achieved a great measure of popularity, nor that it is less authoritarian than one might think. But it does demonstrate that it has created sufficiently solid and broad foundations not to have to resort to extreme methods except on rare occasions. A veiled or explicit threat of repression is often enough to discourage any notions of active opposition, while the systematic maintenance of the fear of change and of communism ensures the passivity required of the mass of the population.

Nevertheless, the communist bogey is losing its usefulness as a justification of the regime's existence, not so much because direct repression has been stepped up, but thanks to the Spanish authorities' greater ability to satisfy the demand for greater material prosperity of those whose support it has not previously been able to solicit. For nearly twenty years, the regime's opportunities in this area were strictly limited by the insolvency of the economy, due to under-development, the destruction wrought by the Civil War, and a more or less deliberate policy of restricting to a minimum changes liable to harm the ruling coalition. For these reasons it has not been possible to solve in a rational and practical manner the problems of the conservative middle classes, despite the fact that they support the governing coalition. All the reward they have received is what G. Germani has called 'surrogate satisfaction', [83] above all in the shape of a state of social stability 'guaranteed' by the regime's hostility to communism.

These sections of society can now be rewarded in a more tangible manner, thanks to a higher standard of living and the greater variety of employment offered by the Spanish economy. They are, moreover, less and less inclined to be satisfied with the symbolic rewards which is all they used to receive in the past.

Several factors have encouraged the middle class to pose new and more specific demands. Perhaps the most important of these factors is the increasingly aloof attitude of the Church towards the Franco regime. The great mass of conservative Catholics is no longer automatically available to Franco. A second factor is the inevitable wear and tear which the Falangist ideals have suffered. Though never put into practice, these ideals were nevertheless preached incessantly until the fifties. Another aspect to be taken into account is the arrival on the scene of a new generation, and the effective example of neighbouring countries now that the frontiers have been opened. Most Spaniards either did not experience the Civil War at all or are too young to remember it. Unlike their parents, they are therefore not attached to the regime by ties of gratitude or by reactionary solidarity, for all that they are members of relatively privileged sections of the population.

Just when the country's rulers became aware of this new situation is hard to tell, but there is no denying that the regime is now going through a period different in kind from its initial stages. Between 1936 and the period 1955–60, Francoism enjoyed the spontaneous support of the Catholics, the wealthy, and of the very many people who continued to nurse ancient grievances against the former republican regime. Little effort was required to retain the loyalty of these groups, which the Franco government could take for granted no matter what happened. All it had to do was to keep alive the fear of the political and social upheaval from which, it said, Spain had not necessarily been 'rescued' for good in 1939.

But the time came when these methods were no longer sufficient to overcome the growing indifference, or even hostility, of the young and of those who considered that the dictatorship had outlived its usefulness and should give way to a government less preoccupied with justifying its own past. Some of the bishops and officials of the Catholic Action, as well as the first representatives of the new technocracy and of Opus Dei, and many executives of the great banks and industrial corporations, seem to have understood at this stage the benefits that could accrue from setting into motion a new process of economic and social modernisation. They also appear to have succeeded in gradually convincing General Franco both of the dangers inherent in the contradiction between a society in the throes of change and an almost ossified political system, and the advantages the regime stands to gain if it can persuade the sections of society most favoured by the country's economic progress to support it more actively.

Accordingly, the authorities are now less concerned with keeping alive negative loyalties nurtured by anti-communism and fears of change, and the regime has not been afraid to make numerous overtures to the members of the Eastern bloc. It has toned down its denunciations of the 'moderate' communists, preferring instead to conjure up a spectre of a leftist menace, posed in particular by the Basque separatists of the ETA. This threat is represented as a danger common to the whole of 'free' Europe, of which Spain is considered to be a part.

The fact that the psychological pressure on Spaniards is now being directed against another target could in a sense help the PCE by moderating the instinctive mistrust it inspires in its political adversaries. Indeed, this new trend could eventually afford the Party more room for manoeuvre, always providing that the persecution to which its members are exposed does really diminish. On the other hand, the immediate effect is to weaken the PCE's unity and influence by transferring to other, more radical, movements the virtual monopoly it used to enjoy in the provision of political training for a working-class élite. Since the end of 1970 the heroes of this struggle against Franco are no longer the communists but the Basque separatists.

## Notes

1 E. Willems, *Dictionnaire de sociologie,* Marcel Rivière, Paris 1961, p. 93.
2 T. Lowi, 'Party, policy and constitution in America' in W. N. Chambers and W. D. Burnham (eds), *The American Party System, Stage of Political Development,* Oxford University Press, Oxford 1967, pp. 238–76.
3 And thus to represent, and to some extent to become integrated in, the political system.
4 G. Lavau, 'Le parti communiste dans le système politique français' in *Le communisme en France*, Armand Colin, Paris 1969, pp. 18–19.

[5] Juan Diz, 'Libertades politicas y socialismo' *Alkarrilketa* 2 (2) [1969], p. 13.

[6] *Le bilan de vingt années de dictature fasciste*, p. 61.

[7] S. Alvarez 'Lenín y el pluripartidismo en el socialismo' *Mundo obrero* 40 (7), 5 April 1970, p. 2.

[8] S. Carrillo, *Nuevos enfoques a problemas de hoy*, p. 179.

[9] J. Diz, op. cit., p. 14. See also S. Carrillo, 'Discurso pronunciado en la Conferencia de los partidos comunistas y obreros de Moscú — Junio 1969' in *Problemas del socialismo*, Editions de la librairie du Globe, Paris 1969, pp. 119—20.

[10] 'Declaración política del comité ejecutivo del PC de España' *Mundo obrero* 37 (10), 1 April 1967, pp. 4—5; 'Declaración del comité ejecutivo del PC de España' *Mundo obrero* 38 (93), 15 December 1967, pp. 4—6; 'Declaración del comité ejecutivo del Partido Comunista de España' *Mundo obrero* 38 (12), 1 June 1968, p. 4.

[11] Ibid., 38 (3), 15 December 1967, p. 5.

[12] S. Carrillo, *Après Franco ... quoi?*, p. 97; 'Santiago Carrillo responde a varias preguntas de *L'Humanité*' *Mundo obrero* 37 (1), 15 April 1965, pp. 4—5.

[13] S. Carrillo, *Après Franco ... quoi?*, p. 122.

[14] S. Carrillo, *Libertad*, p. 61.

[15] 'Declaración del Partido Comunista de España' *Mundo obrero* 39 (15), 2 September 1969, p. 1.

[16] S. Carrillo, *Après Franco ... quoi?*, pp. 132—33. See also 'Problemas de la organización del futuro Estado democrático de España' *Nuestra bandera* 44—45, June 1965, pp. 11—29.

[17] S. Carrillo, *Nuevos enfoques ...* , pp. 175—7.

[18] Ibid., p. 178.

[19] S. Carrillo, *Après Franco ... quoi?*, p. 119.

[20] Ibid., p. 117.

[21] 'Aspectos de la lucha por el socialismo' *Mundo obrero* 39 (18), 22 October 1969, p. 7.

[22] S. Carrillo, *Nuevos enfoques ...* , p. 182.

[23] Ibid., pp. 109—21.

[24] The PCE also recognises Navarre as a 'political and ethnic entity' which should have its own form of government (*Informes y resoluciones del pleno ...* , p. 76).

[25] Economic and Social Councils would also be set up at the regional and autonomous province level.

[26] S. Carrillo, *Après Franco ... quoi?*, pp. 156—7.

[27] Ibid., pp. 94—5.

[28] S. Carrillo, *Nuevos enfoques* ... , pp. 123 and 126.

[29] S. Carrillo, *Après Franco ... quoi?*, 161–2. See also *Nuevos enfoques* ... , pp. 121–2.

[30] *Le bilan de vingt années de dictature franquiste*, pp. 50–1.

[31] S. Carrillo, *Après Franco ... quoi?*, pp. 157–9.

[32] 'Declaración del Partido Comunista de España' *Mundo obrero* 32 (11), June 1962, p. 8.

[33] S. Carrillo, *Discurso ante una asamblea de militantes del Partido*, p. 38

[34] 'Communicado sobre una entrevista de representantes del PCUS y del PC de España' *Nuestra bandera* 56–57, 3rd quarter 1967, pp. 162–3.

[35] 'Declaración común del Partido Comunista de España y el Partido Comunista Marroqui' *Mundo obrero* 28 (7), 15 March 1958, pp. 1–2.

[36] 'La agresión israelo-imperialista a los pueblos árabes' *Nuestra bandera* 54, 2nd quarter 1967, p. 77.

[37] 'Contra la agresión de Israel ¡Solidaridad con la justa causa de los pueblos árabes! Declaración del Partido Comunista de España' *Nuestra bandera* 54, 2nd quarter 1967, p. 162.

[38] S. Carrillo, *Après Franco ... quoi?*, p. 127.

[39] 'Declaración del Partido Comunista de España' *Mundo obrero*, 1 July 1964, p. 3.

[40] S. Carrillo, *Après Franco ... quoi?*, p. 128.

[41] Culminating in the 'pro-Chinese' secessions and the expulsion of F. Claudín.

[42] S. Carrillo, 'La lucha por el socialismo hoy' *Nuestra bandera* 58 (supplement), June 1968, p. 20. Roger Garaudy uses exactly the same terminology as the PCE Secretary-General in his analysis of the 1968 strikes (R. Garaudy, *Pour un modèle français du socialisme*, Gallimard, Paris 1968, pp. 9, 115 and 310).

[43] S. Carrillo, *Après Franco ... quoi?*, pp. 95–6.

[44] E. García, 'Le Parti communiste consolide ses rangs' *Nouvelle revue internationale* 8 (120), August 1968, p. 176.

[45] 'Resolución del comité ejecutivo del Partido Comunista de España' *Mundo obrero* 39 (10), 24 May 1968, p. 3.

[46] 'Santiago Carrillo responde a varias preguntas de L'Humanite' *Mundo obrero* 37 (1); 15 April 1967, p. 5.

[47] '¡Frente al gobierno opusdeista! ¡Ofensiva de las fuerzas obreras y populares! ¡Pacto por la libertad!, *Mundo obrero* 39 (20), 20 November 1968, p. 3.

[48] S. Carrillo, *Nuevos enfoques* ... , p. 115.

[49] J. Echalar, 'Navarra por las libertades democráticas' *Nuestra ban-*

*dera* 53, 1st quarter 1967, pp. 55—6; S. Carrillo, *Nuevos enfoques* ... , pp. 112—13; 'Declaración del comité ejecutivo del Partido Comunista de España' *Mundo obrero* 41 (4) 19 February 1971, p. 2.

[50] 'Por un Partido comunista de masas ...' *Nuestra bandera* 54, 2nd quarter 1967, p, 134.

[51] F. Melchor, 'Comunistas y católicos' *Nuestra bandera* 56—57, 4th quarter 1967 — 1st quarter 1968, p. 90.

[52] Julio, 'La guerra popular es invencible' *Mundo obrero* (m.l.), 2(12) July 1966, p. 8.

[53] '¿Boicot del referendum?' *Vanguardia obrera* 2 (18), November 1966, p. 3.

[54] '¡Votaremos en blanco!' *Mundo obrero* (m.l.) 2 (11), June 1966, pp. 1—7.

[55] Cf. 'El Frente unido' *Mundo obrero* (m.l.), June 1966, pp. 1—7.

[56] 'Espagne: franquisme sur la défensive' *Action* 39, 21 February 1966, p. 3.

[57] J. J. Linz, 'L'opposizione in un regime autoritario, il caso della Spagna' *Storia contemporanea* 1 (1), March 1970, p. 98.

[58] Ibid., p. 85.

[59] Such as the one caused in the spring of 1970 by the general in command of the Staff Academy, who said in a speech at a passing-out parade that the government was not paying officers adequately.

[60] Violent action is mostly the work of young libertarians or the Basques of the ETA rather than of dissident communists.

[61] Discernible, that is, as distinct from the latent function of lending legitimacy to the regime, which the communists fulfil willy-nilly.

[62] For a definition of authoritarian regimes, the distinction between authoritarian and totalitarian governments, and the role of opposition movements in authoritarian regimes, see J. J. Linz, 'An authoritarian regime: Spain' in E. Allardt and I. Littunen (eds) *Cleavages, Ideologies and Party Systems*, the Academic Bookstore, Helsinki 1964, pp. 231—341; A. Inkeles, 'Totalitarianism and ideology' in C. E. Friedrich (ed.), *Totalitarianism*, Harvard University Press, Cambridge 1954, p. 89; G. A. Almond and G. B. Powell, *Comparative Politics*, Little Brown and Co., Boston, Toronto 1966, pp. 217 and 280—84; and M. Duverger, *Institutions politiques et droit constitutionnel*, pp. 389—93. It should be noted, however, that there is no agreement on the conservative, rather than the truly fascist, nature of the Franco regime. Thus, in drawing a distinction between the deeper historic significance and the institutional forms of right-wing totalitarian and authoritarian systems, Gino Germani takes the view that 'the fundamental aims and historical orientation of Franco's regime

are typically fascist'. He maintains, moreover, that until recently the regime had a number of purely authoritarian features. See G. Germani, 'La socializzazione politica dei giovani nei regimi fascisti: Italia e Spagna' *Quaderni di sociologia* 18 (1–2), January, June 1965, p. 16.

[63]    E. Feit uses this expression to describe the ruling coalition on which General Primo de Rivera's dictatorship was based and on which the political system of Ghana is also built. But it seems to us that it applies equally well to Franco Spain (E. Feit, 'The Rule of the "Iron Surgeon". Military government in Spain and Ghana' *Comparative Politics* 1 (4), July 1969, p. 490).

[64]    A survey – quoted in the preceding chapter (see p. 159 above) – shows that 53 per cent of the sample interviewed wanted freedom of expression restored; 62 per cent favoured a return to the party system, and 19 per cent preferred the formula of political associations of the type acceptable to the regime (*Le Monde*, 5 February 1970, p. 5, and *Ya*, 27 March 1970, p. 5). But other opinion polls conducted by the Spanish Institute of Public Opinion among a similar sample indicate that at the end of 1966 only 10 per cent of the upper middle class and 6 per cent of the working class thought that democracy and freedom should be the principal aims of politics. On the other hand, 45 per cent of the former and 59 per cent of the latter thought that what mattered most was domestic peace – in other words, the continuation of the present situation ('Cuestiones de actualidad politica' *Revista española de la opinión pública* 9, July to September 1967, pp. 185–225).

[65]    *Informe de la CIA sobre el P.C. español*, Madrid, 5 June 1970, p. 9.

[66]    'Desarticulación de una organización clandestina en Cádiz' *Ya*, 8 February 1970, p. 11.

[67]    'Les mouvements catholiques laïcs en Espagne' *IDOC international* 3, 1 June 1969, pp. 18–19.

[68]    J. Bardavio, *La estructura del poder en España*, Ibérico Europea de Publicaciones, Madrid 1969, p. 117.

[69]    General Franco did so again in a speech at Valencia on 16 June 1970.

[70]    J. A. Navarro, *Historia de la masonería española*, Ediciones antisectarias, Burgos 1938, pp. 5 and 14.

[71]    *¿Que pasa en España?*, CEDESA, Madrid 1959, unpaginated.

[72]    Communist defectors seem to have been relatively few in number. The best known among those who have openly sided with the regime include Enrique Castro Delgado and Oscar Pérez Solís. The former, appointed member of the Central Committee in 1937, died in Madrid in 1962, on the best of terms with the Falangist leaders, having regularly contributed to the Catholic *Ya* under the pseudonym Jorge Manrique. The

latter, having been Secretary-General of the PCE in 1923 and 1924, died twenty years later in Valladolid, where he became the Grey Eminence of the local Falange.

[73] The daily *Madrid* produced a two-page spread about Sánchez in one of its Sunday supplements. This included an interview with the sculptor's wife, who was presented as having the serenity of one who knows she has done her duty and justified her existence! J. M. Ballester, 'Exiliado en Moscú, Alberto hizo su obra pensando en España' *Madrid domingo*, 13 June 1970, pp. 1–2.

[74] Despite its title, this law has hardly ever been used against Freemasons, few if any of whom have been arrested.

[75] A tribunal set up in 1955 in succession to the 'Special Military Court against Freemasonry and Communism'.

[76] 'Tiene unas manos como un comunista'. 'Este niño tiene las manos como un comunista' (expressions picked up in Estremadura and among rural immigrants on the outskirts of Madrid).

[77] An expression still used by an immigrant Galician domestic in Paris.

[78] Under the heading 'powers of patronage' some authors include both the state's functions of economic redistribution and its role as the dispenser of honours and privileges.

[79] Any explicit criticism of the regime, especially if put in writing and distributed in more than five copies, is liable to land its author before the Public Order Tribunal. The military tribunals remain responsible for dealing with any active displays of opposition, under the 1941 'Decree on Terrorism and Banditry', amended in 1960 and revalidated in 1968.

[80] According to official statistics, the number of persons detained for offences against the internal or external security of the state was 1,143 in 1954, 649 in 1960 and 170 in 1964, while the number of those charged before civil or military courts for the same offences rose to 932 in 1964. (Instituto Nacional de Estadística, *Estadísticas judiciales de España. Año 1964*, Sucesores de Rivadeneyra, Madrid 1965, pp, 12, 101 and 190). Unofficial sources give somewhat higher figures. According to R. Sánchez-Mazas, the number of political prisoners was 1,510 in January 1959. (R. Sánchez-Mazas, 'España encadenada' *Combate*, June 1959, p. 17, quoted by J. J. Linz in L'Opposizione ...' (article quoted above) p. 66). The total is said by B. Welles to have been 611 in December 1962 and 520 in 1964 (B. Welles, *Spain, the Gentle Anarchy* op. cit., p. 188). The communist press spoke of 683 political detainees in 1963, 468 of whom were in Burgos jail ('Relación de los presos políticos existentes en el penal de Burgos ...' *Mundo obrero* 31 (9), 15 April 1961, p. 3; '¡Tomad vuestra causa en vuestras manos!' *Mundo obrero* 31 (24), 1 December 1961, p. 3).

[81]  Miguel Núñez, a communist leader long imprisoned in Spain together with his wife, has stated: 'Although torture is still used in certain circumstances ... there is no doubt that it is difficult nowadays to resort to the worst forms of it'. Cf. S. Vilar, *Protagonistas de la España democrática; La oposición a la dictadura 1939–1969*, p. 241.

[82]  In 1968, the USSR devoted 9·3 per cent of its national product to defence; the USA 9·2 per cent; Portugal 6·2 per cent; Britain and France 5·3 per cent. Italy 2·7 per cent; Belgium 2·4 per cent; and Luxembourg 1 per cent (figures furnished by the Institute of Strategic Studies of London and reproduced in 'Gastos de defensa de diversos países' *Ya*, 23 April 1970, p. 18).

[83]  G. Germani, article cited above, p. 13.

# Conclusion

Any attempt to draw up a balance sheet of the part played by communist movements during the thirty-five years of the Franco dictatorship would entail making a rough summary of the preceding chapters. It might be more worthwhile, therefore, to ask the two questions which would seem basic now that we have arrived at this concluding stage of our study. The first, of interest mainly to 'practitioners' and 'specialists' of politics, concerns the effects on a party of prolonged clandestine existence. The second, which concerns Spaniards in the first place — whether communists or not — concerns the role the PCE and the groups which have broken away from it could play in the various possible contingencies which might ensue upon the demise of the Franco regime.

There is in fact little to add as regards the political part played by the communists in the underground situation in which they have operated for three decades. Relegated to the sidelines by the regime even more completely than the other opposition groups which it could not 'assimilate', the communists stand outside the present political system and exert no influence, open or covert, on it. They cannot even help serving willy-nilly as a justification for the methods employed by the government. Their one important role is to bring up a fresh generation of potential working-class leaders and to keep alive a working-class awareness in Spain. In all other respects, one is almost tempted to agree to the cruel proposition, put forward in a book published some years ago in Spain, that 'Spanish communism has every appearance of being a minority opposition group which runs an agitation and propaganda machine without greatly believing that it has even the slightest chance of success'.[1]

The internal effects within the various communist groups, of an underground life deserve somewhat more comment. By virtue of its long clandestine existence, the PCE typifies the transformations and distortions caused by clandestine activity stretching over many years, if only by the way it has grown almost to take such conditions for granted. The distortion most frequently mentioned nowadays, which applies to most clandestine groups that have both leaders in exile and an organisation in the home country, are the frequent clashes which occur between the émigré Party machine and the militants who have stayed behind. One need only recall in this connection the more or less open crises due to this situation within the Greek and Turkish communist organisations and within some of the similarly constituted national liberation movements in Third World countries. It even looks as if the PCE has been less affected than others by this phenomenon, since it has at least managed to maintain a fairly clear lead within the Spanish communist movement.

Underground life also accentuates the split which nearly always appears to occur in communist movements between the workers on the one hand and the intellectuals on the other. This phenomenon is due both to persecution and to the fragmentation resulting from it for security reasons. Not even minimal contacts between the two sides can be established in the absence of adequate distribution of theoretical and ideological literature, and also because so few cells include elements from different social strata. Cells consisting mainly of workers are for the most part completely isolated, both physically and ideologically, from the little groups of communist students, artists, teachers, doctors or lawyers.[2]

The parallel isolation of the intellectuals is not unconnected with the proliferation of internecine quarrels and divisions which stem from their excessive tendency to indulge in verbal battles and futile speculation. It is true, of course, that the expulsions and splits resulting from this cause are by no means peculiar to clandestine parties. Parties operating in the open also have their dissidents, whose numbers have indeed grown steadily in recent years. But considering how few members the PCE has, it would seem that the groups the Party has expelled, or which have broken away from it, are proportionately larger than in the neighbouring countries, where the communists do not labour under the handicap of illegality. The same was true of the PCE towards the end of the Primo de Rivera dictatorship — during the Party's first clandestine period — and later under the Second Spanish Republic.[3] The same applies today, when the 2,000 dissident communists of all varieties are equal in number to at least ten or fifteen per cent of the PCE's total strength including émigrés, against only one per cent in France and five per cent in Italy.[4]

The PCE's example also shows that underground life tends to aggravate the bureaucratic practices typical of all tightly organised parties. One reason is that the officials and leaders of underground movements, unlike those of overt ones, can never hope to attain public office by election or appointment. They therefore cling even more grimly to their positions in the party hierarchy, which alone give them status and prestige and are a way of life for them.[5]

Underground conditions also make it more difficult to replace the leaders and senior officials at the top of the émigré Party apparatus. With the leading figures of the underground network inside Spain being frequently replaced as a result of arrests and other hazards of persecution, the émigré leaders of old standing are virtually the only ones to have acquired sufficient national and international prestige for their tasks. Most of them were appointed before, or shortly after, the Party went underground and have held on to their offices — not always to the entire satisfaction of the membership — merely because they have no rivals enjoying a reputation comparable to their own.[6]

Let us finally mention another form of adaptation to a clandestine existence, that is characteristic of the PCE but perhaps less marked in other underground communist parties. This is the Spanish communist leaders' chronic propensity to concern themselves less with their Party's role in Spain than with its position in the international communist movement.

It is certainly not surprising that the leaders of small parties, especially when they have to work underground and know that their hold on the population and their activities in their own country are greatly restricted, should find a kind of compensation abroad for their lack of importance at home. However, in the PCE's case this tendency seems to have been aggravated by nostalgia for a former greatness which both officers and rank-and-file militants who went through the Civil War seem to find it hard to forget. Able to do but little in Spain, they save face by keeping an honoured place in the hierarchy of the world's communist parties.

The principal object of the Comintern's care and attention between 1931 and 1938, and later during their Party's first years underground, when they were treated as the equals of the French and the Italians, the Spanish leaders at that time perhaps acquired a strongly international outlook. Later, they sought to repay these favours by giving priority to the slogans of the cold war at the expense of the day-to-day struggle against the Franco regime. While their behaviour towards the USSR may since have altered, they remain just as preoccupied with the international status of their organisation as ever. By taking up a relatively outspoken position among the European parties to have criticised Russia's subjection of Czechoslovakia, maintaining frequent contacts with the Romanian Communist Party and even officially expressing a wish for a reconciliation with the Chinese,[7] as well as establishing contacts with the EDA and the Greek Communist Party within Greece,[8] the PCE is doing more than asserting its independence — it is virtually resorting to a form of blackmail, which is its reaction to the increasingly open hostility of the CPSU and the parties which have stayed loyal to it. One may, however, question the wisdom of these tactics, which have produced reactions dangerous to the Spanish communists. The first of these were the contacts established in Moscow between López Bravo and Kovalyev in January 1970 and the emergency deliveries of Polish coal to Spain during the Asturian miners' strike the same month,[9] quickly followed by Soviet support for Enrique Lister's act of secession — an action which amounted to a direct attack on the PCE.

Our second question, which concerns the part the communists could play in any successor regime, would have seemed somewhat academic only a few years ago, in view of the incontestable, if often deplored, durability of Franco's rule. Today this no longer applies, thanks to the possibilities opened up by the revival of social and political agitation, and even more by the growing probability of General Franco's replacement as Head of State.

Franco, who entered his eighty-second year on 4 December 1973, can not stay in power much longer, if only by reason of his age. Moreover, certain hypotheses about Spain's political future have now become clear-cut and plausible. An official successor was designated in the person of Prince Juan Carlos on the occasion of the proclamation of the Monarchy in July 1969. A law on 'political associations' seems, despite some initial hesitation, about to be promulgated. It may allow, if not the setting up of true parties, at least the establishment of groups which could act as a substitute for them for Spaniards wishing to commit themselves politically, especially should such associations be given an electoral part to play in the selection of members of the Cortes.[10] True, these associations would be formally required to join the *Movimiento* and to subscribe to its basic principles; but, as one Cortes Deputy has put it: 'The principles of the national Movement are open to a variety of interpretations and must not be monopolised by any one group ...'.[11] It is also possible that the proportion of elected members of the Cortes, now only one-fifth,[12] will be increased in future.

These minor changes, taken together, could, if no serious accident occurs to undo them during the next few years, result in the establishment of an authoritarian regime with a democratic facade in the Orleanist manner. Such a 'grey' regime, with a young monarch as its symbol, vaguely liberal and close to an Albert de Mun-style Christian socialism, would also be anxious to retain the support of the army. The latter is likely in future to follow increasingly the ideas of conservatively-minded technocrats. Under such a regime real power would remain in the hands of governments little different from the last ministries of General Franco. A legal opposition would presumably be tolerated, and perhaps even created — as Kemal Atatürk created one. There would thus come into being a degree of consensus between a 'modernist' right wing not far removed from the Opus Dei line, a Falangist element with reformist pretensions, a Christian

Democrat grouping, probably without an explicitly Christian label, and a moderate socialist wing.

Leaving aside the Falangists, whose revolutionary verbiage has long lost all credibility, none of these groups would seriously aim at challenging the *de facto* political supremacy of the economic power-holders; all would basically be appealing, though in somewhat different terms, to the same section of the electorate: the middle class, which has been the main beneficiary of economic progress and of the opening towards Europe. There would almost certainly be less repression and control over the media, and perhaps even a real amnesty. However, the development of trade unionism which is to be expected would only partially offset the political neutralisation of the working class. Such a political structure would — a few details apart — conform to the blueprint drawn up by the most important of the Opus Dei technocrat-ministers, Laureano López Rodó, according to whom 'the number one aim is to reach a per capita income of 1,000 dollars; the rest, whether social or political, will follow naturally'. [13]

Other forecasts for the post-Franco era seem less well-founded, although some could conceivably come true as a result of contingencies which are well within the bounds of possibility. While any idea of the Falange experiencing a genuine revival can be dismissed out of hand, it is by no means difficult to envisage the coming to power of a military regime even more repressive than the present one. Even Falangists of good will might well view such a regime askance. Such a situation could arise as a reaction against the disrepute into which the present government has fallen due to repeated political and financial scandals. Nor would an intervention by the army be inconceivable in the event of worker and student unrest such as might follow Franco's disappearance. It can also not be ruled out — in view of the precedent set by the military when it made its pressure felt prior to the proclamation of the state of emergency in January 1969 — that the army may act even before the Caudillo's formal replacement as Head of State.

There remains the option of democracy, be it of the bourgeois or the socialist variety. For this to come about in either form, social upheavals in Spain or very far-reaching international events, the nature and likelihood of which are equally difficult to foretell exactly, would have to take place. The only international development which might have justified some hope of a restoration of democracy in Spain was the defeat of Fascist Italy and Nazi Germany. But the Franco regime held out, perhaps only because of the hesitation of the victors. In these circumstances, it is difficult to see how a development as gradual and easily controllable as the economic opening towards Europe — which on the face of it ought to be accompanied by an alignment of Spanish political institutions with those of the European Economic Community — could lead to really significant changes. It is far more likely that association with, or even entry into, the Common Market would instead encourage an evolution towards a pseudo-democratic technocratic system, liberal in economic affairs but keeping 'order' in the social and political spheres. Both the myth and the reality of Europe are in fact capable of furnishing, at one and the same time, the ideological justifications, as well as the material advantages, required for the success of such a policy.

As for the likelihood of political and social upheavals far-reaching enough to drive the existing regime into a corner and to offer an opportunity to the republicans, socialists and communists to seize power — in the event of their being able to come to an agreement among themselves — that is even more improbable. The failure of the French effort in 1968, which after all took place under a regime much less skilled in the art of repression than the Spanish one, would appear to confirm this view and the same might be said of the capacity for resistance that the Franco regime has shown in the face of the countless strikes and student troubles the country has witnessed almost without interruption since 1962. In this connection, it would seem that the nationwide reaction to the Burgos trial in 1970 in fact strengthened, rather than weakened, the regime.

Those who hope for some unforeseeable but decisive event — and those to whom that hope is all they have to live for — will of course never rule it out completely. If that hope were to come true, and only then, there might be a place for the PCE in Spanish political life. Of the alternatives to the Franco regime considered here — a 'grey' technocratical-cum-monarchical regime, a military dictatorship, and a new republic — only the last named would be likely to offer the communists an opportunity to regain legal status and to play an acknowledged political part in their own right.

In such a case, the PCE would be one of a probably fairly wide spectrum of parties, which would include national, regional and autonomist groups of various hues. Taking this idea as his point of departure, Linz does not think it too far-fetched to point to the example of Italy after the overthrow of fascism, and suggest that Spaniards might vote in the same way as Italians belonging to the same social categories. The electoral model he has built on these assumptions gives 40·9 per cent of all votes to the communist and socialist left, with 25 per cent of the vote going to the PCE itself, against 36·9 per cent polled by the Italian Communist Party. [14] The Christian Democrats would collect 40·5 per cent of the Spanish vote, compared with 42·4 per cent in Italy.

But for all its ingenuity, and interesting though it is — without even questioning whether electoral attitudes in the two countries can in fact be equated — this method fails to take account of a vital element of uncertainty in the whole situation, namely the anarchists. Yet, this aspect may prove of decisive importance for the communists' hopes of gaining electoral support under a regime which would allow freedom to political parties. Should one assume, as Linz appears to do, that the libertarian tradition is moribund, that it is no longer likely to work against the communist and socialist far left and will not lead to the creation of a rival organisation? Would it not be unwise to underestimate the chances of a revival of the anarchist movement, possibly in a new form? Traces of the anarcho-syndicalist ideology are to be found today in clandestine organisations and trade union bodies purporting to follow a left-wing Christian line. A senior official of the Falangist vertical syndicates declared in 1961 that supporters of anarchism still accounted for 60 per cent of all workers aged over forty, while 30 per cent were socialists and 10 per cent communists. [15]

However, such calculations are in any case academic in present circumstances, in view of the great uncertainty surrounding the prospects for a multi-party democracy which would accord the communists legal status. All the other scenarios for the replacement or transformation of the Franco regime exclude, to all intents and purposes, the possibility of the PCE's legalisation; they do, however, offer Spanish communism some hope of being able to assert itself.

No return to a system allowing for the existence of a multitude of parties including the PCE is imaginable under a post-Franco military dictatorship. Such a development would do nothing, as far as the communists are concerned, to change the situation they have been in since 1939; in fact, their persecution might become even more savage.

On the other hand, if an authoritarian monarchy were to succeed Franco by constitutional means and without a noticeable break, their future, and that of Spain as a whole, might be less daunting. There would in that case, of course, be no question of any legalisation of the PCE as such. However, the introduction of a degree of pluralism, the germ of which is contained in the draft of the Bill on political associations, would probably involve a certain relaxation of the constraints which today apply to clandestine groups. It is even conceivable that the organisational framework offered by the associations — if they ever see the light of day — might at some time allow the launching of a movement, not unlike the Greek EDA or the Turkish Workers' Party, within which communists might be able to play a discreet but lawful part in the political life of their country. The 'grey' regime of which we have spoken would in that event become a little more 'democratic', in the sense that it would no longer completely exclude the working-class masses from political life.

It is in fact not inconceivable that those who wield the reins of economic power might one day wish to find people to speak to who could control the social unrest the police are no longer able to restrain. If that were to happen, the 'protection' offered by a regime which is too authoritarian and unacceptable to the working class would become unnecessary, and even harmful, to the development of the country. The communists would then be tacitly allocated the role of defenders of the underprivileged which they have so long demanded for themselves. They could play this part in the trade union context or within a political association, but in either case they would have to accept the moderating role assigned to them. [16]

## Notes

[1] S. Santiago de Pablo 'El marxismo en los exiliados comunistas españoles' in *Situación y revisión contemporánea del marxismo*, p. 191.

[2] This remark is less applicable to Catalonia and the Party in exile.

[3] In mid-1936, the membership of the POUM was said to be equal to almost one fifth of the PCE's.

[4] According to A. Kriegel, *Les débats théoriques et idéologiques*, Foundation nationale des sciences politiques, Paris 1968, p. 59.

[5] We are not here discussing officials who are tempted away from the Party, since their elective office becomes in any case very precarious the moment they are expelled. This holds true for all countries. We are only considering the normal case of the disciplined official for whom, if his party is a clandestine one, there is no promotion except within the Party itself.

[6] It must be admitted that the leaders dispute that the PCE has become bureaucratic. They point to the size of the Executive Committee, which had twenty members in October 1970, and the Central Committee, which had 111 members at the same date. These are exceptionally large numbers for a clandestine party. They also argue that party officers from Spain itself hold dominant positions in these bodies (see I. Gallego, 'El centralismo democrático en el Partido' *Nuestra bandera* 65, 3rd quarter 1970, pp. 18—24). However, the 'democratic' character of a party is not necessarily measured by the size of its representative bodies but rather by the part these bodies play, especially when, by the very reason of their num-

bers, their members can meet only very rarely and never at full strength.

[7] Cf. Santiago Carrillo's four-hour speech on 19 April 1970 at the Parc des Sports at Ivry to mark the fiftieth anniversary of the PCE.

[8] A meeting took place between EDA and PCE representatives during the first half of January 1970. The Spanish delegation was led by Carrillo. Soon afterwards, *Mundo obrero* mentioned a message addressed to the Spanish Communist Party by the Greek Communist Party within Greece ('El 50 aniversario de nuestro Partido' *Mundo obrero* 40 (10), 25 May 1970, p. 5).

[9] This meeting in Moscow produced a protest from the PCE Executive Committee. Five years earlier, on 31 August 1965, rumours of a resumption of relations between Moscow and Madrid had led to a meeting, between Dolores Ibarruri and Santiago Carrillo on the one hand, and Ponomarev and Suslov on the other, to clarify the matter. In his speech on 19 April 1970, Carrillo condemned the deliveries of Polish coal during the Asturian miners' strike. He also said that the Polish and Hungarian governments had broken promises made to the PCE by restoring consular relations with Spain. But he said nothing about Romania, which had done the same thing.

[10] Though the original draft of the Bill, published late in the spring of 1970, does not assign this function to the political associations, an amendment suggested, by Manuel Fraga Iribarne, the former Minister of Information, does contain such a proposal.

[11] 'Cuatro políticos ante el asociacionismo' *Madrid*, 18 June 1970, p. 12.

[12] 108 'representatives of families' are at present elected by members of the public under the terms of the Constitutional Act of 10 January 1967.

[13] M. Niedergang, 'Vive déception chez les phalangistes après le remaniement ministériel' *Le Monde*, 31 October 1969, p. 2; S. Paniker, *Conversaciones en Madrid*, Editorial Kairos, Barcelona 1970, p. 310.

[14] J. J. Linz 'The Party System of Spain, Past and Future' in S. M. Lipset and S. Rokkan, (eds), *Party Systems and Voter Alignments,* op. cit., pp. 268–71. It should be noted that J. J. Linz's theories are very largely invalidated by the results of a survey, also inspired by the Italian electoral model. (This only dealt with bank staff, on the basis of a national sample of 1,117 employees.) Answering a question about the party they would choose if they found themselves in the position of an Italian voter, only 1·3 per cent of those interviewed answered that they would vote communist. This compares with 36·4 per cent favouring the Christian Democrats; 18·7 per cent the Social Democrats; 8·2 per cent the left-wing socialists; 5 per cent the Liberals; 2·7 per cent the monarchists; and 0·9 per cent the

neo-fascists. Of those questioned, 6·7 per cent would have abstained; 16·1 per cent did not know for whom to vote, and 3·5 per cent refused to answer. A less directly personal question, i.e. which political group enjoyed the sympathy of the colleagues of the person questioned, did not show any significant increase in the number of communist sympathisers, which was a mere 2·3 per cent. ('Actitudes socialistas entre los empleados de la banca' *Mundo social* 180, 20 September 1970, pp. 25—6.) On the other hand, in a recent nationwide poll, publication of which was forbidden, 40·9 per cent of the people questioned answered that they supported the communists and left-wing socialists, four per cent the Social Democrats, 40·5 per cent the Christian Democrats and 13 per cent the Liberals.

[15] Quoted by B. Welles *Spain, the Gentle Anarchy*, p. 211. The same senior Falangist asserts that at the time of the official elections to the syndicates in 1957, half those elected were former militants of the CNT and UGT. He also thought that 2,000 of the 400,000 delegates elected in 1960 were 'known communists' (p. 131).

[16] The PCE is officially opposed to the draft Bill on political associations 'Después de Burgos' *Mundo obrero* 41 (4), 19 February 1971, p. 2).

# Bibliography

The documents here listed represent a selected choice, except for list no. 3, in which we tried to include the largest possible number of studies dealing specifically with the history or present condition of the Spanish communist movement. By contrast, the other lists include only a small proportion of the works we could have quoted. Only those which contain a substantial amount of information on the subject, as well as those which in our judgement are the most important — either by virtue of their content or because they typify a source used in a particular field (this applies particularly to lists 1, 9, 10 and 11) — are mentioned below. The documents are listed in the alphabetical order of their authors or, if anonymous, in alphabetical order of titles. French translations of publications in Spanish or English have been preferred to the original texts, insofar as they exist and we are aware of their existence.

## 1. General studies and articles on the Spanish working-class movement, the Spanish Second Republic and the Civil War*

Bécarud, Jean, and Lapouge, Gilles, *Anarchistes d'Espagne*, Collection 'R', André Balland, Paris 1970, 164 pp.

Bolloten, Burnett, *The Grand Camouflage, The Spanish Civil War and Revolution* (introduction by H. R. Trevor Roper), The Pall Mall Press, London 1968, XII + 350 pp.

Brenan, Gerald, Spanish Labyrinth, Cambridge University Press 1950.

Broué, Pierre, and Témime, Emile, *La Révolution et la guerre d'Espagne*, Les Editions de Minuit, Paris 1961, 544 pp.

Bullejos, José: *España en la Segunda República*, Difusión Ruedo ibérico, Mexico 1967, 183 pp.

Claudín, Fernando, *La crisis del movimiento comunista, I: De la Komintern al Kominform*, Ruedo ibérico, Paris 1970, 704 pp.

Delperrie de Bayac, Jacques, *Les Brigades internationales*, A. Fayard, Paris 1968, 472 pp.

* Publications including a substantial number of pages dealing with the Spanish communists.

211

Díaz del Moral, Juan, *Historia de las agitaciones campesinas andaluzas* (*El libro de bolsillo* 68) Alianza Editorial, Cordoba, Madrid 1967, 510 pp. New edition of an older work.

Ercoli, M. (Palmiro Togliatti), *The Spanish Revolution*, Workers' Library Publisher, New York 1936, 112 pp.

*Guerra y revolución en España 1936—1939, Obra realizada por una comisión presidida por Dolores Ibarruri e integrada por Manuel Azcárate, Luis Balaguer, Antonio Cordón, Irene Falcón y José Sandoval*, 2 vols Editorial Progreso, Moscow 1966, 320 and 296 pp.

Jackson, Gabriel, *The Spanish Republic and the Civil War 1931—1939*, Princeton Paperbacks, Princeton University Press, Princeton 1965, XIV + 578 pp.

Jutglar, Antoni, 'Notas para la historia del socialismo en España' *Revista de Trabajo* 7 (3), 1964, pp. 21—47.

Lamberet, Renée, *Mouvements ouvriers et socialistes (Chronologie et bibliographie). L'Espagne (1750—1936)*, Les éditions ouvrières, Paris 1953, 207 pp.

Longo, Luigi, *Le brigate internazionali in Spagna*, Editori Riuniti, 1956, XXIV + 409 pp.

Lorenzo, César M., *Les anarchistes espagnols et le pouvoir, 1868—1969*, Editions du Seuil, Paris 1969, 431 pp.

Maurín, Joaquín: Revolución y contrarevolución en España, *Ruedo ibérico*, 1966, 290 pp. Contains an additional chapter on the origins of communism in Spain, in addition to the material in the 1935 and 1957 editions.

Mintz, Frank, *L'autogestion dans l'Espagne révolutionnaire*, Bélibaste, Paris 1970, 190 pp.

Nenni, Pietro, *La Guerre d'Espagne*, (translated from the Italian by Jean Beaumier: (*Cahiers libres* 1—2) F. Maspero, Paris 1959, 297 pp.

Ramos Oliveira, Antonio, *Historia de España*, 3 vols Compania general de ediciones, Mexico 1952, 639, 652 and 647 pp.

Thomas, Hugh, *Histoire de la guerre d'Espagne*, 2 vols, (*Le livre de poche* 2191—2192), Robert Laffont, Paris 1961, 448 and 542 pp.

Trotsky, Leon, *Ecrits 1928—1940,* vol III, P. Frank, Paris 1959, 581 pp.

Trotsky, Leon, *Leçon d'Espagne*, Collection marxiste, Pionniers, Paris 1946, 77 pp.

## 2 General information on groups opposed to the Franco regime

Blanc, Jacques, and Gabel, André, 'Un syndicalisme de classe: les CO' *Le*

*Semeur* 1, 1967—1968, pp. 108—17. Deals with the workers' committees.

Cerón, Julio, 'El Frente de Liberación Popular ha sido la gran oportunidad de los últimos años' *Cuadernos de Ruedo ibérico* 13—14, July—September 1967, pp. 201—3.

Dessens, André: 'Les tendances politiques et le régime' *Articles et documents 1919—1920*, 30 August—6 September 1968, pp. 9—12. Translation of an article by José Antonio Valverde: 'Estos son los cerebros de las corrientes políticas' *Actualidad española* 854, 16 May 1968.

Flores, Xavier, 'El exilio y España' in *Horizonte español 1966* vol. II, Ediciones Ruedo ibérico, Paris 1966, pp. 29—38.

Fuentes, Enrique, 'La oposición antifranquista de 1939 a 1955' in *Horizonte español 1966* vol. II, Ediciones Ruedo ibérico, Paris 1966, pp. 1—28.

Gallo, Max, *Histoire de L'Espagne franquiste*, Robert Laffont, Paris 1969, 493 pp.

'Groupes ètudiants et politiques' *Le Semeur* 1, 1967—1968, pp. 56—9. Key to the abbreviations of names of organisations.

Hermet, Guy, 'Les Espagnols devant leur régime' *Revue française de science politique* 20 (1), February 1970, pp. 5—36.

Linz, Juan J., 'An Authoritarian regime: Spain' in Erik Allardt and Yryö Littunen (eds), *Cleavages, Ideologies and Party Systems*, the Academic Bookstore, Helsinki 1964, pp. 291—341.

Linz, J. J., 'L'opposizione in un regime autoritario: il caso della Spagna' *Storia contemporanea*, 1 (1 and 2), March and June 1970, pp. 63—102 and 219.

Payne, Stanley G., *Franco Spain*, Thomas Y. Crowell, New York 1967, XVIII + 142 pp.

Raymond, J., 'Limites des oppositions politiques' *Le Semeur* 1, 1967—1968, pp. 9—24.

Ridruejo, Dionisio, *Escrito en España* Editorial Losada, Buenos Aires 1962, 253 pp.

Semprún, Jorge, 'La oposición política en España: 1956—1966' *Horizonte español 1966* vol. II, Ediciones Ruedo ibérico, Paris 1966, pp. 39—55.

Vilanova, Antonio, *Los olvidados: los exilados españoles en la segunda guerra mundial*, Ruedo ibérico, Paris 1968, 432 pp.

Welles, Benjamin, *Spain, the Gentle Anarchy*, F. A. Praeger, New York 1965, 386 pp.

Wingeate Pike, David, *Vae Victis, Los republicanos españoles refugiados en Francia, 1939—1944*, Ruedo ibérico, Paris 1969, 140 pp.

## 3  History of the communist movement in Spain: studies dealing with Spanish communist organisations*

Adam, Michel, *Etude sur les thèmes de l'opposition communiste en Espagne de 1945 à 1963*, Paris, 1965, 353 pp. multigr. Mémoire DES science politique, under the direction of M. Duverger.

Bahne, Siegfried: *Origine et débuts des partis communistes des pays latins (1919–1923)* (*The Jules Humbert-Droz Archives* vol. I) D. Reidel Publishing Co., Dordrecht 1969, 620 pp.

Cattell, David T., *Communism and the Spanish Civil War* (University of California publications on international relations no. 4), University of California Press, Berkeley, Los Angeles, 1955, XII + 290 pp.

Comín, Colomer, Eduardo, *Historia del Partido comunista de España, Abril 1920–Febrero 1936. Primera etapa*, 2 vols, Editora nacional, Madrid 1967, XVI + 652 and 765 pp.

García Palacios, Luis, *Los dirigentes del Partido Comuniste al desnudo*, Imprenta de Juan Puevo, Madrid 1931, 63 pp. A pamphlet attacking the PCE and its Secretary-General at the time, Jose Bullejos.

*Historia del Partido Comunista de España*, Editions sociales, Paris 1960, 287 pp.

*Historia del Partido Comunista de España (Versión abreviada)*, Editora política, Havana 1964, 285 pp.

Lazitch, Branko, *Les partis communistes d'Europe. 1919–1955*, Les Iles d'Or, Paris 1956, 255 pp. Written by a militant anti-communist.

Lazitch, Branko, 'Les écoles de cadres du Komintern' in J. Freymond (ed.), *Contributions à l'histoire du Komintern*, Droz, Geneva 1965, pp. 111-27.

Linz, Juan, 'The Party System of Spain: past and future' in Seymour Martin Lipset, and Stein Rokkan (eds), *Party Systems and Voter Alignments*, The Free Press, New York 1967, pp. 197–282. The last few pages contain a study of the PCE.

Martín López, Enrique, 'Análisis de contenido de la declaración del Partido Comunista de España (Junio de 1964)' *Revista de Trabajo* 8 (4) 1964, pp. 181–233.

Pestaña, Angel, *Consideraciones y juicios acerca de la Tercera Internacional*, Editorial ZYX, Santiago de Chile, Madrid 1968, 49 pp. (*Colección Lee y Discute* 37) Published version of a report by a leading anarchist on the Second Congress of the Comintern.

* Confidential papers produced by police or intelligence services, such as the CIA, are not listed here.

Santiago de Pablo, Luis, 'El marxismo en los exiliados comunistas españoles' in *Situación y revisión contemporánea del marxismo*, (*Anales de moral social y económica* 13) Centro de estudios sociales de la Santa Cruz del Valle de los Caídos, Madrid 1966, pp. 175–92.

Sorel, Andrés, *Búsqueda, reconstrucción e historia de la guerrilla española del siglo XX, a través de sus documentos, relatos y protagonistas*, Colección Ebro, Editions de la Librairie du Globe, Paris 1970, 253 pp.

'Spain' in *Yearbook on International Communist Affairs*, The Hoover Institution on War, Revolution and Peace, University of Stanford, Stanford 1967, pp. 144–8.

## 4 First-hand accounts, memoirs, interviews

Castro Delgado, Enrique, *J'ai perdu la foi à Moscou* (translated and adapted from the Spanish by Jean Talbot), Gallimard, 1950, 352 pp.

Ehrenburg, Ilya, *Corresponsal en España*, Editorial Tiempo contemporáneo, Buenos Aires 1968, 213 pp.

El Campesino, General [Valentín González], *La vie et la mort en URSS (1939–1949)* (as told to Julian Gorkin; translated by Jean Talbot), Les Iles d'Or, Librairie Plon. Paris 1950, 222 pp.

'(L') Express va plus loin avec Jorge Semprún' *L'Express*, 8–14 December 1969.

Fischer, Louis, *Men and Politics, an Autobiography*, Jonathan Cape, London 1941, 639 pp.

Gudell, Martín, *Lo que oí en la URSS*, Ediciones estudios sociales, Mexico 1946, 401 pp. Account of a journey to the USSR by a CNT delegation towards the end of 1936.

Hernández, Jesús, *La grande trahison* (translated by Pierre Berthelin), Flasquelle, Paris 1953, 255 pp.

Hidalgo de Cisneros, Ignacio, *Virage sur l'aile (souvenirs)* (translated from the Spanish by L. Viñas), Les Editeurs français réunis, Paris 1965, 415 pp. Memoirs of a communist general.

Humbert-Droz, Jules, *L'oeil de Moscou à Paris*, (*Archives* 2) Julliard, Paris 1964, 269 pp.

Ibarruri, Dolores, *Mémoires de La Pasionaria* (*El único camino*; translated from the Spanish by François-Marie Rosset), R. Julliard, Paris 1964, 445 pp.

Koltsov, Mikhail, *Diario de la Guerra de España*, Ruedo ibérico, Paris 1966, 486 pp.

Krivitsky W. G., *I Was Stalin's Agent*, Hamish Hamilton, London 1939, 297 pp.

215

Lister, Enrique, *Nuestra guerra*, Editions de la Librairie du Globe, Paris 1966, 299 pp.

Martínez Prieto, Horacio, *Facetas de la URSS*, Madrid 1933, 194 pp. Account of a journey to the USSR in 1933 by an anarchist militant.

Mora, Constancia de la, *Fière Espagne, Souvenirs d'une républicaine* (translated from the Spanish by C. Dalsace and L. Viñas), Editions Hier et aujourd'hui, Paris 1949, 448 pp. Memoirs of a communist aristocrat.

Núñez, Mercedes, *Cárcel de Ventas*, (Colección Ebro), Editions de la Librairie du Globe, Paris 1967, 104 pp.

Paniker, Salvador, *Conversaciones en Madrid*, Editorial Kairos, Barcelona 1970, 369 pp. See particularly the interviews with Ramón Tamames, J. L. Aranguren, E. Tierno Galván, M. Fraga Iribarne.

Pestaña, Angel, *Informe de mi estancia en la URSS, (Documentos para la historia obrera) (Colección Lee y Discute* 29), Editorial ZYX, Santiago de Chile, Madrid 1968, 52 pp. Published version of the report which gave the reasons for ending the CNT's short-lived membership of the Communist International.

Prieto, Indalecio, *Cómo y porqué salí del Ministerio, Intrigas de los Rusos en España*, Imprimerie nouvelle, Paris 1939, 84 pp.

Razola, Manuel, and Constante, Mariano, *Triangle bleu. Les Républicains espagnols à Mauthausen, 1940—1945*, Collection Témoins, Gallimard, Paris 1969 196 pp.

Ríos, Fernando de los, *Mi viaje a la Rusia sovietista*, Alianza editorial, Madrid 1970, 256 pp. A new edition of the report submitted by the leader of the socialist majority opposed to membership of the Communist International after his return from Moscow in 1921.

Rodríguez Chaos, Melquesidez, *24 años en la cárcel*, Colección Ebro, Editions de la Librairie du Globe, Paris 1968, 253 pp.

Rojo, Vicente J., *Así fué la defensa de Madrid (Colección ancho mundo* 21) Editorial Era, Mexico 1967, 267 pp.

Sanz, Gonzalo, 'Recuerdo de aquellos días', *Mundo obrero* 217, 13 April 1950, p. 20. The establishment of the original two Communist Parties as rememembered by a veteran militant.

*(Le) Stalinisme en Espagne* (Testimonies by revolutionary militants rescued from Stalin's jails. Collected by Katia Landau. Preface by Alfred Rosmer.) (*Spartacus*, monthly booklets, new series, 11) Cerbonnet, Paris (no date), 48 pp. Souvenirs of POUM militant and communist dissident survivors of Spanish republican prisons and concentration camps.

Vilar, Sergio, *Protagonistas de la España democrática. La oposición a la dictadura 1939—1969 (Depositario: Librería española, Paris)*, Ediciones sociales, Barcelona, Paris, Madrid 1969, 745 pp. Series of interviews with members of clandestine opposition groups.

## 5 Official or semi-official PCE documents published since 1964 (Programmes, reports of meetings and policy statements; books, articles, statements and speeches by the Party's leaders)

'(La) Agresión israelo-imperialista a los pueblos árabes', *Nuestra bandera* 54, 2nd quarter, 1967, pp. 73–7.

Alvarez, Santiago, 'Le Parti communiste et le mouvement ouvrier' *Nouvelle revue internationale* 3 (103), March 1967, pp. 111–25.

Alvarez, S., 'Del encuentro de Budapest a la conferencia de Moscú' *Nuestra bandera* 58, 3rd quarter 1968, pp 75–9.

Alvarez, S., 'L'alliance des catholiques et des communistes' *Nouvelle revue internationale* 9, September 1968, pp. 125–44.

Antón, Francisco, 'Notre travail à la campagne' *Nouvelle revue internationale* 3 (103), March 1967, pp. 126–34.

Antón, F., 'Une alternative démocratique à la dictature franquiste' *Nouvelle revue internationale* 3 (115), March 1968, pp 118–25.

Azcárate, Manuel, 'Realidades españolas en el diálogo cristiano-marxista' *Nuestra bandera* 54, 2nd quarter, 1967, pp. 107–11.

Azcárate, M., 'Práctica y teoría en el diálogo católico-marxista' *Realidad* 14, July 1967, pp 35–47.

*(Le) Bilan de vingt ans de dictature fasciste, les tâches immédiates de l'opposition et l'avenir de la démocratie espagnole*, Rivet, Limoges 1959, 84 pp.

[Carrillo]: *Informe sobre problemas de organización y los estatutos del Partido. Presentado por el camarada Santiago Carrillo (V° Congreso del Partido Comunista de España)*, No place, date or pagination. Contains the text of the Party statutes, only slightly amended in 1960.

Carrillo, Santiago, *Sobre algunos problemas de la táctica de lucha contra el franquismo*, no place, 1961, 30 pp.

[Carrillo], *La situación en el movimiento comunista. Informe presentado por el camarada Santiago Carrillo. Pleno ampliado del Comité central del PC de E*, November 1963, French Communist Party, Paris 1964, 47 pp. Diatribe against the faction led by F. Claudín.

Carrillo, S., *Discurso ante una asamblea de militantes del Partido (19 de abril de 1964)*, French Communist Party, Paris 1964, 48 pp.

Carrillo, S., *Después de Franco ¿que?, La democracia política y social que preconizamos los comunistas*, Editions sociales, Paris 1965, 173 pp.

Carrillo, S., *Après Franco ... quoi?* (translated from the Spanish), Editions sociales, Paris 1966, 191 pp. Translation of the last-mentioned work.

Carrillo, S., *Nuevos enfoques a problemas de hoy*, Editions sociales, Paris 1967, 205 pp.

Carrillo, S., 'Cuba, marzo 1968' *Nuestra bandera* 58, 2nd quarter 1968, pp. 49—74.

Carrillo, S., 'La lucha por el socialismo hoy' *Nuestra bandera* (supplement to no. 58) June 1968, 48 pp. Reflections on the events in France in May 1968.

Carrillo, S., 'Más problemas actuales del socialismo' *Nuestro bandera* 59, 1968, pp. 41—53. The PCE's position after the invasion of Czechoslovakia.

Carrillo, S., *Cuba 68*, Colección Ebro, Editions de la Librairie du Globe, Paris 1968, 72 pp.

Carrillo, S., ¡Libertad! *Nuestra bandera* 60, December 1968—January 1969, pp. 6—11. The covenant for freedom.

Carrillo, S., *La lucha por el socialismo hoy. Más problemas actuales del socialismo. Sobre el conflicto chino-soviético. Discurso pronunciado en la Conferencia de los partidos comunistas y obreros de Moscú — Junio 1969*, Editions de la Libraire du Globe, Paris 1969, 128 pp. See particularly the last text.

Carrillo, S., 'La democracia en el Partido leninista' *Mundo obrero* 40 (7), 5 April 1970, p. 6.

Carrillo, S., 'Libertad y socialismo', Editions sociales, Paris 1971, 104 pp. Report to the September 1970 Central Committee plenum.

'Coloquio sobre los problemas de la universidad' *Realidad* 10, June 1966, pp. 5—45.

'Conférence de presse de Santiago Carrillo à Rome' *L'Humanité*, 14 February 1969, p. 2.

'Contra la agresión de Israel: Solidaridad con la justa causa de los pueblos árabes! Declaración del Partido Comunista de España' *Nuestra bandera* 54, 2nd quarter 1967, pp. 135—47.

'(Une) Déclaration du Parti Communiste d'Espagne' *L'Humanité*, 7 September 1968, p. 3. Condemnation of the Soviet forces' intervention in Czechoslovakia.

Diz, Juan, 'Le Parti communiste dans les universités' *Nouvelle revue internationale* 3 (103), March 1967, pp. 135—47.

Diz, J., 'Libertades políticas y socialismo' *Alkarrilketa* 2 (2) pp. 13—15.

*Dos meses de huelga*, French Communist Party, Paris 1962, 189 pp.

*(Un) Futuro para España: la democracia económica y politica. Prólogo de*

218

*Santiago Carrillo*, Colección Ebro, Editions de la Librairie du Globe, Paris 1967, 325 pp.

García, Eduardo, 'En torno a una auténtica política de reclutamiento' *Nuestra bandera* 3, 1st quarter 1967, pp. 106–11.

García, E., 'Une avant-garde dans la lutte du peuple' *Nouvelle revue internationale* 3 (103), March 1967, pp. 100–10.

García, E., 'Le Parti communiste consolide ses rangs' *Nouvelle revue internationale* 8 (120), August 1968, pp. 169–83.

[Ibarruri], *Informe del Comité central presentado por la camarada Dolores Ibarruri, (V° Congreso del PC de España)* French Communist Party 1954, 125 pp.

*Informes y resoluciones del pleno del Comité central del Partido Comunista de España (Agosto de 1956)*, Ediciones Boletín de Información, Prague 1956, 281 pp. De-stalinisation in the PCE.

Lister, Enrique, *El pueblo español lucha por la paz*, Colección Ebro, Editions de la Librairie du Globe, Paris 1968, 109 pp. The struggle against the American bases.

M. A. [Manuel Azcarate], 'Aspectos del diálogo católico-marxista' *Realidad* 11–12, November–December 1966, pp. 5–23.

'Más de 40 millones recaudados en la campaña de los treinta millones' *Mundo obrero* 39 (15), 2 September 1969, pp 4–6.

Melchor, Federico, 'Comunistas y católicos' *Nuestra bandera* 56–77, 4th quarter 1967 – 1st quarter 1968, pp. 83–92.

Mije, Antonio, 'La educación y la práctica internacionalista del PC de España' *Nuestra bandera* 60, December 1968 – January 1969, pp. 29–33.

'Nuestro programa. Por una república democrática' *Mundo obrero* 24 (2), 31 December 1954, p 2.

'(Le) Parti communiste d'Espagne appelle à la riposte populaire et nationale' *L'Humanité*, 30 January 1969, p. 3. PCE declaration on the state of emergency.

Pla, Nuria, 'Juventud: lo pro-soviético y lo anti-soviético' *Nuestra bandera* 59, 3rd quarter 1968, pp. 29–31. After the invasion of Czechoslovakia.

'Por un Partido comunista de masas. Resolución del CE del PC de España' *Nuestra bandera* 54, 2nd quarter 1967, pp. 123–41.

*Programa del Partido Comunista de España ... (V° Congreso del Partido comunista de España)*, French Communist Party Paris 1955, 31 pp.

'¿Qué hay tras la inmolación de Jan Palach?' *Mundo obrero* 39 (3), 5 February 1969, p. 7.

219

'Resolución del Comité Ejecutivo del Partido comunista de España: *Mundo obrero* 39 (10), 24 May 1969, pp. 1–8. The covenant for freedom.

Sangre obrera sobre el Amur' *Mundo obrero* 39 (7), 3 April 1969, p. 8. The Sino–Soviet confrontation.

Suárez, Victor, 'Les commissions ouvrières en Espagne' *Nouvelle revue internationale* 2 (126), February 1969, pp 133–53.

[Uribe], *Informe sobre el programa del Partido presentado por el camarada Vicente Uribe (V° Congreso del Partido Comunista de España)*, no place, date or pagination.


## 6.  PCE documents first published before 1954

Antón, Francisco, 'El programa de la victoria sobre el franquismo' *Mundo obrero* 217, 13 April 1950, pp. 10–11. The programme approved at the 1945 Central Committee plenum.

Carrillo, Santiago, 'Por la República y la legalidad constitucional: todos unidos a la lucha' *España popular*, no place, 1945, 15 pp.

Carrillo, S., *Los niños españoles en la URSS. Conferencia pronunciada por el camarada Santiago Carrillo ... el dia 6 de septiembre de 1947 ...* , Publicaciones *Mundo obrero*, (supplement no. 89) Paris, II + 31 pp.

Checa, Pedro, *Qué es y cómo funciona el Partido comunista (Algunas normas de organización), Con los estatutos del PC de España*, Ediciones Mundiales, Madrid 1936, 32 pp.

'Declaración del secretariado del Partido Socialista Unificado de Cataluña sobre la conducta política de Juan Comorera' *Mundo obrero* 195, 10 November 1949, p. 2.

Díaz, José, *Nuestra bandera del Frente Popular*, Ediciones Europa-America, Madrid, Barcelona 1936, 144 pp. Speeches, articles.

Díaz, José, *Tres años de lucha. Por el Frente Popular, por la libertad, por la independencia de España*, Ediciones Europa-America, Paris 1939, 703 pp. Speeches, articles. Reissued 1970.

Gallego, Ignacio, 'Salvaguardar al Partido de los zarpazos del enemigo' *Mundo obrero* 217, 13 April 1950, p. 12. The 'traitors' of the Stalinist era.

Ibarruri, Dolores, *En la lucha. I: Palabras y hechos 1936–1939*, Editorial Progreso, Moscow 1968, 368 pp. Speeches and articles published in *Mundo obrero* and *Frente rojo*.

Modesto, Juan, 'Progreso y perspectivas del movimiento guerrillero (Intervención ... en el III° pleno del Partido Comunista de España en Francia, celebrado en París los días 19, 20, 21 y 22 de marzo de 1947), *Nuestra bandera*, no date, 14 pp.

'Por una España republicana, democrática e independiente. Las sesiones del III° pleno del PC de E en Francia' *Mundo obrero* 59, 27 March 1947, pp. 1–4.

Soria, Georges, *Trotskyism in the Service of Franco, Facts and documents on the Activities of the POUM*, International Publishers, New York, 48 pp. Attempted justification of what was done to the 'Trotskyites' of the POUM.

Uribe, Vicente, 'Todos unidos por la reconquista de la república (Discurso pronunciado en Méjico el 29 de enero de 1945)' *España popular*, no date, 13 pp.


## 7   Recent documents published by dissident communist organisations or individuals (since 1960)

*Adulteraciones del equipo de Santiago Carrillo (Segunda edición aumentada)*, Ediciones *Vanguardia obrera*, Madrid no date, 243 pp. Maoist pamphlet.

'Carta sin respuesta' *Mundo obrero (M.L.)* 2 (11), June 1966, pp. 4–5. Attack on the PCE by another pro-Chinese group.

Claudín, Fernando, 'Dos concepciones de la vía española al socialismo' in *Horizonte español 1966*, vol. II, Ediciones Ruedo Ibérico, Paris 1966, pp. 59–100.

Claudín, Fernando, *El subjetivismo de la política del Partido comunista de España (1956–1964)*, ENP del PCE (ML), Madrid, no date, 88 pp. The Claudín report, as published by the PCE (ML).

'El Frente Unido' *Mundo obrero (ML)* 2 (11), June 1966, pp. 1–7. Tactics advocated by the Marxist-Leninists.

Julius, 'La izquierda socialista y el Partido Comunista' *Cuadernos de Ruedo ibérico* 12, April–May 1967, pp. 112–14.

'Materiales del II° Pleno del Comité Central del Partido comunista de España (ML)' *Revolución Española* 4, 1st quarter 1968, pp. 1–145.

Naranco, Juan, 'La agricultura y el desarrollo económico español' *Cuadernos de Ruedo ibérico* 13–14, June–September 1967, pp. 6–46. 'Claudinist' criticism of the PCE's programme for agriculture.

Partit socialista unificat de Catalunya (Executive Committee), *Aportació a la historia política social i nacional de la clase obrera de Catalunya*, Publicacions Treball Modern, Paris, no date, 46 pp. 'Comorerist' version of the 1949–1950 PSUC crisis.

Prieto, Carlos, 'La tactique du Parti communiste a contribué a l'affaiblissement des commissions ouvrières' *Le Monde*, 18 February 1970, p. 5.

'Sobre la lucha de clases y la insurrección armada' *Mundo obrero (Internacional)*, December 1968, pp. 13–16. Programme of one of the most recent dissidents, See also '¿Existe el partido de la clase obrera?' and 'La línea divisoria' in the same issue pp. 1–7 and 7–13.


## 8 Biographies of leaders; profiles of militants*

*Crime ou châtiment? Documents inédits sur Julian Grimau García,* Madrid 1963, II + 126 pp. Julian Grimau, according to Franco's propaganda.

Dolores Ibarruri *Nuestra bandera* 5, April 1950, pp. 245–65.

'José Díaz, *Nuestra bandera* 5, April 1950, pp. 227–43.

Pla, Nuria, 'José Díaz (1895–1942)' *Nuestra bandera* 53, 1st quarter 1967, pp. 115–46.

'Respuestas ...' *Nuestra bandera* 55, 3rd quarter 1967, pp. 69–76. Concise biographies and character sketches of some militants.

Velarde Fuertes, Juan, 'Enrique Castro Delgado (1906–1965' *Revista de Trabajo 8* (4), 1964, pp. 237–40.


## 9. Reminiscences, novels

Alvarez de Toledo, Isabel [Duchess of Medina Sidonia], *La grève* (translated from the Spanish by L. Vergnes), Bernard Grasset, Paris 1970, 275 pp.

Goytisolo, Juan: *Pièces d'identité* (translated by M. E. Coindreau), Collection du monde entier, Gallimard, Paris 1968, 379 pp.

Izcaray, Jesús, 'Las guerrillas de Levante' *Mundo obrero*, 4 September to 13 November 1947.

Izcaray, Jesús, '30 días con los guerrilleros de Levante' *Mundo obrero*, 6 May to 26 August 1948.

Izcaray, Jesús, *Las ruinas de la muralla*, Colleción Ebro, Editions de la Librairie du Globe, Paris 1965, 273 pp.

Ramírez, Luis, *Nuestros primeros veinticinco años*, Ruedo ibérico, Paris 1964, 295 pp.


* See also S. Vilar's book in list no. 4.

## 10. Marxism in Spain; Catholics and Marxism

Aranguren, José Luis L., *El Marxismo como moral, (El libro de bolsillo 10)* Alianza Editorial, Madrid 1968, 191 pp.

'Del diálogo a la lucha revolucionaria. Entrevista con el Padre José María Gonzáles Ruiz, *Cuadernos de Ruedo ibérico* 12, April—May 1967, pp. 43—4.

Díaz, Elías, 'La filosofía marxista en el pensamiento español actual' *Cuadernos para el diálogo* 63, December 1968, pp. 9—13.

Ramírez Molina, Eulogio, '¿Anticomunista el cristiano?' *Cuadernos para el diálogo* 55, April 1968, p. 29.

Velarde Fuertes, Juan, 'Una nota acerca de Trotsky y sus ideas sobre la realidad económica y social de España' *Revista de Trabajo* 8 (4), 1964, pp. 29—38. Trotsky's ideas examined by a trade unionist on the left wing of the Falangist movement.

## 11. Miscellaneous documents on the political attitudes of the Spanish public *

Aguilo, Federico, *Emigration et syndicalisme*, Dossiers 'Masses ouvrières', Les Editions ouvrières Paris 1968, 72 pp.

'Cuestiones de actualidad política' *Revista española de la opinión pública 9*, July—September 1967, pp. 187—225.

'Informe sobre España' *Mundo* 1566, 9 May 1970, pp. 11—14. How political public opinion surveys are carried out in Spain. Comprehensive results of a large-scale poll of this kind.

*Mañana votará el 67 por 100 del censo. Se quiere votar y no se sabe a quién*, Madrid, 19 November 1966, pp. 3—4. See also *Análisis de unas elecciones. Influencia de la propaganda del factor religioso y de la ocupación*, Madrid, 21 November 1966, p. 3; *No hay voto sin información. Participación en las últimas elecciones*, Madrid, 25 November 1966, p. 3; *Con vistas al referendum. Actidudes en las recentes elecciones*, Madrid, 2 December 1966, p. 3. A survey by 'Data SA' on the eve of the November 1966 municipal elections.

Martínez Alier, Juan, 'El reparto' *Cuadernos de Ruedo ibérico* 13—14,

---

\* When preparing this book, we did not have available to us the latest issue of *Informe sociológico sobre la situación social de España,* published by FOESSA. The value of the documents listed above varies considerably.

June—September 1967, pp. 47—65. What the agricultural labourers of Córdoba think of land reform today.

Martínez Alier, Juan, *La estabilidad del latifundismo*, Ediciones Ruedo ibérico, 1968, 420 pp.

Miguel, Amando de, 'Estructura social y juventud española: el modelo teórico de cultura política' *Revista del Instituto de la juventud,* 3 January 1966, pp. 81—106; 'Estructura social y juventud española: impacto político y interés por la política' *Revista del Instituto de la Juventud* 5 June, 1966, pp. 63—81; 'Estructura social y juventud española: participación política' *Revista del Instituto de la Juventud,* 6 August 1966, pp. 15—38. A survey conducted in 1960—61 of a sample 1,318 young males, according to the procedure outlined by G. Almond and S. Verba in their book 'The Civic Culture'.

'Opiniones sobre cuestiones nacionales' *Revista española de la opinión pública* 18, October—December 1969, pp. 265—302. Attitudes to the Cortes, the Falangist movement, vertical 'syndicates', political parties and associations, and freedom of expression.

'Opiniones sobre problemas nacionales e internacionales (Otoño 1968)' *Revista española de la opinión pública* 17, July—September 1969, pp. 187—257. Attitudes to the communist countries and to the Soviet intervention in Czechoslovakia.

Ramírez, Luis, 'Visión actual de la guerra civil (encuesta)' in *Horizonte español 1966* vol I, Ediciones Ruedo ibérico, Paris 1966, pp. 253—79.

Tezanos, José Félix, and Domínguez, Rafael, 'Encuesta sociopolítica realizada en la Universidad de Madrid' *Cuadernos para el diálogo* 5, May 1967, pp.96—9.

'(El) Verdadero rostro del clero español' *Vida Nueva* 722, 21 March 1970, pp. 7—34.


12.   Principal periodicals used *

*Acción comunista* (mouthpiece of a group which broke away from the FLP)
*Acción estudiantil* (FLP, Madrid)
*Alkarrilketa* (*PC de Euzkadi* — Basque Communist Party)


* Only Spanish communist and extreme left socialist periodicals are listed here. These are for the most part underground publications, often issued in mimeographed form. Spanish-language periodicals published in France by the CGT and the French Communist Party are also included.

*Avance* (Alvárez del Vayo faction)
*Comuna* (FUDE, Madrid)
*El comunista (Movimiento ML)*
*El quehacer proletario* (PCE [Int.], Madrid)
*Hora de Madrid* (PCE, Madrid)
*Horizonte* (PCE  Communist Youth)
*La verdad* (French Communist Party)
*La voz del campo* (PCE)
*Lucha obrera* (Partido obrero revolucionario [trotskysta])
*Mundo obrero* (PCE)
*Mundo obrero (Internacional)* (PCE [Int.])
*Mundo obrero (ML)* (PCE [ML])
*Nuestra bandera* (PCE)
*Nous horitzons* (PSUC)
*Realidad* (PCE, semi-official)
*Revolución española* (?)
*Treball* (PSUC)
*Unidad* (CGT, in Spanish)
*Vanguardia* (PCE, Madrid students)
*Vanguardia obrera* (PCE [ML])
*Vanguardia socialista revolucionaria* (PSOE, extreme - left)
*Voz obrera* (PCE, Germany)

# Glossary

ACO — *Acción católica obrera* (Workers' Catholic Action).

AS — *Alianza sindical* (Trade Union Alliance). Underground trade union body founded in February 1960 by the émigré trade union organisations UGT, CNT and STV.

ASO — *Alianza sindical obrera* (Workers' Trade Union Alliance). Underground trade union breakaway group from above, including socialists and anarchists in Spain itself, as well as Catholic elements. Founded in October 1962; anti-communist.

AST — *Acción sindical de trabajadores* (Workers' Trade Union Alliance). Underground Christian revolutionary trade union organisation founded in 1966; co-operates with communists.

ASU — *Agrupación socialista universitaria* (Socialist University Association). Founded in 1957 by young socialists under Dionisio Ridruejo. Now the USD — *Unión social demócratica* (Social Democratic Union).

BP — *Buró político* (Political Bureau).

BPS — *Brigada político-social* (Political and Social Brigade). The organ of political repression in Spain.

CC — Central Committee.

CCOO — *Comisiones obreras* (Workers' Councils).

CE — *Comité ejecutivo* (Executive Committee).

CEDA — *Confederación española de derechas autónomas* (Spanish Right-wing Confederation). Conservative Catholic party under the Spanish Second Republic; created by Gil Robles.

CGTU — *Confederación general de trabajo unitario* (United General Labour Confederation). Set up by the communists between 1932 and 1934. Later merged with the UGT.

CNT — *Confederación nacional del trabajo* (National Confederation of Labour). Anarcho-syndicalist body founded in 1911. now in exile.

CPSU — Communist Party of the Soviet Union.

CUDE — *Confederación universitaria democrática de estudiantes* (Democratic Confederation of University Students). Set up in 1933; superseded in 1966.

DRIL — *Directorio revolucionario ibérico de liberación* (Iberian Revolutionary Liberation Directorate). Active mostly in Portugal; involved particularly in the hijacking of the liner Santa Maria; set up in 1959.

ETA     *Euzkadi Ta Azkatasuna* (Land and Freedom of the Basques). Basque revolutionary movement split into several factions; set up in 1959.

FAI     *Federación anarquista ibérica* (Iberian Anarchist Federation). Underground anarchist organisation founded under the dictatorship of Primo de Rivera; very influential from 1931 to 1939.

FELN     *Frente español de liberación nacional* (Spanish National Liberation Front). Left-wing revolutionary group; pro-Alvárez del Vayo.

FET y de las JONS     *Falange española tradicionalista y de las juntas de ofensiva nacional sindicalista* (Spanish Falange of Nationalists and of the Juntas of National Syndicalist Offensive). Official name of the Falange since the 1937 merger decree.

FIJL     *Federación ibérica de juventudes libertarias* (Iberian Federation of Libertarian Youth). Consists of anarchists who resort to violent action against Francoism. Has claimed responsibility for most attempts on life and kidnappings in recent years.

FLP     *Frente de liberación popular* (Popular Liberation Front). Set up in 1958 by left-wing Catholic intellectuals and students; split into several factions. Advocates socialist revolution.

FUDE     *Federación universitaria democrática española* (Spanish Democratic University Federation). Student organisation set up in Madrid in 1961. Originally under strong PCE influence; now dissident.

HGP     *Huelga general política* (Political General Strike). PCE slogan.

HNP     *Huelga nacional pacífica* (Peaceful National Strike). PCE slogan.

HOAC     *Hermandades obreras de Acción católica* (Catholic Action Workers' Fraternities). Catholic workers' organisation set up in 1948, joined by many present-day trade union activists.

IDC     *Izquierda democrática cristiana* (Christian Democratic Left). Founded by J. Ruiz-Gimenez, generally following the line of *Cuadernos para el diálogo*; part of the opposition tolerated by the regime; has been drifting away from its original Christian orientation.

| | |
|---|---|
| JSU | *Juventudes socialistas unificadas* (United Socialist Youth). Came into being in 1936 as a result of a merger of the Socialist and Communist Youth organisations. |
| OSO | *Oposición sindical obrera* (Communist Workers' Opposition). Underground trade union body set up by the PCE in 1962. |
| PCE | *Partido comunista de España* (Communist Party of Spain). Sometimes abbreviated PC de E. |
| PCE | *Partido comunista español* (Spanish Communist Party). First communist organisation founded by the Socialist Youth; later merged with the PCOE to form the PCE. |
| PCE (Int.) | *Partido comunista de España (Internacional)* (Communist Party of Spain [International]. Dissident communist group formed in 1967—68. |
| PCE (ML) | *Partido comunista de España (Marxista-Leninista)* (Communist Party of Spain (Marxist-Leninist). Maoist body set up in 1964. There has also been another PCE (m.l.) |
| PCOE | *Partido comunista obrero español* (Spanish Communist Workers' Party). Set up by a dissident faction of the PSOE. Later merged with the PCE to form the present PC de E. |
| POR (T) | *Partido obrero revolucionario (Trotskysta)* (Revolutionary Workers' Party [Trotskyite]). Underground Trotskyite organisation, advocating the policies of J. Posadas. |
| POUM | *Partido obrero de unificación marxista* (Marxist Workers' Party of Unification). Brought into being in 1935 by various dissident and Trotskyite factions, mostly in Catalonia. At that time under the influence of A. Nin and J. Maurín. |
| PSOE | *Partido socialista obrero español* (Spanish Socialist Workers' Party). Socialist party founded by Pablo Iglesias. |
| PSUC | *Partit socialista unificat de Catalunya* (United Socialist Party of Catalonia). The PCE's Catalan branch, set up in 1936. |
| SDEUB | *Sindicato democrático de estudiantes de la Universidad de Barcelona* (Barcelona University Democratic Students' Union). Student body set up in 1966. |
| SDEUM | *Sindicato democrático de estudiantes de la Universidad de Madrid* (Madrid University Democratic Students' Union). Came into being in 1966—67. |
| SEU | *Sindicato español universitario* (Spanish University Union). The old official university syndicate, now replaced by APE — *Associaciones profesionales de estudiantes* (Professional Associations of Students). |
| SIM | *Servicio de investigación militar* (Military Investigation Ser- |

vice). The Republic's military security branch during the Civil War.

STV     *Solidaridad de trabajadores vascos* (Basque Workers' Solidarity). Basque Christian trade union organisation formed in 1911; affiliated to ASO.

UDC     *Unión democráta cristiana* (Christian-Democratic Union). New name of J. Ruiz Giménez' IDC, introduced in 1965.

UDE     *Unión democrática de estudiantes* (Democratic Students' Union). Student organisation set up in 1957, later replaced by FUDE.

UFD     *Unión de fuerzas democráticas* (Union of Democratic Forces). Coalition of the old republican parties minus the communists.

UGT     *Unión general de trabajadores* (General Workers' Union). Socialist-inclined trade union organisation founded in 1888. Now in exile.

UJC     *Unión de juventudes comunistas* (Communist Youth Union). Set up in 1962 by the PCE to take the place of the JSU.

USD     *Unión social demócrata* (Social-Democratic Union). Successor to the Partido social de acción demócrata (PSAD). Founded in 1956 by Dionisio Ridruejo. So called since 1964.

USO     *Unión sindical obrera* (Workers' Trade Union Association). Underground trade union body set up in 1961 by socialist-oriented activists from the ACO. Later reintegrated in the ASO.

VOJ     *Vanguardia obrera juvenil* (Young Workers' Vanguard). A Catholic Action movement founded by Jesuits, from which some of the ASO militants come.

# Index

234

237

MAR 2 6 1981